INFINITE GRACE

DIANE GOLDNER

INFINITE GRACE

*where the worlds of science
and spiritual healing meet*

HAMPTON ROADS
PUBLISHING COMPANY, INC.
for the evolving human spirit

Cover design by Marjoram Productions
Cover image copyright © PhotoDisc, Inc.

For information write:

Hampton Roads Publishing Company, Inc.
134 Burgess Lane
Charlottesville, VA 22902

Or call: 804-296-2772
FAX: 804-296-5096
e-mail: hrpc@hrpub.com
Web site: http://www.hrpub.com

If you are unable to order this book from your local
bookseller, you may order directly from the publisher.
Quantity discounts for organizations are available.
Call 1-800-766-8009, toll-free.

Library of Congress Catalog Card Number: 98-73919

ISBN 1-57174-125-9

10 9 8 7 6 5 4 3 2 1

Printed on acid-free paper in the United States

God does respond when you deeply pray to Him with faith and determination. . . . You don't realize how wonderfully this great power works. It operates mathematically. There is no "if" about it.

Paramhansa Yogananda
Founder, Self Realization Fellowship

The most interesting phenomena are of course in the new places, the places where the rules do not work—not the places where they do work! That is the way in which we discover new rules.

Richard Feynman
Physicist, Nobel Laureate

To The Reader

This book is the result of four years of intensive investigation. What you are about to read are the true experiences of healers, their clients, and the scientific studies in this area.

Healing is not a panacea, as you will see, but it is a doorway into a new paradigm.

I have focused on one interrelated group of healers—a soul band if you will. This is not an endorsement, but an exploration. There are many other healers practicing and teaching in the United States at many skill levels. No matter who the healer is, or what the healing style, however, the same principles apply, just as the laws of electricity and magnetism are the same in Europe and Asia. I have also focused on the contemporary pioneers of science who are studying the effects of mind and spirit, and who are documenting these phenomena in the laboratory.

I could not have written this book without many deeply personal conversations with healers, scientists, and people on their healing journeys—whether that journey is being guided by cancer, heart disease, AIDS, infertility, or heartache, which comes in so many forms.

I also have had to enter the trenches, so to speak. I ended up having many experiences with spiritual energy. In the course of my investigations, I have come to understand that infinite grace is the birthright of each and every one of us; even our suffering is a path to bring us home.

I did not know what I would find when I began my research. I was taken by surprise many times. I hope that reading this book will be as enlightening for you as writing it has been for me.

Diane Goldner

Table of Contents

Part One

One

Initiation

NORMALLY, DR. JONATHAN KRAMER, a radiologist at the Berkshire Medical Center in Pittsfield, Massachusetts, began his day at 8 A.M. and often worked for the next ten hours without a break. But December 2, 1996, was no ordinary day. Kramer, thirty-eight, was about to face his own mortality.

Kramer was a classic "type A." Lean and athletic, with short brown hair and a friendly open face, he had a take-charge manner that inspired confidence. He was an achiever, although you couldn't locate the quality any one place on his five foot, ten inch frame. It was perhaps best expressed in his effortless motion. He thrived on pushing himself as hard as he could. And although he worried about things, he thought of himself as leading a charmed life.

He had been a clinical instructor in radiology at Harvard Medical School until he left Beth Israel Medical Center in Boston in 1993 to go into private practice at Berkshire. When he wasn't competing in a triathalon or tearing up the basketball court, he wrote scholarly papers for publications such as *The American Journal of Neuroradiology* and *Stroke*, contributed to radiology textbooks, and taught continuing medical education classes at Harvard. Getting married two years earlier to Maria, a psychotherapist, had hardly slowed his pace. The birth of their daughter, Raphaela, in 1995, only made him feel more urgent about providing for his new family.

Kramer thought of the radiology department as the nerve center of the hospital. Like clockwork, when a patient had a problem, doctors ordered pictures of the brain, the heart, the spine, the legs, the stomach, the lungs, wherever the trouble seemed to be. The internists and other specialists worked with the patients, but it was radiologists like Kramer who typically made the diagnosis. He spent his days doing delicate invasive procedures like angiograms and mylograms. He always took the sickest patients, the ones most at risk for complications. Kramer liked that kind of challenge. The other doctors were just as happy to let him have them.

Working hard came naturally to Kramer, the son of a neurologist father and a mother who had survived the Holocaust to become an executive secretary who took shorthand in six languages. He had graduated from Downstate Medical School, in Brooklyn, New York, in 1982 and had done his residency and fellowship at Downstate Medical Center. The center's doctors treated so many gunshot wounds and poor people deprived of regular medical care that European governments sent up-and-coming army doctors there to train in battlefield medicine. The physicians there saw everything. And they learned fast. Kramer loved it. He could not have dreamed of a better place to earn his stripes.

But now he had the disquieting feeling that he was about to face a different kind of challenge. For the last few days he had not felt well. It wasn't anything dramatic. On Saturday he had gone for a four-mile run. When he got home his heart was beating fast, and it was still beating fast the next day. An elevated heart rate was not normal in a man his age—or for that matter, any age. His appetite hadn't been so great, either. During Thanksgiving dinner, his father-in-law had asked if something was wrong. Kramer usually ate more than anyone else.

Kramer lived with Maria and Raphaela in an old colonial house with lots of doors and windows at the end of a dead-end dirt road in Pittsfield, Massachusetts, the kind of house Kramer had always dreamed of owning. It was in the center of town, but it was on two-thirds of an acre of wooded land. It was just five minutes from Berkshire where Kramer worked. From the windows of the hospital, he could even see the Taconic and Berkshire mountains off in the distance. He did not want anything to upset this beautiful life he had worked so hard to create.

By midmorning Kramer couldn't stand the suspense. Something was very wrong; he wanted to know what. He had had a physical on Monday, but the internist couldn't find anything. All his tests had come back normal except for the sedimentation rate of his red blood cells, which was elevated. But that didn't mean much; the sedimentation rate could be raised by almost anything, including arthritis. Tomorrow he faced an appointment with an infectious disease doctor. Working in a hospital, Kramer could have picked up tuberculosis or the Epstein-Barr virus. He knew the doctor would need chest X-rays. So he ordered his own.

When the processor spit the film out, he and the technologist saw it at the same time: a white mass next to the heart, between the heart and the root of the lung vessels on the right side. He watched the technologist's jaw drop. "Oh God," Kramer thought. But then he had a second thought: "Thank God." Something about his life was going to have to give now. He'd known for a long time that he needed to make some kind of change.

A few hours later, the oncologist diagnosed Kramer with Hodgkin's lymphoma. Working with radiation might have caused it, which was a frightening thought—the very thing Kramer had always feared. Yet if you had to have cancer, Hodgkin's disease was one of the most treatable.

The next morning, tests confirmed the diagnosis: Kramer's cancer had reached Stage 3B. His oncologist told him the odds were 75 percent in his favor. That also meant, Kramer realized, that he had a 25 percent chance of dying. He started chemotherapy almost immediately. Altogether he would get twelve rounds of ABVD (adriamycin bleomycin vinblastine dacarbazine), an aggressive blast of poison to be injected every two weeks. But it was no guarantee. He still might die.

On January 6, after his second shot of chemo, just a month after his diagnosis, Kramer flew to Los Angeles with Maria and Raphaela to see the Reverend Rosalyn Bruyere, one of the most powerful spiritual healers in the West. Some might dismiss the trip as a desperate effort by a man facing death. After all, haven't terminally ill patients been seeking miracles for centuries? But Rosalyn Bruyere was not peddling miracles.

With auburn hair, a big aura, and a big sense of humor, Bruyere is literally and metaphorically larger than life. Born just after the end of World War II, Bruyere knows more about the anatomy of the human aura than almost anyone practicing energy healing today, at least in the West. In more than thirty years of practice, she has laid hands on thousands of people suffering from everything from cataracts and arthritis to cancer and AIDS. She also is a scholar and practitioner of the esoteric teachings of nearly every faith, including the religions of ancient Egypt, Hinduism, various Native American tribes, the Bonpo of Tibet, and Christianity.

Bruyere, the founder of the Healing Light Center Church in Los Angeles, keeps a low profile, but she has quietly treated some of the top stars in Hollywood, including Cher, Barbra Streisand, James Coburn, Frank Zappa, director Martin Scorsese, and, at the very end of his life, Sammy Davis, Jr. When Ellen Burstyn needed someone to teach her hands-on healing for the movie *Resurrection*, she turned to Bruyere, who acted as a technical adviser on the film. Bruyere has also been called on to counsel children abused by a satanic cult; to help, unofficially, in police work; and to use her clairvoyance to locate bombs when Los Angeles hosted the Olympic games.

Stories of Bruyere's healing prowess are legion. I myself have seen her separate the fused spinal vertebrae of a young minister when doctors urged surgery, release the pain of a student's rectal surgery and the underlying childhood sexual abuse that Bruyere believed caused the pain, and elicit a long-repressed childhood incident in a young man merely because of the way the pattern of his aura shifted during a lecture. Students study with her for years without consistently getting the same effects in their own healing practices.

"An everyday healing for Rosalyn is mind-blowing for everyone else," says Deborah East Keir, a registered nurse who has studied with Bruyere for more than a dozen years. Yet Bruyere never promises or predicts an outcome. She advises clients to follow their doctors' orders, urges them to have necessary surgeries, and never claims healing is a panacea for all physical ailments. Students of hers are no different from the rest of us: They have open heart surgery and hysterectomies. Bruyere herself sometimes limps from an arthritic hip. "On a good day," she likes to say, "you get a healing."

Bruyere has influenced most of the healers in the United States, including many of the nurses who have studied Healing Touch, one school of energy healing. Even Barbara Brennan, who runs the largest school for "healing science," briefly studied with Bruyere and teaches the techniques she learned from her. Recognition of her gift crosses color lines and nationalities. The Sioux and the Hopi consider Bruyere a medicine woman. And the Bonpo, a pre-Buddhist Tibetan group, regard her as the living embodiment of a 4,000-year-old prophecy. Unlike some other American teachers, Bruyere has never trademarked or labeled her techniques, which derive from ancient traditions; she believes that anyone can channel the techniques and that these techniques cannot be owned by any one person.

Bruyere has been poked and wired and tested and quizzed by scientists at UCLA and at the Menninger Clinic, where biofeedback was developed. Nobody has definitively measured subtle energy, what the Chinese call *chi*, or life force. But when Bruyere works on patients, she sometimes has voltage surges in the electrical potential on her skin that scientists cannot explain. Her brain wave pattern is typically theta, the pattern associated with a deep sleep state, but one that is also found in long-time meditators, yogis, and healers. "She lives and walks around in the dream world," says Nancy Needham, a healer in New Hampshire and an elder in Bruyere's church.

Such laurels would mean nothing to Kramer's by-the-book colleagues at Harvard and Berkshire Medical. In 1997, Dr. Andrew Weil launched the program for Integrative Medicine at the University of Arizona, where Bruyere now guest lectures on energy anatomy each year. A handful of pioneering hospitals, including the University of Pittsburgh Medical Center and Stoney Brook in New York also have begun to offer energy healing and spiritual counseling in integrative and complementary care programs. But for a mainstream doctor or scientist at most hospitals to talk about "subtle" or "spiritual" or "bio" energy still is a little like being back in Galileo's day and suggesting that the Earth revolved around the sun. You could lose your funding, your job, and your reputation—the modern version of excommunication. Kramer knew this as well as anyone else. But he also felt that there was something to this *chi*.

In his first year of medical school, Kramer had gone to the annual American Medical Students Association meeting in Denver. On a whim, he had signed up for an afternoon course on healing through prayer. At the time he had a compound fracture in his finger from a basketball injury. The doctors had told him he needed surgery, but they had said the best he could hope for was 50 percent use of the finger. The healer who spoke at this lecture, Hank Kowalsky, offered to help. He put a hand on Kramer's shoulder while six or so devout Christians gathered around and prayed to Jesus, which made Kramer a little uneasy. He had been raised in the Jewish faith, and had not previously had any direct experiences of other religions.

"He did his thing for about ten minutes," recalls Kramer. "Within seven or eight seconds of these people doing their prayers, I felt heat in my finger. It went to the base of the finger, but didn't go up my arm." Kramer attributed these effects to hypnosis or suggestion. But the feeling persisted the next day, and the day after. And, strangely, his finger healed completely—without an operation.

In his senior year of medical school, after a fellowship at the world-renowned Queens Square Neurological Institute in London, he met up with a cousin who taught him about chakras (energy vortices that run perpendicular to the spine and, according to Hindu tradition, that take in information and energy from the environment). Then he tried a chakra exercise with a friend; she keeled over from the force and started crying. When he heard about Bruyere in 1991, he decided to attend a workshop she gave in Williamstown, Massachusetts.

At first, Kramer felt like an intruder. Bruyere's group was composed overwhelmingly of women; more than a few seemed angry at men. But he was mesmerized by Bruyere's view of how physical illnesses were connected to emotional, mental, and spiritual issues.

These were things he had never read about in any medical book. Yet they had a compelling logic.

Ever since, he had taken an intensive course with Bruyere once or twice a year. As a doctor, he longed to see someone jump off the table after a healing session and throw away their crutches. That never happened while he was in class. But he had seen Bruyere shrink Kaposi's sarcoma lesions right before his eyes. He had also seen her help a registered nurse with multiple personality disorder integrate her personality fragments over several years, at one point even watching Bruyere perform an exorcism in which she danced with a snake-like energy she released. And he had watched Bruyere work on a man so riddled with cancer that doctors had advised the man's wife to make the funeral arrangements. The next day the man looked infinitely better, and the following year and the year after that, he was very much alive. Kramer knew Bruyere was the real thing even if he didn't understand, as a scientist, exactly how *chi* worked.

At the same time, a part of him held back. He was just curious. Experimenting. Watching. Waiting. Once, while Bruyere was channeling "Master Chang," who she claims is a 4,000-year-old Bonpo leader, Kramer asked about his career. "He said I could practice healing by focusing a healing intention or prayer on the patient whose film I was reading," Kramer recalls. "He suggested twenty minutes a day, two minutes a patient, ten patients a day." Kramer never really did it.

But he did occasionally use subtle energy. When he did angiograms, he always prayed, asking for his hands to be guided. He had done 1,200 angiograms on people's heads and only had one complication, when he was supervising a fellow in training. The average doctor had a 1.5 percent complication rate, or 18 in 1,200. "I really haven't had any," says Kramer. "I consider that unusual. I thank my guides."

Strangely, during that early channeling, Master Chang predicted that in four and a half years, Kramer's life would change. That was in May 1992, exactly four and a half years before Kramer was diagnosed with cancer. A friend reminded him of Master Chang's words just six months before the diagnosis by sending him a tape of the channeling.

So he didn't totally believe. But he felt there was something to it. Either way, he was up against the wall. He had nothing to lose.

Bruyere's Healing Light Center Church in Sierra Madre, California, is at the edge of the desert foothills that rise above Los Angeles. The garden apartment complex blends in with the leafy suburban surroundings. It was built in the 1920s to house a tuberculosis sanitarium and rests on a former Native American healing ground. On Easter Sunday Bruyere delivers a sermon in the inner courtyard. And late in the quiet of a summer afternoon, you can literally hear the vines grow; they sometimes stretch twelve inches in a single Southern California day. The spot was carefully chosen by Bruyere, who is ever conscious of the energy not only of people, but of places, things, and situations.

Bruyere's small but cozy healing room is decorated with Egyptian papyrus scrolls and figurines, books on Native American and Egyptian religion and art, and pictures of friends and family, including Cher, the actress, and Cher's mother. But it is the massage table in the center of the room that is the focal point. Bruyere usually keeps a stuffed leopard on the table, which she uses underneath clients' knees to make them more comfortable.

Bruyere, who travels around the United States and Germany to teach healing, doesn't see many patients any more. But she makes sure to maintain a small practice to keep her hands in, and her skills growing. She doesn't believe in being strictly an academic, a healer emeritus.

Kramer arrived late in the afternoon with Maria and Raphaela. He was tightly wound. Raphaela, sitting with Maria, quickly began to amuse herself with some of Bruyere's invaluable sacred objects—toys to her. Bruyere, a doting grandmother to her own grandkids, didn't mind. Her attention was on Kramer. The actual work would be easy. She had done it thousands of times. But she also knew that the real issues weren't physical. On some level, so did Kramer.

"This is pretty big stuff when your body tells you that your job is killing you in a very specific way," says Bruyere. "You're pretty much going to have to deal with all your core assumptions." She sees body, mind, and soul as inextricably linked. She saw the tumor as a message from Kramer's soul.

When Bruyere put her hands on his chest and his abdomen, the energy field around her fingers extended deep into Kramer's body. Kramer had never felt the tumor growing inside him. But now it was as if Bruyere had electrified it. He experienced a tugging sensation, a localized tightness where the mass was, with the sensation radiating up the right side of his neck. With these "energy fingers," Bruyere says she could feel the energy of the tumor, get acquainted with it, and bring it up to the same energy state as the rest of his body, thus transforming it.

"All tumors feel alike," she says. "They're slightly hot, slightly confused, slightly aggressive. They're extraordinarily quiet. If I was going to use the word noise, it would be 'electronically,' where there's some static. You feel you're holding something that doesn't belong here." Visually, she says she could see "a black hole" in his chest.

The cancer was speaking very specifically, lodged next to his heart. "It was the result of doing a practice his heart wasn't in. That's why it affected his heart," she says. "He was full of his own biases and his own notions of reality, many of which didn't serve him very well."

As Bruyere ran *chi* into the tumor, Kramer talked about his longings and his frustration, as if the tumor was holding these pieces of his consciousness. "I think this is about my career," he would say. "Ah ha," Bruyere would answer, as she continued to run energy into his system, raising the energy state of the cancer cells as she did. "I was thinking of getting out of radiology. But I'm so stubborn," he added. She listened. She didn't set the agenda, but she went with him wherever he needed to go.

"I should have learned this lesson a long time ago," Kramer said. He had been toying with energy healing for years, thinking it was real but keeping his distance, afraid to do something that his colleagues would think was foolish and compromise his standard of living. He was afraid to follow his own heart. And Bruyere answered, "You're right. You're stubborn." She allowed him to voice all his fears and anxieties, his guilt and his shame, going all the way back into his childhood.

"The cancer is going to be done with you much sooner than you're done with it," she told him. Hearing those words for him was like drinking in joy. His whole body relaxed. For the first time since the diagnosis, he felt confidant that he would survive. Bruyere had worked with so many cases of cancer, Kramer felt he could trust her opinion. Plus, when Bruyere channeled energy, she included an energy that can only be described as love. It touched him at a level that chemotherapy could never reach.

Each day, for a week, Kramer came back. They often had the same conversation, or variations of it. They talked about how he was diagnosing illnesses but was powerless to make a difference in the patients' outcomes. He did not have direct contact with the patients. Even if he did, in many cases there was not much a medical doctor could do for them. In the brain, where he often worked, there are not many things a Western physician can fix.

Bruyere could see that his absolute faith in science and medicine was being shattered. He had devoted his life to medicine. But the radiation from his job very likely had helped cause his cancer. Now medicine couldn't necessarily save his life. And deep down he had never felt completely fulfilled by technological medicine, although he had reached the top of his profession.

At times, he cried. "I was petrified. I was scared beyond description," he says. "It was the tension breaking. I was relieved that she was working on me. I had faith in her. I had been studying with her for five years, almost six years."

As Bruyere charged Kramer's aura—using subtle energies scientists have yet to measure directly—she also engaged in a dialogue with the tumor. She says that in the beginning it's the same conversation with every tumor. "The conversation is like this: What are you doing here? Why did you come? Is there something you want to tell us? How can we help you? And what that tumor says back is, 'I belong here. I need to be here. I'm serving a purpose.'"

"You assure [the tumor cells] that it's not true," Bruyere continues. "You say, 'You're lost. You don't belong here.' It's actually a very strange kind of conversation," she admits. "I do it so automatically, I've never given it much thought. But it is strange, isn't it?"

Bruyere then "told" the tumor telepathically that it was time to change. She ran a high frequency of subtle energy into the tumor cells, higher than they could tolerate. The tumor cells then transformed into healthy cells or were otherwise consumed by the body, she says.

At the same time, Bruyere claims, she brought the subtle frequencies of the chemotherapy and the tumor "closer" and made them more "attractive" to each other—to make the chemo "smarter" and more efficient. "I think chemotherapy is pretty much a proven technology," she says. "My biggest fear for Jonathan was that his biological system would somehow get the idea that medicine had betrayed him and that medicine was now dangerous. And I didn't want him to have that in there. I thought that was too dangerous a message for his body to carry."

On the last day, she also talked to Kramer and Maria about their marriage. She could see the strain the cancer was putting on them. The level of fear Kramer was facing and the level of change he would have to go through before he emerged in a new psychic space were going to continue to stress the marriage, she warned them. She told Maria that she needed to take care of herself if the marriage was going to survive, advising, "As a partner, you have to pretend you are just as sick, and get just as much support." And she counseled them both, "Try to stay connected in sweetness."

After returning to Pittsfield, Kramer had his first follow-up X-ray on January 15, 1997, less than a month into his six-month course of chemotherapy. The tumor was gone. He had had just two shots of chemotherapy. He says every oncologist he has talked to—and he has talked to at least a half-dozen—has said it was a very rapid response.

As a doctor, he confesses, it was hard to believe. Typically, people who have a six-month course of chemotherapy have a follow-up CAT scan in three months. "They like to see some kind of response [to chemo] after three months," Kramer says. "Mostly after six months, it's gone."

Kramer, however, was not leaving anything to chance. He

finished his chemotherapy, losing his hair temporarily. Even so, he says, part of him did not want the chemotherapy treatments to end; he was terrified the cancer might come back. Occasionally, he felt the tugging sensation where the mass had been and worried that the tumor had returned. Bruyere assured him it was just scar tissue. Laying hands on him, she put an energy "cushion" around the scar. He has not felt it since.

Without double-blind studies there is no way to prove what effect Bruyere's treatment had, says Kramer. "Who knows what saved my life. Was it Rosalyn or chemo? All I know is it was an extraordinarily quick response. But," he admits, "I'm certain Rosalyn had a big hand in this."

Kramer says he feels the tumor has played an important role, putting him on the right path, and helping him to become more whole. He was forced to leave his radiology practice because continued exposure to radiation could stimulate a recurrence of lymphoma. Yet he has not stood still.

Five months after completing chemotherapy, Kramer flew to Los Angeles to attend a practicum, taught by Bruyere, on healing terminally ill patients. On the plane Kramer was called on by the airline personnel to minister to a fellow passenger. The passenger, a former professional football player, then in his sixties, appeared to be in cardiac distress. Kramer worried that the man was going "to code"—have a heart attack. The passenger's pulse was 140 beats a minute, compared to the 70 beats a minute it should have been. His blood pressure was markedly elevated, too. He had discomfort in his chest. He also had a personal and family history of heart disease.

Kramer gave the man a nitroglycerin pill from the airplane's emergency medical kit. Instead of putting it under his tongue, the man swallowed it and refused to take another. Without medicine, Kramer could only watch the man's condition, helplessly. A half hour passed without any change in the man's vital signs. Then Kramer had an idea. He put his hand on the man's heart and ran *chi* into it. Within ten minutes, the man's heart rate had dropped to 92 beats per minute and his blood pressure went from 186/130 to 150/108 millimeters of mercury.

"The scientist in me says, 'I don't know what to think of this,' " Kramer says. "But," he adds, "there's a good chance I prevented him from having a cardiac arrest."

Kramer still doesn't know exactly what's next. Somehow, he wants to marry his skills as a medical doctor and an energy healer. But he doesn't know yet how that will look. He still has questions. "I want to be as good at energy healing as I am at radiology," he says. "I want to understand it scientifically, too."

Kramer is far from alone. More and more people, including doctors, want to understand *chi*. "Sometime in the next 100 years, subtle energy will be the basis of medicine," predicts Bruyere. "It will be where people start from, before they learn about physical anatomy or biochemistry. Some people think energy is a metaphor. But it's real. It connects all the dots."

Leading scientists are beginning to believe what healers and mystics have always said: the forces of mind and spirit are as real as gravity and atomic power. Yet this mysterious energy that most people can't touch or see still makes a lot of people nervous. The implications, after all, are enormous. If subtle energy and consciousness are as powerful as recent research and the experiences of people like Dr. Kramer suggest, the world will never be the same again. Love, it turns out, may be one of the most powerful physical forces in the universe.

Two

Child's Play

Some people hoped it might be an April Fool's Day joke when the *Journal of the American Medical Association* (JAMA) published a study on Therapeutic Touch on April 1, 1998. The study was poorly designed. The lead author was a prepubescent child. The three adult coauthors were part of Quackwatch and other anti-Therapeutic Touch groups, suggesting they might have a bias. Yet the study was no joke. It was an illustration of how, even in science, maintaining the status quo can be more important than truly investigating a subject.

Therapeutic Touch, or TT, as it is often called, is a simple form of laying on of hands practiced by many nurses. Practitioners simply pass their hands over a patient's body, without actually touching the patient, to smooth out the patient's energy field. Nurses use TT to calm patients and ease their pain. Some say they can feel the energy field and even sense "hot" and "cold" spots within it.

In controlled studies, TT has been found to increase hemoglobin levels and to reduce tension headache pain, and anxiety states. Some 43,000 nurses around the world have been trained to practice TT since the early 1970s. It was developed by Delores Krieger, Ph.D., a professor of nursing at New York University, with spiritual healer Dora Kunz. A nurse can be certified in TT after a weekend workshop, but nursing schools often devote more time to it.

Emily Rosa of Lakeland, Colorado, the daughter of nurse Linda Rosa, decided to study TT for her fourth-grade science project. She wanted to see whether TT practitioners could actually feel an energy field. If they could not, she theorized, it would be proof that the human energy field did not exist.

She rounded up twenty-one practitioners. Each one took a turn behind a screen and put their hands through two slots in the screen. Emily then placed her hand a few inches above one of the practitioner's hands and asked the practitioner to identify which hand experienced her hand's energy field. The practitioners did not do very well. In 280 tests, they identified the correct placement of Emily's hand just 44 percent of the time. Even if they had guessed, they should have been right 50 percent of the time. Young Emily concluded that Therapeutic Touch was a hoax.

Dr. George Lundberg, the editor in chief of *JAMA*, agreed. "I don't claim to be an expert on Therapeutic Touch," he told me a few months later. "I had never heard about it until Emily's paper arrived." But what he read shocked him. Nurses were claiming to calm patients and to reduce their pain by using a "touch" technique where they did not even touch the patient. "There is no physiological basis that makes sense," he said. "And the whole thing is so completely counterintuitive." He realized many physicians had no idea that their nursing colleagues were doing something so absurdly unscientific. He said he felt he had a moral responsibility, both to his physician readers, and to the American public, to educate them. "I did believe [the study] called into question the whole thing."

When he published the study, Dr. Lundberg underscored it with an editor's note stressing that: "Practitioners should disclose these results to patients, third-party payers should question whether they should save their money unless or until additional honest experimentation demonstrates an actual effect."

Emily became the youngest person ever to publish in a leading scientific journal and an overnight sensation. She appeared on the network news shows. The *New York Times* ran a front-page story complete with a color picture of Emily, her hair neatly pinned with barrettes. The paper praised her method as "devilishly simple." It noted that she had thrown the field of alternative medicine into "tumult."

It was a strange conclusion for either *JAMA* or the mass media to reach from just one study, and one conducted by a young child at that. Emily's study did not even examine whether Therapeutic Touch had a clinical effect. Even more curious, her study flew in the face of previous research of an almost identical nature.

The research, published in 1995 in the peer-reviewed journal, *Subtle Energies*, did have some key differences worth noting: it found that untrained college students could sense subtle energy, it was conducted by senior university researchers, and it was far more rigorous in its design than Emily's project. In the study, psychologists Gary Schwartz, Ph.D., and Linda Russek, Ph.D., at the University of Arizona, found that sixty-one blindfolded college students could sense when an investigator's hand hovered a few inches above their right or left hand in 66 percent of 1,464 trials.

In follow-up studies Drs. Russek and Schwartz found that 58 percent of the time blindfolded students could even guess when an experimenter was merely gazing at the back of the student's head or lower back. The implication, they believe, is that the "magic" of subtle sense perception is not in the touch but in the mere intention to do something. Indeed, they speculated that the reason Emily Rosa's study had a-lower-than-chance success rate might have been because of some form of negative intention. Perhaps her intention had been colored by a belief that Therapeutic Touch was fraudulent.

Curiously, in their studies Drs. Russek and Schwartz also found that the subjects who performed the best believed in the existence of God or a higher power, extrasensory perception, and the survival of consciousness after death. Their data suggests that those who believe in subtle or spiritual energy are more likely to perceive it. These studies were presented in June 1998 at the Society of Scientific Exploration and are being published in the *Journal of Scientific Exploration*.

Drs. Russek and Schwartz teach energy medicine to the post-graduate doctors in the Program for Integrative Medicine run by Andrew Weil, M.D. Oddly, despite their qualifications, when they wrote a letter to the editor of *JAMA* citing their research results shortly after Emily's study came out, Dr. George Lundberg and his editorial team declined to publish the letter. Months later, Dr. Lundberg was still pleased that he had published the eleven-year-old's study. He claimed not to know anything at all about any research by senior investigators with a different outcome. And he insisted that he still found Emily's study to be "quite convincing." In fact, he called both the study and his decision to publish it, "good science."

Right now there is a big secret in America. It has to do with the power and potential of subtle energy. More and more people are in on the secret. But lots of people are not. We all hear about the latest pill, Viagra, which makes some men potent again. It earned the company who developed it millions of dollars just in the first few months of sales. Prozac, an anti-depressant, racks up more than $2 billion in sales per year. But we do not hear about the studies that are being conducted that suggest people with cancer, AIDS, heart disease, emotional distress, and a myriad of other conditions also might benefit from treatments that do not come in the form of a pill.

There is, after all, no big business to champion energy healing. The American Medical Association (AMA), the largest trade association of doctors, has no special reason to investigate spiritual healing. Although it publishes research through its journal, the organization is, after all, a business trade association, dedicated to the financial and professional well-being of its members. Indeed, the AMA has for nearly a century tried to present itself as the "one true" medical profession.

In 1987 a federal judge even found the organization guilty of violating the Sherman Antitrust Act in its efforts to eliminate chiropractic as a profession, as Larry Dossey, M.D., editor of *Alternative Therapies*, noted in a report to the National Institutes of Health in 1992. Many leading doctors, of course, are in the vanguard of the new move for integration of alternative and allopathic therapies. But not the AMA.

Americans spent $21.2 billion on services provided by alternative medical practitioners in 1997, according to a study published in *JAMA* in 1998. The study found that American doctors are rapidly losing ground, and billions of dollars a year, to alternative practitioners. Indeed, visits to alternative practitioners exceeded visits to all U.S. primary care physicians. Most of these Americans were college

I. Subtle Sense Perception

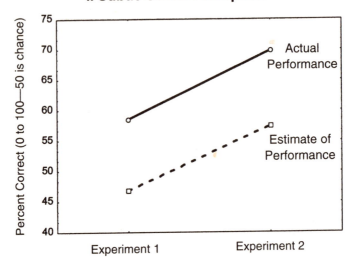

Blindfolded subjects sensed a nearby hand 58% of the time in Experiment 1, and 70% of the time in Experiment 2. (*Subtle Energies*, Vol. 6 No. 3) Courtesy of Russek and Schwartz.

II. Subtle Sense Perception

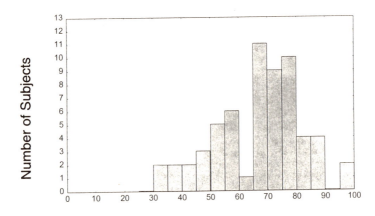

Percent Correct

If performance was at chance or below (like Rosa et al), the bars would center at the 50% or below range. Instead, many subjects were above 70% correct, eight subjects got between 80% and 90% correct, and two subjects got between 95% and 100% correct. (*Subtle Energies*, Vol. 6 No. 3) Courtesy of Russek and Schwartz.

III. Subtle Sense Perception:
Staring versus the Intention to Stare

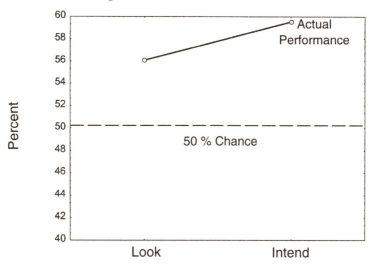

This graph shows that the accuracy of telling whether someone was staring at the back of subjects' heads or the small of their backs was 56%, and 59% for simply the intention to stare. (*Journal of Scientific Exploration*, 1999) Courtesy of Russek and Schwartz.

IV. Subtle Sense Perception:
Relationship to Spiritual Beliefs

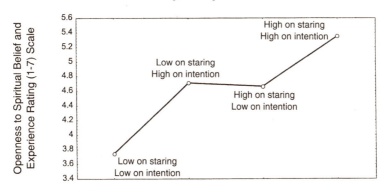

Subjects who were good in detecting actual staring and intended staring had the highest spiritual scores, and subjects who were poor in detecting actual and intended staring had the lowest spiritual scores. Those with high spiritual belief and experience are better in detecting eye gaze and intention. (*Journal of Scientific Exploration*, 1999) Courtesy of Russek and Schwartz.

educated and made more than $50,000 a year. They were not the fringe, but rather people who could afford to buy the best care in the world. Most of them did not even bother to discuss their alternative treatments with their doctors. Lead author David Eisenberg, M.D., of Beth Israel Deaconess Medical Center in Boston, predicted use of such treatments would only increase over time. In fact, energy healing had already risen in popularity since an earlier study in 1990.

Right now there are two sets of information, the party line and the facts. If you happen to be suffering from a brain tumor and are part of the Washington power establishment, you or a family member might hear about energy medicine from none other than the head of the National Institutes of Health's Office of Alternative Medicine. And a local doctor, out of the goodness of his heart, might telephone just to recommend a particular spiritual healer.

If you are a famous movie star or pop singer you are also likely to get on the inside track. TV star Tracy Nelson, daughter of the late rock singer Rick Nelson, granddaughter of America's most famous TV couple, Ozzie and Harriet Nelson, and a lead actress in the series *Father Dowling*, had weekly sessions with a Los Angeles healer, Maria Bartolotta, who trained with Rosalyn Bruyere, while Nelson underwent seven months of chemotherapy and radiation to combat Hodgkins Lymphoma in 1988. "It was wonderful that I could be touched and held and I could feel the energy work," says Nelson.

During chemotherapy, Nelson, who is five feet, seven inches, shrank to eighty-seven pounds. She believes the healings helped her through the ordeal and also helped preserve her fertility. "They told me I would not be able to have children," recalls Nelson, who now has a six-year-old girl. "My periods never stopped. The doctors didn't understand that. My oncologist said I was very lucky."

Nelson believes healing also helped her body grow a vestigial spleen after doctors surgically removed the original organ. "When I had my second MRI, all the doctors were standing around the monitor. . . . They said, this is your spleen. It's growing back. My doctor was fairly shocked. The oncologist said maybe the surgeon didn't get it all. The surgeon was irate. He said, 'Of course I got it all.' All I know is I have a little baby spleen. I really credit [the healing]." She says she still goes for healing sessions every other week because they boost her health and her psyche. "It's not as woo woo as it seems. It's all energetic and biochemical. . . . As soon as the AMA figures out how to make money from it, they'll be involved."

Power has a way of drawing to it what it needs. It might even be the definition of power. If you just happen to be one of the ordinary folk, you may never get the latest information. It is not readily available. If someone told you about spiritual healing, you would have every reason to doubt its validity. How can you make an educated decision in an information vacuum? And if you decided you had nothing to lose (maybe because nothing else worked) how would you distinguish between one healer and another, between the real McCoy and a quack?

It took me several years of serious investigation to put the pieces together. Even the National Institutes of Health, which is supposed to be a clearing house for information, seemed curiously uninterested in discussing or acknowledging energy healing. In response to an April 1998 Freedom of Information Act request, the Office of Alternative Medicine (OAM) Deputy Director Geoffrey Cheung, Ph.D, stated in a letter that the office had never sponsored research on energy healing or even discussed the subject in internal meetings.

By then, a researcher who had been funded by the office had forwarded me a copy of the report he had filed, the first study on energy healing the OAM ever funded. (The grant for the study is also, it turns out, listed on the Office of Alternative Medicine's web pages.) I also had a copy of "Alternative Medicine: Expanding Medical Horizons." This is a nearly 400-page report based on a series of workshops sponsored by the Office of Alternative Medicine in 1992 in which spiritual energy healing and energy medicine were discussed in detail. It is obtainable from the Government Printing Office by anyone willing to spend $20 .

Dr. Wayne Jonas, the OAM director through 1998, declined to be interviewed about spiritual healing for this book. But Mary Moran, the wife of Congressman James Moran, Jr. of Virginia, says that over dinner the OAM director personally encouraged her and her husband to try sessions with healer Mietek Wirkus for their baby daughter, who had a brain tumor, along with the standard treatments of chemotherapy and radiation. Mary Moran says what influenced her to follow his advice was that Dr. Jonas was not speaking from blind faith. He cited NIH research and other studies.

When she was diagnosed with the cancer in 1994, doctors had given three-year-old Dorothy Moran only a 10 percent to 20 percent chance of being alive on her fifth birthday, after taking advantage of all available allopathic treatments. After chemotherapy, Dorothy went into remission for several months. But in October 1995 doctors found a new spot on her brain. She had a six-week course of radiation, a treatment that doctors warned could potentially cause brain damage. Moran pulled out all the stops. She added energy healing sessions, huge doses of vitamins, and acupuncture treatments to her daughter's regimen. Pictures taken after the radiation showed the spot had disappeared. Moran, who took her daughter for energy healing sessions every other week for two years, says, "I am not hung up on what worked."

Energy healing did not necessarily save Dorothy's life. Indeed, another child who received standard care along with energy sessions at the same time as Dorothy, and from the same healer, Mietek Wirkus, suffered a relapse. But something worked. The girl's cancer has now been in remission for three years. In December 1998 Dorothy was a healthy, happy seven-year-old. "To see her," Mary Moran says, "you would never guess this kid had been sick."

Mrs. Moran reports that she, too, had a few treatments of her own during the family crisis. "I was depressed at the time," she explains. "It was almost an epiphany type of experience. I remember I told him I felt at one point—you don't know what it is—but I felt like I almost glimpsed heaven. . . . It fills you with faith."

The truth is that, despite what *JAMA* and the mass media report, studies on energy healing do exist. Just as important, the preliminary results are making a few top researchers and doctors sit up and take notice.

The field is still in its infancy. Researchers only began studying the effects of spiritual healing in the laboratory in the 1960s, and under great financial and professional duress. These studies do not generally get federal or private funding because spiritual healing has not been considered an appropriate topic for scientific research. For the same reason, they do not advance a scientist's career. Nor does research in this area make scientists rich, since there is no patent to file.

The phenomenon being studied goes by many names. Sometimes it is called spiritual energy because whatever is involved is nonmaterial. But it is also called bioenergy or biomagnetism, because it involves biological systems; intentional influence, because whatever is transmitted is directed by intent; and psi healing, because it is of the psyche or mind. Right now, these terms are largely interchangeable. Each term emphasizes a different aspect of what is probably an extremely complex dynamic.

By 1998 more than 177 controlled studies of energy healing had been completed. Of these studies, 72.9 percent found significant effects in the judgment of Dr. Daniel Benor, an American psychiatrist who reviewed them in *Healing Research: Holistic Energy Medicine and Spirituality* and *Subtle Energies*.

Dr. Benor began collecting the data after a colleague invited him to witness a healing session by MariEl healer Ethel Lombardi in 1980. Dr. Benor says he was a total skeptic—until he saw her work. "She brought about a change in one hour in a young man that I couldn't explain," he recalls. He says Lombardi did not even touch the lesion under the young man's nipple, which was the ostensible reason for the session. "As she was doing the laying on of hands, she said you have some unfinished business with your father," says Dr. Benor. "She'd never met him before. He nodded and started sobbing. She looked at me and winked, as if to say, 'Top that in psychiatry.'"

Dr. Benor says he palpitated the lesion before and after the session. He claims that it shrank by a half-centimeter and grew softer after the healing treatment. "Imagine. This woman cut through, in no time, what it would take me years or at least months of work to do as a psychiatrist," he says. "So I started looking at the research."

The studies, which he gathered over nearly a decade, show that healing treatments affect the growth of hemoglobin, cancer cells, bacteria, human hormones, and enzyme levels in vitro. They also demonstrate that healing influences the growth and health of fungus, plants, and animals. Other studies found that healing reduced hypertension. One study even documented reduced symptoms in a group of men who had suffered heart attacks and had been prayed for in distant healing sessions. Some of these studies involved healers holding the organism to be treated in their hands. Others measured healers' abilities to influence organisms by intention from another room or even another city.

In one of the most compelling studies conducted on human subjects, published in *Subtle Energies*, researcher Daniel Wirth found that noncontact Therapeutic Touch more than doubled the rate of wound healing. First, Wirth had a doctor make identical skin wounds in forty-four people, using a skin biopsy instrument. They were told the wound would be monitored, but not that they would receive any treatment. Next, each day for sixteen days, the subjects came in. They had to put their arms through a screen so that they could not see what was happening. Both the control and treatment group went through the same procedure, but the treatment group received a five-minute noncontact Therapeutic Touch session. The other group received no treatment.

On the day the incision was made, the wounds averaged 58.88 millimeters in diameter. On the eighth day, the wounds of the treatment group averaged 3.9 millimeters, compared to 19.34 millimeters for the control group. On the sixteenth day, the wounds of thirteen of the twenty-three people in the treatment group had completely healed. All those in the control group still had wounds. Statistically, the probability that the results were due to chance were one in one thousand.

Most of these studies were published in alternative journals, which do not carry the same weight as *Science*, the *New England Journal of Medicine*, or the *Journal of the American Medical Association*. Thus the studies automatically have less credibility. But researchers in this area note that this is a "Catch-22." The most prestigious magazines do not publish research on subtle energy healing, so the validity of the research cannot be judged by that rejection alone. Other studies were conducted as research dissertations or not published at all and carry even less scientific credibility.

What makes many of these studies so interesting, however, is that plants and animals and fungus and enzymes presumably do not respond to the power of suggestion. If they do, that alone is certainly interesting news for science. Many doctors, like JAMA editor George Lundberg, dismiss healing effects as a measure of the placebo effect. It is a comforting explanation for what is going on. It keeps the established order intact. But in light of these studies, it may not be a valid criticism.

Some doctors, like Larry Dossey, editor of *Alternative Therapies*, author of *Healing Words*, and the former chief of staff at Humana Hospital in Dallas, Texas, consider these studies irrefutable proof of the power of spiritual healing. Dr. Dossey, who lectures at medical schools around the country on the subject, calls their existence "one of the best kept secrets in medical science." Dr. Benor is equally impressed. "If psi healing were a medication, it would be accepted as a potent treatment by mainstream science," he asserts. "This is especially so in view of the absence of side effects." (In England, where Dr. Benor lived and worked for ten years, he says healing is already covered in some instances by the National Health Office.)

Other American doctors who have looked at the research record are intrigued but less convinced. And most doctors—and most of the public—remain unaware that such studies even exist.

Researchers involved in studying healing and consciousness do not believe that subtle is necessarily synonymous with inconsequential. "If someone yells at you, you may not pay much attention," explains David Muehsam, a researcher who has studied *chi gong* healers at Mount Sinai Hospital in Manhattan. "But someone can whisper something to you that changes your whole life. You could be whispering—and saying just the right thing."

If anything, subtle seems to be equivalent to fundamental. The effects of healing often seem to happen at a level below what scientists can comfortably measure right now. We do not yet have laboratory instruments that directly measure soul qualities such as love, desire or intention. Yet we know that love, desire, and intention shape our lives, along with many other soul qualities, such as clarity, precision, harmony, courage, and trust. They influence our choice of spouse, our choice of career, the way we feel about ourselves, the way we treat our friends, children, parents, and partners—even what we have for breakfast, lunch, and dinner. Love, desire, and intention even are main ingredients in the creation of our children, our art, our music, and our literature.

Studies show that love, desire, and intention are also the very tools of spiritual energy healing. For instance, researcher Glen Rein of Quantum Biology Research Labs, studied Dr. Leonard Laskow, a gynecologist who now teaches healing. Rein investigated Dr. Laskow's ability to affect DNA synthesis of tumor cells in vitro using five different healing intentions.

When Dr. Laskow held an intention for the cells to "return to the natural order and harmony of the normal cell line," he found a 39 percent inhibition in tumor cell growth. Allowing God's will to manifest resulted in an 21 percent inhibition. A visualization in which he saw only three cells in the petri dish found an 18 percent inhibition. A visualization in which he saw many cells resulted in an increased growth of tumor cells by 15 percent. Unconditional love had no effect on the rate of cell growth—without any guiding intention, it was completely neutral. In a second experiment the intent for normal cell growth had only a 20 percent inhibitory effect, while combining that intention with a visualization doubled the inhibitory effect to 40 percent.

"The results suggest that certain healing states and contents of consciousness are more effective than others," Dr. Benor wrote, adding that the results could be healer specific or even cell specific. Rein would not allow Dr. Benor to independently review the data while it was pending publication in a peer-reviewed journal, so Dr. Benor did not include the study in the category of research yielding statistically significant data.

Dr. Benor deemed still other studies to be too poorly executed to be considered significant, even when the researchers reported statistically significant results. In another group of studies, subtle effects occurred. Intuitively, one might feel they were related to the healing treatments. But the effects, while suggestive, did not yield statistically significant data.

One particular series of studies sheds some light on just how significant these seemingly subtle influences of mind can actually be. Marilyn Schlitz, Ph.D., a medical anthropologist and researcher at The Institute for Noetic Sciences, and William Braud, Ph.D., of the Mind Science Foundation in San Antonio, Texas, did a series of fifteen experiments involving distant intentional influence of emotions, measured by recording fluctuations in the electrical signals at the skin. (Electrodermal fluctuations reflect emotional changes and are the basis of lie-detector tests.) Ordinary subjects were asked to use desire and intent to create specific influences on a person in another room, such as to calm them down or make them anxious. The researchers measured whether they had succeeded by recording the electrodermal fluctuations of the distant subject.

All fifteen experiments had statistically meaningful results. Four other investigators, repeating these studies, also got meaningful results. In a meta-analysis of all 19 studies, the intentional influence caused only a 3 percent shift away from the random results of the control periods. But the probability that this shift was caused by chance was 1.4 million to 1.

A 3 percent shift from random may seem terribly insignificant. But in meta-analysis, scientists use something called an "effect size" and the effect size here was .25. Again, it may not sound like much, until you consider that a major study on aspirin's ability to prevent heart attacks was stopped early because the researchers felt it was unethical to withhold the drugs from the control group, as Dean Radin, Ph.D. notes in *The Conscious Universe*. The effect size for aspirin was only .03. Doctors also stopped a study of propranolol for the same reason. The effect size for that drug was just .04.

It seems from this research that subtle influences may be more powerful than many more gross phenomena—in the same way that the atomic energy in a few pounds of uranium has a lot more impact than a ton of TNT. Radin, former director of the Consciousness Research Lab at the University of Nevada, Las Vegas, notes that if a healing treatment with a .25 effect size was added to a medical treatment that ordinarily produced a 37.5 percent survival rate, the new survival rate would become 62.5 percent. "Some psi effects recorded in the laboratory are much larger than many people realize," he writes. "When we add a distant mental 'treatment' with an effect size of .25 to a conventional treatment, the majority of a population that would have died would instead become a majority that would live."

When it comes to energy medicine, scientists may be doing the first studies that measure a dimension of reality that is so fundamental to our existence that we sometimes forget it exists or assume it is beyond our abilities to measure or harness. Many in this still tiny group of pioneering scientists believe that soul qualities such as intention, love, and desire may actually help to direct the sticks and stones and biochemistry of our physical world, just as subatomic particles direct atoms and molecules.

Dr. Schlitz completed another, not yet published, experiment that sheds additional light on just how pervasive the influence this level of being may actually be. In this study, she found that the subtle level of desire and intention does not just influence cancer cells in vitro, but also the experimental environment.

Dr. Schlitz and a skeptical colleague, Richard Wiseman, Ph.D., a psychologist at the University of Herfordshire in England, both ran the exact same study on intentional distant effects from Dr. Wiseman's lab. Dr. Schlitz's result showed a statistically significant result. Dr. Wiseman's did not. When they repeated the exercise in Dr. Schlitz's lab, Dr. Schlitz again got statistically significant results. Dr. Wiseman did not.

It turns out in the world of subtle energy research, the intent, desires, and beliefs of the experimenter may be just as important as the intent, desire, and beliefs of the healer. Indeed, it may explain, in some cases, why one study of spiritual healing shows an effect and another does not. "Under well-controlled circumstances, we're finding differences based on the intention and expectations of the experimenter—differences in empirical outcomes," explains Dr. Schlitz. "I think it's a significant study. . . . It deconstructs the whole assumption we make about objectivity in science."

I think the evidence for healing is extremely compelling," Dr. Schlitz adds. "It's just whether you call it energy or not." She believes a better word is "intentionality." (Energy can be defined as the capacity to do work or make a change. But electromagnetic frequencies dissipate over time and space.)

Some scientists believe the implications of these recent findings are revolutionary. "Once you're into this place where the mind and spirit exist, the thoughts and person doing the experiment are an issue," explains William Gough, M.S., president of the Foundation for Mind-Being Research in Los Altos, California, which brings together high-level physicists and consciousness researchers. "If a person worries about what his colleagues are going to think or say, it can affect the experiment. Now that's kind of wild. That's why this whole thing is very threatening to science. I don't know how many people will say that."

New studies continue to be conducted, albeit at a slow pace because of the lack of funding. Not all of them demonstrate significant results, of course. Of those already completed, the study the NIH funded is also of some interest. It caught the attention of OAM director, Dr. Jonas, according to healer Mietek Wirkus.

In 1995, with a grant of $30,000, microscopic in the world of medical research, Steven Fahrion, Ph.D., then a Menninger Clinic researcher, studied the effects of hands-on subtle energy healing on ten patients with basal cell carcinoma. Each received six healings lasting between fifteen and thirty minutes over three weeks from Mietek Wirkus, of Bethesda, Maryland, and a former government-licensed healer in his native Poland, and Ethel Lombardi, a highly regarded Chicago healer. Dr. Fahrion took photographs and measurements, using a millimeter ruler of each carcinoma before the study began and after each treatment.

After three weeks, four of the ten patients showed tumor reduction or elimination. One man, who had been exposed to arsenic while working with bug spray for plants, had had 300 basal cell carcinomas removed during his life, in surgeries every two or three months. After the energy treatments, no further carcinomas developed for the year that he was tracked. "The only thing he could attribute [the change] to was the treatment," says Dr. Fahrion. "He'd done nothing else different."

The other three patients' carcinomas began to reappear later.

"We feel they needed more treatment," Dr. Fahrion stated in his report. Six other patients had equivocal or no noticeable results. Dr. Fahrion noted that those whom the healers perceived as having a more balanced energy field in the initial assessment had the best outcome.

Two of the patients whom the healers had assessed as being the most depressed were among those who did not show any improvement. One of these was a woman whose son had recently been murdered. The healer who worked with her predicted she would die in a few months. "She couldn't access energy," the healer told Dr. Fahrion. Instead of dying, Dr. Fahrion reported, she was less depressed by the following year.

Dr. Fahrion concluded that a larger, more comprehensive study was necessary. "The findings of significant effects were modest," he noted in his final report. "This study needs replication with better standardization of camera-client distances and the use of color film and a longer treatment period." Three years later, such a follow-up to the original pilot study has not yet been funded.

One more study, the first ever of distant healing and AIDS, which was published in the *The Western Journal of Medicine* in December 1998, also bears highlighting.

In this study, half of forty end-stage AIDS patients received distant healing sessions for an hour a day, six days a week, for ten weeks. The study found that distant spiritual healing treatments reduced the number of illnesses in twenty AIDS patients, the number of doctor visits, the length of hospitalizations, and the amount of medicines required compared to twenty people in the control group. The healers and patients never met, and the patients had no idea that long-distance healing sessions were taking place.

The *New England Journal of Medicine*, the journal *Science*, and the *British Medical Journal*, all turned down publication of this study. Some of the doctors and scientists who reviewed it found fault with the statistical analyses. Others dismissed the entire premise of the research as being inappropriate.

Adjunct associate scientist at California Pacific Medical Center Fred Sicher, who ran the study with Elisabeth Targ, M.D., clinical director of psychosocial oncology research at California Pacific, says he is not surprised. To scientists subscribing to a Newtonian view of reality, reading the study would be a little like a thirteenth-century European, sure that the Earth was flat, going on a trip around the world.

"There is resistance to these findings. It's controversial stuff," says Sicher. The study had the backing of California Pacific president and CEO, Martin Brotman, M.D. But one researcher notes that even at California Pacific, "as many scientists became aware of these results, they became threatened. They walked around saying, 'Oh God, we've turned into a flaky outfit.'"

Three

Shifting Paradigms

I understand why Emily Rosa and the editors of *JAMA* thought energy healing had to be a hoax. The first time I watched a healing I thought I might be witnessing a mass hallucination. In January 1995, as part of my investigation of healing for a magazine, I watched a sophomore class demonstration at the Barbara Brennan School of Healing, the biggest school for energy healing in the world. Some 150 students, ranging from medical doctors to psychologists, and from housewives to a colonel in the U.S. Army Reserve, sat in rapt attention in the ballroom-turned-lecture hall of a Central Islip, New York, hotel.

Brennan, a bubbly blonde woman then in her late fifties, called a student, a twenty-eight-year-old musician and son of a physician, to the makeshift stage to be the client. Soon Brennan was discussing the "plate" or "shield" over his heart. Much to my amazement, others seemed to know exactly what she was talking about. I couldn't see a thing.

I never saw the "plate" over the student's heart. I never saw Brennan lift "it" out, even though others did. For all I could see, she just waved her hands about, claiming to be doing this and that. Could everyone around me have been brainwashed? I wondered. When I talked to the student a few weeks later he told me he felt the healing had subtly improved his relationship with his father. But that wasn't something anyone could measure. No one had documented changes in his blood counts or the rhythms of his heart or brain with EKGs and EEGs. There was nothing tangible to convince me something had happened.

It wasn't much better the next few times I observed workshops where healers did demonstrations and taught healing techniques. At the urging of several healers, I even laid hands on a few people. I could not even sense the chakras. Nor could I affect a person's blood pressure, or inspire an epiphany if you held a gun to my head. Yet I watched healers stir revelations in people as they lay on the table, seemingly just by laying hands on them. I also followed some cases in which doctors and medical tests verified changes in medical conditions after healings.

I might as well have been transported from the eighteenth century, a time when electricity and magnetism had not yet been "discovered," into a twentieth-century living room where the television was on in full color, and the electric lights were burning bright. That is how much like magic the effects of subtle energy seemed to me.

Finally, in February 1995 I decided to see what it would be like to have a treatment myself. My attitude was: prove it. Dianne Arnold, a cheerful, blonde woman in her 40s, was then a newly-minted graduate of the Brennan school and a former general partner in a brokerage firm. She seemed like a down-to-earth person as she led me upstairs to the parlor room of her Brooklyn town house. As she sat me down on her couch, she asked me to describe my "presenting complaint." Although I have suffered from frequent migraine headaches for most of my life, I didn't think of myself as having any physical problems. But like so many people, I certainly wanted to be happier. I especially wanted to understand my romantic relationships better.

Arnold seemed to feel that she could help. (I was dubious. I had been through years of psychoanalysis. I understood some of the causes of my anxiety, but I had not changed in any fundamental way.) I lay down on the table in her small healing room and closed my eyes. After a few minutes I had the strangest sensation of something spinning inside of me, but not in my body. I sat up with a start. Arnold was holding a pendulum over my abdomen, which esoteric literature describes as the location of the third chakra. I had felt my chakra spin. (I never before or since have had such an experience.) It turned out to be the highlight of the session. Other than that, I just felt so relaxed, it was almost like I had been drugged.

By the end of the session, I even wondered if I had made up the sensation of my chakra spinning. Nevertheless, I tried a few more sessions. They were all pleasant. I drifted off into a kind of sleep. I was in a good mood afterwards. Arnold described being guided to draw flowering vines on my "etheric" body during one session. After another, she told me three goddesses came and did the healing while she stood and "held the space." She had never heard of one of the Goddesses. "She says her name is Sweet Mother," Arnold reported. She had a lovely poetic imagination. I had to give her that. But I was losing patience. I did not see any particular benefit. The fifth session, which I assumed would be my last, was the turning point. I almost walked out on it.

On that visit Arnold announced that she would work on my neck. "You have quills in your neck," she said. I looked at her: Was she utterly crazy? Then it occurred to me she was speaking metaphorically. "There really are quills," Arnold insisted. "Someone's been throwing barbs at you when you try to speak your truth. The quills are on the right side," she continued. "That means that they were thrown by men."

I got up to leave. But something made me stay to give healing one final test. As I lay on the healing table, I fell into that state of pleasant, slightly drugged relaxation (which I now know is a sign I have entered an altered state of consciousness from the energy). Then Arnold reached my neck. I suddenly experienced the most irritating stinging sensation. "Whatever you're doing, that hurts," I announced as calmly as I could. The sensation was so annoying I wanted to kill her. Even so, I wondered if it was the power of suggestion at work.

"I'm just removing the quills," she said. "It'll be over in a minute."

"Are the 'quills' going to come back?" I asked, sarcasm in my voice, after the session ended. I couldn't help it. I had felt something. But certainly not imaginary quills. "Not unless you let them," she said.

I didn't give these "quills" another thought. I left this woman's house certain I would never return. I flew to Colorado to ski with my brother and his family. At the end of a lovely week, my brother and I got into an argument. I'm sorry to say this, but it was not especially unusual. In the middle of our exchange, however, I suddenly became aware that he was far more nasty than he needed to be. "You can't speak to me that way," I said quietly. "If you do, I will never visit you here again." I had never held my ground like that before. He was furious. (He remained angry with me for more than a year, but our relationship has since become smoother and more mutually respectful.)

Only when I was on the plane returning to New York did I remember the "quills." My brother had thrown a barb at me, and I didn't let it stick. Suddenly, I felt in my bones that the way I responded was connected to the energy session. It was as if I was a computer and someone had gone in and reset my programming ever so slightly, smoothing out a glitch. To me, it was both subtle and astonishing. It was only then that I became convinced that energy healing was real.

Later a few of the earlier sessions that I had dismissed turned out to be extremely significant, too. I learned over time that subtle energy affected me more like a letter or a poem or a song than a pill, in the sense that its significance and impact unfolded over time. Indeed, when I was taken to meet a Hindu guru, I did not notice any effect for many months, although the impact turned out to be profound. But I found that even seemingly basic healings sessions often made more sense a day or a week or even months later, as the energy and consciousness percolated its way through my system.

Eventually, I had many other experiences, in the course of my research on subtle energy healing that I would have said were impossible until I had them. One of the biggest shocks was my first long-distance healing session, in which I literally felt a healer run energy through my body and release a migraine headache—the kind that, for me, usually lasts for several days and is impervious to prescription medication—although at the time we were on opposite coasts. How could someone 3,000 miles away affect my system? It's one of the great mysteries of spiritual healing, although a few scientists have some interesting ideas.

Belief is like a container. It shapes our understanding of reality. Change the belief and reality changes, just as when you pour water from a bottle into a pot it will change its shape.

We do not change our beliefs as easily as water changes its shape. Most of us prefer to have things stay just the way they are. We cannot conceive of things being any different, even when the evidence stares us in the face. In the course of my reporting I have seen many examples of this in myself and in others.

Almost everyone I interviewed for this book had trouble, at first, believing that subtle energy was real. When she began to see auras, Rosalyn Bruyere thought she was going crazy. Deb Schnitta, a registered nurse and Flow Alignment and Connection energy practitioner in Pittsburgh, Pennsylvania, was so frightened when energy started running through her hands that she went to see someone for help. "Make this stop," she pleaded. And the person she consulted replied, "I can't. But I can help you understand it."

Meanwhile, Alan Hayes, a forensic accountant by training and now also a healer, recalls going to a weekend workshop taught by Barbara Brennan just to please his then-wife, and getting on a table only because "my accountant mind kicked in. I paid so many hundreds of dollars, if I didn't volunteer, I wouldn't get my money's worth." When a healer laid hands on him, he says, "I could feel his hands inside my body. It was an astonishing event."

Some people could not seem to believe subtle energy was real, even though it seemed to affect their system. Once, a family friend, a retired *Wall Street Journal* editor, decided to go see a healer. After a routine cataract operation, he developed a raging infection in the eye, which his doctor failed to notice for ten days. The doctor treated the eye infection but warned him that his sight in that eye was probably gone forever. The retired editor was so devastated he was willing to trying anything—even something as "out there" as healing. He realized he did not have much to lose.

After the session, this normally shy, retiring intellectual told me he thought he was going to hear the angels in heaven play their trumpets at any minute as he had his healing. The day after the session, the editor's sight began to return, which his doctor (unaware of the healing) called "miraculous." But, the doctor warned, the pressure in the eye from fluid buildup was still dangerously high.

The editor went back for another healing session. In a follow-up visit to his doctor, he learned the pressure in his eye had dropped. By now, the editor was nearly a convert to energy medicine. Then his retina detached. The doctor attributed it to all the insults the eye had received during surgery, infection, and examinations. Despite his earlier euphoria, the editor concluded that healing was bogus, the results he had gotten mere coincidence. He never had another session. He had an operation to repair the retina. He has vision in his eye, but it is no more clear than before he ever had the cataract operation.

On another occasion, I held a state of grace and unconditional love (something I learned in the course of my research) for a highly successful person who had recently been given a diagnosis of a potentially fatal illness. This person was so upset at the thought of dying, and of all the things that could have been done differently during a long and beautiful life, that sleep was all but impossible. According to the spouse, who was also present, the person became calmer than in many years (let alone since the diagnosis). If that comfort had come in the form of a pill, this person would have begged for more. But going to a healer was out of the question.

Other people learned about energy healing as a last resort. "I don't believe in it. I don't not believe in it. It's the end result I look at," says a Manhattan businessman whose heart condition temporarily stabilized after several healings. "I find it amazing. People look at me like I'm crazy when I talk about it. So I don't talk about it."

A professor at an Ivy League business school who pursued spiritual healing, instead of radiation, as a surgical follow-up, watched his PSA test for prostate cancer rapidly become normal. Before his illness, he says, "I had no clue, not a clue that this exists. And anything that would have crossed my path, I would have dismissed this stuff out of hand. . . . A paradigm is a very powerful frame of reference which affects what you see." Now, he says, "I don't mind thinking differently than some very smart people. . . . I'm going to keep learning. I don't begin to sense the outer limits of this stuff."

Nancy Reuben, M.D., a Harvard medical school graduate, recalls being told by a psychic early in her medical career to get one of her kidneys checked out. She dismissed the advice. Four years later, she lost the kidney but in the process of became a convert to energy medicine.

"We are energy," she says. "So it makes sense to work on the level of energy. Physical medicine is important, too. Ideally, I'd be practicing in a complementary care center."

Many prominent scientists still cannot accept the existence of subtle energy. It does not fit into the Newtonian model of reality, on which science, especially medicine, is currently based. For instance, when Harvard Medical School researchers Dr. Herbert Benson, and Dr. David Eisenberg, went to China in 1983, they were treated to several demonstrations of *chi gong*. As Dr. Eisenberg recounts in *Encounters with Qi*, a *chi gong* master sent *chi* (the same as *qi*), without touching, to Dr. Eisenberg, another Harvard medical doctor and Ph.D., and Dr. Benson's own son. They all reported distinct tingling sensations. Dr. Benson had, by then, spent much of his career studying the effects of meditation (considered in Eastern traditions to be a form of internal *chi* or consciousness control). But he dismissed the experiences of his colleagues and son as the power of suggestion.

When a *chi gong* master then lit a fluorescent bulb with his bare hands, Dr. Benson, who now runs Harvard's annual conference on Spirituality and Healing In Medicine, concluded it was probably a form of static electricity or fraud. Besides, he knew that to talk about what they were seeing would be a form of scientific suicide. As Dr. Eisenberg recalls in *Encounters*, Dr. Benson warned, "If you tried to publish a description of this sort of observation in any scientific journal, critics would skin you alive, and they'd have a right to."

More than a decade later in *Timeless Healing: The Power and Biology of Belief*, Dr. Benson remained wary of the existence of *chi*. His own brief study of a spiritual healer had mixed results, he noted. Even as he undertook such research, he admitted, "I was always hesitant to start such studies, worried that I might take my interests in remembered wellness too far and jeopardize my credibility in the field."

A paradigm is a set of beliefs shared by almost everyone in a particular group at a given time. Collective beliefs are powerful indeed, so powerful that few people can see past them. For instance, as Dr. Larry Dossey points out, in the 1840s obstetrician Ignaz Philipp Semmelweiss came up with the radical idea that if doctors washed their hands fewer women would die in childbirth. The hygienic measures he instituted brought deaths from the complications of childbirth from 9.92 percent to 1.27 percent a year. But he was laughed out of Vienna and hounded out of medicine. What, after all, would a doctor washing *his* hands have to do with preventing fever in a patient?

Even when, a few decades later, Louis Pasteur suggested that microbes caused infectious disease, the idea was far from acceptable. The Academy of Medicine in France expelled Pasteur, while a fellow scientist was so offended he challenged Pasteur to a duel.

Indeed, the list of scientists' resistance to new ideas is almost endless. As Dr. Dossey also noted in the premiere issue of *Alternative Therapies*, when Kepler proposed in the 1600s that tides were caused by the gravitational pull of the moon, Galileo declared, "These are the ravings of a madman! Kepler believes in action at a distance!" When Guglielmo Marconi, the inventor of radio, proposed that invisible waves moving through space could carry information across long distances, his friends briefly had him committed.

Meanwhile, Ernst Mach, a physicist whose work inspired Einstein, thought the theory of relativity was ridiculous. And the man who developed the modern theory of the atom, Thomas Rutherford, dismissed the concept of atomic power as "moonshine." Lord Kelvin, the scientist who gave the world the Kelvin temperature scale, was sure that X-rays were a hoax. And when the French Academy of Science invited a demonstration of the phonograph, a scientist leaped from his chair, seized the exhibitor and shouted, "I won't be taken in by your ventriloquist!"

Max Planck, one of the founders of quantum physics, noted in his autobiography that science progresses funeral by funeral. "A new scientific truth does not triumph by convincing its opponents and making them see the light, but rather because its opponents eventually die, and a new generation grows up that is familiar with it."

Right now, a small but growing group of leading doctors, scientists and healers, from Nobel laureate physicist Brian Josephson, Ph.D., at Cambridge University to Dr. Dossey to Robert Jahn, Ph.D., dean emeritus of Princeton's School of Engineering and Applied Science, believe we may need to go through a paradigm shift to advance into the next phase of our development. Consciousness studies, of which spiritual and intentional healing are subcategories, has become an emerging science. Studies of consciousness cross nearly every discipline: from psychology to physics to artificial intelligence to medicine.

Apollo 14 Astronaut Edgar Mitchell is a pioneer in the area. On the return from his historic flight to the moon, he says he experienced "the presence of divinity." He founded the Institute of Noetic Sciences in Sausalito, California, in 1973. The Institute funds research into the nature of consciousness, including energy healing and distant healing.

The University of Arizona recently created a Center for Consciousness Studies, the first in the nation, supported by a $1.4 million three-year grant from The Fetzer Institute. And the Princeton Engineering Anomalies Research (PEAR) lab at Princeton University has been studying consciousness, especially human mind-machine interactions for twenty years.

In controlled experiments, scientists are finding that what the mystics have always said is true: We—our minds and our spirits—are intimately involved in the creation of physical reality. "Nothing less than a seriously expanded model of reality, one that allows consciousness a proactive role in the establishment . . . of the physical world will be required," asserts Dr. Jahn, now a professor of aerospace engineering at Princeton and director of the PEAR lab, who has been overseeing one of the longest-running empirical experiments on the nature of consciousness. Dr. Jahn believes that energy and matter and information may all be different forms of the same thing.

He and PEAR lab manager Brenda Dunne, along with many other scientists studying healing, and healers themselves, believe these changes have implications that go far beyond how we will practice medicine in the future. These recent scientific findings, say Dr. Jahn and Dunne, hold "sweeping implications for our view of ourselves, our relationship to others, and to the cosmos in which we exist."

"The whole field of alternative medicine is a big part of this picture. It's a big part, because it touches everybody. It's a way of communicating these ideas in a meaningful way," adds William Gough, president of the Foundation for Mind-Being Research in Los Altos, California, who previously oversaw research and funding in fusion and physics for the Atomic Energy Commission, the Electric Power Research Institute, and the United States Department of Energy.

The new research comes not a moment too soon. After all, spiritual and mystical experiences are among the most pervasive of all phenomena, as Dr. Jahn and Dunne note in *Margins of Reality*, a book about the relationship of science and spirituality, and the convergence they are documenting in laboratory experiments.

Even today, in an age when many people worship science as a religion, millions of people report mystical experiences such as near-death experiences, visitations from angels, psychic visions, and guidance from spiritual forces and beings. A survey published in *Time* magazine in 1996 found that 82 percent of Americans believe in the healing power of prayer; 77 percent believe that God sometimes intervenes to cure people who have a serious illness. Thousands have recovered from addictions by turning over their troubles to a "higher power," as taught by Alcoholics Anonymous and other support groups. Mothers since the dawn of time have "known" when their children are in danger. And millions of people extract meaning from their dreams and make decisions based on their "gut."

Many of our greatest scientists have been mystics, note Dr. Jahn and Dunne. Isaac Newton, who developed the theory of gravity, was a mystic and alchemist. He regarded the ultimate power in the universe to reside in "the mystery by which mind could control matter." And Albert Einstein, the father of atomic energy, often invoked God. "The most beautiful and most profound emotion we can experience is the sensation of the mystical," he noted. "It is the sower of all true science."

The search for metaphysical illumination, "is the only place science has ever been," asserts Brenda Dunne, manager of the

PEAR lab. "If you look at history, there's always been an underground stream. . . . It's an underground current. But it's actually pushing science."

The concept of God and other mystical beliefs were also woven into the very fabric of the United States by the founding fathers, who were Free Masons, students of metaphysics. To this day, thanks to them, "In God We Trust" is stamped on our money, along with representations of the third eye of spiritual insight and the pyramid, both symbols of power from Egyptian mysticism. It was their way of setting the intention for a nation where people would be free to realize their full potential, according to healer and spiritual historian Rosalyn Bruyere. "It was quite calculated," she says.

Nevertheless, for centuries, we in the West have divided the world into spiritual phenomena and natural phenomena, as if all phenomena were not natural. To put it another way, we came to believe that some natural laws were more God's laws than others. Faith and spiritual experiences were dismissed as delusions that had no basis in fact. Scientists drew their conclusions about spiritual reality in a most unscientific way: without ever using the scientific method. They drew a line and said spirit was outside of science and the scientific method altogether. This strange division between worlds has guided all of our scientific inquiry and has created many of the filters through which most of us experience our day-to-day life.

Many historians trace the split between science and spirituality back to the Middle Ages, when scientists were sometimes persecuted by the Catholic Church. For instance, thirteenth-century Franciscan monk Roger Bacon, whose experiments led to the invention of eyeglasses and telescopes, spent twenty-two years in jail, accused of practicing magic. Astronomer Giordano Bruno was burned as a heretic. Galileo was threatened with excommunication for teaching that the Earth revolved around the sun.

Especially after seventeenth-century mathematician Rene Descartes divided the world into mind and matter, scientists increasingly focused on the material world. Even Sigmund Freud, M.D., who first identified the unconscious mind as a powerful force affecting people's lives, dismissed religion as "infantile helplessness" and "regression to primary narcissism." (Carl Jung, M.D., his one-time protégé, however, went in the other direction, writing openly about reincarnation, symbolism, the collective unconscious, and many other mystical experiences.)

Scientific rationalism even influenced religion. "The religious groups had to be creatures of the Enlightenment," explains David Baird, minister of the Putnam United Methodist Church in Putnam, Connecticut. Even today, Reverend Baird notes, "The training we get is ninety-nine percent intellectual, theological and philosophical. There is very little on the cultivation of the spirit." For the last few centuries, he notes, many religions have "tried to package religion in a way society could accept." When he did hands on healing as a Lutheran minister, he recalls, "People felt it was getting into magic. They thought I was leaving orthodox Christianity."

Scientists have at times tried to rectify the split, according to Jahn and Dunne. In the late 1880s, for example, a group of leading scientists, including Marie Curie (who discovered X rays), William Crookes (inventor of the cathode ray tubes used in televisions), and Nobel laureates J. J. Thompson (discoverer of the electron) and Lord Rayleigh (a physicist), argued that paranormal events ought to be followed up with scientific study. Together with intellectuals such as philosopher and Harvard professor William James and writer Mark Twain, they founded two sister organizations, the Society for Psychical Research in London and the American Society for Psychical Research in Boston.

In the end, it was the "hardest" science of all—physics—that paved the way back to the mystical experience that lies at the center of existence. At the dawn of the twentieth century, physicists were patting themselves on the back for having solved nearly all the questions regarding the nature of physical reality. That is when the material world began to unravel.

In 1905 Albert Einstein, then working in a Swiss patent office, published his revolutionary equation $E=mc^2$. In one stroke, he showed that mass (matter) and energy (electromagnetic frequencies) are two different forms of the same thing. Matter, it turns out, is just condensed energy, as Michio Kaku, a professor of theoretical physics at the City College of the City University of New York, explains in *Hyperspace*. Or, put another way, everything is a manifestation of light (energy), including us.

Around the same time, other discoveries gave birth to quantum physics. Since the seventeenth century, when Sir Isaac Newton described the forces of nature, scientists have imagined the physical world to be as predictable as a machine. Even today, if you kick a ball at a specific speed in a specific direction, a scientist can describe with mathematical certainty when and where it will land.

Then quantum physicists peered inside the atoms, which are considered the building blocks of matter. They found mostly empty space. Inside of matter, tiny wave particles vibrate at astonishingly high frequencies. We only look solid. The subatomic world, it turns out, is an ever changing pattern of organic flux and motion. Light waves can behave as photon particles. What we think of as electron particles can just as easily become waves. Waves are infinite. They spread out in space. (Just think of a candle light in an otherwise dark room.)

Consequently, at the subatomic level reality is not fixed. Things are just more, or less, likely. Subatomic wave particles can even "tunnel" through supposedly impenetrable barriers. They show up in places where technically they are not "allowed." According to quantum physics, "there is a finite probability that seemingly implausible events can happen," explains professor Kaku.

These findings changed the way scientists understood physical reality. "This is a horrible thing," the late Noble laureate Richard Feynman once said, only half-jokingly, of the uncertainty that exists. "Philosophers have said before that one of the fundamental requisites of science is that whenever you set up the same conditions, the same thing must happen. This is simply not true, it is not a fundamental condition of science."

Quantum weirdness hardly ends there. Photons can behave as waves or particles. When a scientist sets up an experiment to study waves, the scientist finds only waves. If he designs an experiment to study subatomic particles, he observes only particles. Merely by setting an intention for the experiment and observing the results, the scientist participates in the creation of reality. And, eerily, subatomic wave-particles seem to respond to the environment.

For this reason, some scientists believe these wave-particles are conscious.

The "weirdest" part of quantum "weirdness" is called nonlocality. When scientists separate a pair of subatomic particles, they continue to communicate instantaneously, as if time and space do not exist. One particle knows instantly what "decision" the other particle makes. If the Big Bang theory of the universe is correct, then all particles (including all people) are thus entangled.

Quantum physics has already been used in the world of macroscopic things to create computers and lasers. Yet many physicists, including Professor Kaku, insist the laws of quantum physics don't apply to multibillion atomic clusters like us. They believe statistical laws take over. Others see it differently. As Gary Zukav writes in *The Dancing Wu Li Masters*, one of the most illuminating texts on quantum physics for nonscientists:

> *The philosophical implication of quantum mechanics is that all of the things in our universe (including us) that appear to exist independently are actually parts of one all-encompassing organic pattern, and that no parts of that pattern are ever really separate from it or from each other.*

Modern descriptions of the universe echo the most sacred religious texts, as Zukav notes. "The universe appears as a single, undivided whole," observes contemporary physicist David Peat. "A human being . . . experiences himself, his thoughts and feelings as something separated from the rest, a kind of optical delusion of his consciousness," Albert Einstein once said. And the late physicist David Bohm, a protégé of Einstein's, hypothesized an "implicate order," or holomovement, out of which the manifest world or "explicate order" evolves, much as healers describe a physical world arising out of a subtle or spiritual domain. In the holomovement, everything is a pattern of conscious light waves.

With quantum physics, the Eastern idea that everything is a play of consciousness suddenly seems like more than a spiritual metaphor. "Consciousness is that by which this world first becomes manifest," asserted one of the original quantum physicists, Nobel Laureate

Erwin Shrödinger. "You can't be sure if all things are made of atoms—it's an assumption," adds Amit Goswami, a professor of physics at the University of Oregon writing in *The Self-Aware Universe*. "Suppose all things, including atoms, are made of consciousness instead?"

Suddenly, the world of spiritual healing doesn't seem so inexplicable, at least to a handful of leading scientists and doctors. If a researcher affects the behavior of photons and electrons just by thinking about them, then why couldn't a person affect the photons and electrons of another person by thinking of that person? "Could the confinement of the mind to the brain be an illusion?" asks Dr. Dossey, one of the first physicians to recognize the relationship between healing and quantum physics.

"What is a healer doing?" asks William Gough, of the Foundation for Mind-Being Research, who developed a model that links healing to nonlocal realms with physicist Robert Shacklett, Ph.D. "Coming in through a subatomic level. Picking up what these electromagnetic fields are doing." In some cases, Gough and Dr. Shacklett hypothesize, healing may start in very high spiritual realms beyond time and space and form, before reaching even the subatomic level. From a scientific perspective, they speculate that this high spiritual realm and the realm of the mind begin at the Planck Length, 1.6×10^{-33} cm. (The Planck Length is twenty orders of magnitude smaller than an elementary particle. It is far beyond the reach of any probe of high energy physics. Physicists believe it is the "bottom" of physical space.)

Then, through intent and resonance, Gough believes, healers "are moving charge and changing the spin of [subatomic particles]. I think that's what's going on." Ultimately, changing the charge on ions in our bodies changes molecular structures, which changes meaning and function. "It changes neuropeptides and their receptors," he asserts. "Since the neuropeptides and receptors are the actual underpinnings of our conscious awareness, we experience changes in our emotions, beliefs, and expectations."

Right now, Gough notes, this is just one theory. Most scientists have not even thought about these issues. Direct experimental proof will not be simple. As Gough notes, no physicist has ever touched or seen a quantum particle directly. What can be measured is the impact of subtle energy on the heart rate, biochemical reactions, and other electromagnetic frequency changes in the body. "I do a healing on you," says Gough. "And there's a change. Your DHEA levels go up. I check your heart rate. It becomes more peaceful. I can see all these changes. Those are the effects."

Biophysicist Elmer Green, one of the founders of biofeedback, is the first, and so far the only, scientist to test the hypothesis that subtle energy is coupled to the electromagnetic spectrum (just as electricity and magnetism are coupled). He was first taught about spiritual law by a spiritualist minister in the 1930s who channeled "The Teacher," and has been a life-long meditator and user of visualization and dreams. Unlike many other modern scientists, he was open to the reality of spiritual dimensions.

In a series of experiments conducted at the Menninger Clinic in Topeka, Kansas, between 1988 and 1993, Dr. Green asked ten "normal" meditators to meditate in a special "Copper-Wall" room. It was designed so that anyone in it would be unable to pull up an electrical charge from the ground or their surroundings. As the subjects meditated, Dr. Green monitored the electrical potentials in their body, attaching wires to their skin.

Then Dr. Green repeated the experiment with fourteen psychically sensitive people, including healers Rosalyn Bruyere, Mietek Wirkus, Ethel Lombardi, and six other nationally known healers. Mietek Wirkus, who told me once that he focuses constantly on Jesus's love and mercy, went first. When he began meditating, the machines monitoring the electrical charge on his skin went absolutely wild. "It was off the scale," recalls research associate Peter Parks. "The equipment was flashing zeros."

The scientists assumed their equipment had broken. But when they inspected they found nothing wrong. The normal meditators had never hit a surge in body potential that came close to approaching four volts (what might be expected from moving an arm or a head). But Dr. Green and his team realized they had to reset the equipment to record a wider range of electrical charges. As the experiment unfolded, the healers produced unheard of surges in their electrical body potential: from 4 volts to 221 volts.

These surges in electrical potential in the body are 10,000 times larger than EKG recordings and 100,000 times larger than EEG recordings. "From a physics point of view, the results are not explainable," says Dr. Green. "Something is going on."

During healing sessions, healers produced even more, and more intense, voltage surges. One healer had sixty-nine body potential surges, ranging from 4.1 to 122.4 volts, with a mean of 14.7. Another healer had eighty-six body potential surges ranging from 4.1 to 162.1 volts, with a mean of 21 volts. One healer who had a flat recording during meditation produced forty-five surges in four therapy sessions.

Dr. Green did not examine the question of whether the healing sessions produced measurable results in the patients, because such studies are so broadly ignored or attacked. "We approached the question as physicists, measuring electricity," he explains. "If a healer has a healing effect on patients, there must be a detectable change in the physiology of the healer. It's hard to argue about volt meters."

Dr. Green believes the dramatic electrical surges he documented in the healers is an indication that healers "have a different 'energy structure' or a different 'energy-handling capability,' than untrained people," he noted in *Subtle Energies*, the premiere peer-reviewed journal on subtle energy research, which Green founded in 1990.

He hypothesizes that four grades of subtle energy exist, just as Hindu literature describes four grades of *prana*. The most "dense" subtle energy, in his view, is electricity. And the spiritual mind, Green speculates, lies beyond the subtle energies. He calls the mind, "the organizing principle at every level of substance. . . . Mind is linked with the body by a set of Maxwell-like equations that manipulate the four subtle energies, and these in turn manipulate the body." And, he adds, "all matter in the physical cosmos—solid, liquid, gas—also has the four subtle energies."

"In fifty years, what we're talking about is going to be old hat," says Dr. Green. "We'll be photographing the aura and have classifications in evaluating healers, and offering classes at universities to teach people."

Gough, too, is convinced that eventually, the old beliefs are "going to go, like the fall of the Berlin Wall. The evidence points in only one direction."

In the meantime, many healers already live in a world in which there is far more to being human than most of us have ever dreamed. They, too, are scientists, according to *Webster's Unabridged Dictionary*, which defines science as "systemized knowledge derived from observations, study, and experiment carried on in order to determine the nature and principles of what is being studied."

Part Two

Four

Anatomy of the Soul

Each year in May Rosalyn Bruyere holds an intensive retreat for healers at the Holy Family Monastery in Hartford, Connecticut. One afternoon of this retreat is set aside as a teaching forum in which people with a particular kind of complaint come in for healings. In 1998 the focus was on healing people with damaged spinal columns.

The recreation room where the group convened had been transformed into a healing sanctuary, with a few hanging Tankas, silk pictures of Tibetan Bonpo masters, and at the front, on the mantle, a series of simple blue candles in glass jars, burning in honor of spirit. There was something else in the room, too, invisible *intent*, bending events to their highest order. The *intent* had been set by Bruyere and her senior ministers even before the intensive began. In fact, if you tried to trace the *intent*, it would lead you back to the first moments when the intensive was actively planned. The students in the room had been "cooking" in that heightened force field now for three days. When they left after five days together, in subtle ways they would not be quite the same as before they came. Neither would the people who came for healings.

A slender man wearing wire-frame glasses and a sober demeanor arrived first, brought by the minister of a nearby Methodist church who had studied with Bruyere more than a decade earlier. The young man was a seminary student who had spent the last twelve years studying to fulfill his dream of becoming a minister. To support his wife and two children, he worked as a janitor, washing floors and doing other menial labor. Because of constant pain, the man's doctors were urging him to have surgery, which he wanted to avoid.

The young man handed Bruyere his MRI pictures. He had three herniated discs in his neck. In addition, five discs in his lower back had calcified and fused together. Bruyere scanned the MRI pictures, which showed how the seminary student's spinal cord grew increasingly squeezed as it moved down from cervical disc four to seven. Bruyere could also *see* the underlying problem. "Oh," she said cheerfully, "there's no room for your soul to come in."

She asked the young man to lie face down on the massage table as 160 of Bruyere's students sat expectantly, waiting for Bruyere's magic to unfold. The healings she did in a group might not happen in a different setting. Bruyere gathered all the energy of the group to use in the healings.

As she set to work at the base of his spine, I could see and feel her heart open, like a sun, and gently take the young man in. She held her graceful fingers, elongated by perfectly manicured nails, over his sacrum for a few minutes. Not finding a pulse, she moved to his feet and sent energy up his entire body through his legs. When she returned to his spine, she called on two senior healers to continue charging the man's field. One took his feet, the other his head. Slowly, Bruyere moved up along the patient's spine, vertebrae by vertebrae, asking him if he could feel the energy as she ran it between her thumb on one side of his spine, and her fingers on the other side. He could not. He could sense his usual physical pain; but to energy he was numb.

To the casual observer, it might seem as if Bruyere was merely moving her hands slowly up his spine. But in fact she was reaching into a dimension where the bones existed as energy and reshaping the damaged vertebrae as her hands played upon his spine. She could literally see the energy of his physical body shimmer beneath her hands. As solid bone, what she did would be impossible. As energy, the vertebrae were easy to remold. The energy she worked with was, in her experience, the matrix on which the cells grow. If

Bruyere successfully reshaped it, new cells would grow off the matrix to conform to the new shape.

When Bruyere reached the seminary student's neck, she gently separated the bones from each other to make room for his spinal cord—and his soul. Again, to the casual observer it would seem as if all she did was make a few slight movements of her fingers, nothing more.

In about half an hour Bruyere had finished her technical work. But she knew the seminary student might still get off the table and recreate the problem all over again. To a healer, the body, after all, is just the densest aspect of one's spiritual, mental, emotional, and physical energy bodies. Bruyere now talked with her patient about the underlying problem—the real cause of his pain.

"You're reaching up to your soul," Bruyere told her patient as he got up from the table. "Your soul is trying to reach your heart. They're working at cross purposes. You have to stop trying so hard."

He nodded. He told her his doctors would be taking another series of MRI pictures soon. "What you want to do for the next MRI to come out well is to let your soul come in," Bruyere advised, gently repeating herself.

The future Methodist minister thanked Bruyere and her students. Then he was on his way. "You can't tell people they create their own reality," Bruyere explained to her students later. "It is not about choice. It's about karma [unconscious patterning]. You can discipline [your energy] to work another way. But it's not a choice. It's not so simple."

The second patient of the day was a young woman in her early thirties, with girlish shoulder length hair, who tackled environmental issues for a living. Spunky, outgoing, and luminously intelligent, she was a one-time Fulbright scholar who earned her Ph.D. at Harvard University. For four years, she said, she had had constant pain from three herniated spinal discs located behind her heart. A friend from college, an ordained minister in Bruyere's church, arranged for her to have this session with Bruyere.

In the cosmology of spiritual healing, nerves are solar—directly related to the soul. But each soul and each injury is unique. This time, when Bruyere asked the woman to lie down she got right to work. Again, Bruyere's heart opened and radiated its light. A delicious warmth enveloped them both and subtly permeated the room. Bruyere began by charging the woman's energy field. "The disc material is like polymer clay," Bruyere said, as her fingers started to work the woman's spine. "Once it is shaped, it tends to hold that shape." A few minutes later, she reported, "I'm hydrating the space between the discs." Her hands moved up the woman's spine. "It's hot over the injury," she exclaimed. "It's sizzling."

Soon, Bruyere stood quietly, her hands firmly planted on the woman's lower back. She did not appear to be doing anything. Instead, I could feel her radiating love. It reminded me of the way young mothers hold their newborn infants. When Bruyere was finished, she helped the young woman off the table.

"There was a split between her emotions and thinking," Bruyere explained after the environmentalist left the room. "She was a professor at [a top University] by the time she was thirty. She's brilliant. I reparented her. I made a lot of space. I did some 'wombology'—for lack of a better word." Bruyere explained that the environmentalist, because of early issues with her mother, distrusted women. As she worked, she said, "There was an energetic dialogue. She said, 'Are you going to hurt me?' And I replied, 'I'm just here.'"

"The discs are cushions," Bruyere continued. "So I asked myself: 'In life, what would it be like for her to be in comfort and have ease in her life?'" Bruyere said she became the embodiment of the comfort and cushioning the environmentalist had never had. "She had a difficult mother," Bruyere summed up. "She wants the Earth to be big and loving. There's a big solar battle going on in her, and it's caught up in her discs. Sometimes," Bruyere added, "you're giving someone companionship in their pain so they are not in their pain alone."

The next morning the environmentalist reported that for the first time in four years, "I woke up without pain." She sounded happy and very surprised. She remained pain free for only a few days. "The whole emotional response eclipsed the physical response," explains Stacy Sabol, a senior minister and healer in the Healing Light

Center Church. The woman is now in counseling to explore her emotions.

The seminary student, too, ended up with a change in his physical condition. Two months after the healing, he went in for a new set of MRI pictures. When his doctors got the results they were baffled by one thing: his lower lumbar vertebrae were no longer fused. Sure that there was some mistake, they ordered a second set of MRI pictures. It confirmed the "inexplicable" change. The seventh cervical vertebrae, however, was still a problem. In December 1998 he had surgery. "He's still feeling inadequate about talking to God," explained Nancy Needham, an elder in Bruyere's church.

All energy healing is based on the idea that energy and consciousness underlies the physical and biochemical structures of the body (and the entire world). Healers say this energy and consciousness surrounds and permeates our bodies. It is more primary than our physical, material self, the template out of which our physical bodies and experiences arise.

"The human energy field isn't just an energy field," explains Barbara Brennan in *Light Emerging*. "It is the person. In fact, it is more the person than the physical body is. . . . You are energy. You are not in your physical body—your physical body is in you."

From the perspective of a healer, when a person gets sick, it is generally an indication that the person's subtle energy and consciousness is not open and flowing. The lack of flow creates energy blocks, which then prevent the cells from getting the frequencies of subtle energy they need. Most physical, emotional, mental, and spiritual "diseases" are a reflection of such energy distortions. Healers work largely at the level of energy. The energy then filters down, if it is for the highest good of the patient's spiritual unfoldment, into the physical plane of reality

At the most basic level, Mietec Wirkus explains, a healer jump-starts a patient's energy system. But when a healer lays hands on a client, he or she literally expands the client's awareness to a new level. "You amp up enough and when the aura gets big enough, something very specific takes place," explains Bruyere. "[The client] is going to make connections once their connections are put back—to information and data they didn't even know was there. An awful lot of character building, forgiving, repairing of old patterns in families happens naturally in the presence of increased energy."

A highly trained healer can hold a very precise state of being and intention. Skilled healers can also go in, as Bruyere did, and move subtle energy around to reshape organs, bones, and other tissues. "You can be much more direct and much more specific," says Bruyere. "You can reach in and move parts around and separate meaning from parts."

The levels of energy are seemingly infinite. All the different levels are also interrelated. For instance, if we have a physical illness, it often causes emotional distress. And emotional distress, such as anxiety or depression, has physical effects. In the same way, according to healers, what happens to us in the physical and emotional worlds also affects the soul and vice versa.

The spiritual world is vast. Many people, even many healers, do not realize that the spiritual realms consist of far more than the physical and auric dimensions. After the auric dimension comes a more subtle causal dimension. Some people call it the Light Body. Other healers access this dimension through states of being such as grace or Divine love, through universal gridlines, and through various Kabbalistic energies. There is also at least one dimension even more fundamental, the unmanifest. Reality changes exponentially with each more subtle dimension.

All these different levels of our being are nested, like a series of Russian dolls, in the same way that subatomic particles, atoms, and molecules and the entire physical structure of our bodies are nested. The most subtle energy is not any further away from you than your own physical body. In fact, the unmanifest is our very core. Some people believe the chakras are the transducers of energy and consciousness between the different dimensions, as well as within a single dimension such as the auric field.

Consciousness first takes on some kind of recognizable anatomical form within the central channel, located along the spine, and the chakras. According to the esoteric literature, the chakras create the seven levels of the auric field. Healers describe seven major chakras—vortices of energy—each located at a spot along the body's spinal column and associated with specific emotional and physical processes. (Minor chakras exist at every joint.) The chakras are the basis of spiritual anatomy, just as our bones and organs are the basis of physical anatomy.

The chakras were first described by Eastern, Egyptian, and Native American spiritual traditions that date back at least twenty thousand years. The experiences of thousands of healers and clients are consistent with the theory of chakras. But their existence has yet to be verified by scientists. Several researchers, including Dr. Becker however, have measured increased electrical activity around the area of the chakras. Healers can perceive these subtle realms because they have trained themselves to move into different dimensions of reality through meditation, energy healings, martial arts, prayer, and other practices. According to a healer, anyone can develop this ability to some degree, just as anyone can learn to paint or sing or master a sport. Proficiency requires a combination of innate talent and years of spiritual training.

The chakras take in energy and information and consciousness that is all around us and process it and distribute it to our physical, emotional, mental, and spiritual energy bodies. "The chakras in your aura are your energy receivers," Barbara Brennan explains in *Hands of Light*. "They look like vortices of energy that, by virtue of their spin, pull energy into them like any whirlpool. After the energy gets sucked into your body, it then flows along the energy lines in your field to your organs. Whenever there is a disruption in your field, your organs don't get the energy they need, and they become weak, eventually allowing access for infection or other physical problems."

Each chakra processes energy and consciousness that corresponds to specific physical, emotional, mental, and spiritual aspects of our being. An experienced healer will get different information from each chakra. "When we touch the auric field of a client, we're touching the client," says Dianne Arnold, a teacher at the Brennan school. "When you're on the fourth level [of the auric field, which is created by the heart chakra] you really start connecting with the person's heart. Some of my students start crying."

There is nothing more inherently mystical about the chakras than about our hearts, lungs, or cells. As Thomas Ayers, Ed.D., a graduate of Brennan's school notes, "Dogs have chakras, too." But chakras are mystical in that they do connect us to each other in profound and intimate ways. Our "vibration" or level of consciousness literally influences the "vibration" and level of consciousness of others. "If my heart chakra is actually open," explains Bruyere, "it should affect you and your whole aura. And if you're my child, even more so, because probably all my children reproduce all the cells of their young life under the influence of my aura."

The first chakra, at the base of the spine, is responsible for overall physical vitality, the health of our bones, and the energy in the legs. It regulates our sense of grounding, which includes our ability to be present and focused and centered on whatever we are doing. It looks red to those with clairvoyant vision. The kundalini—spiritual energy—also lies coiled like a snake in this chakra until it is "awakened" and thus begins to rise through the other chakras. The first chakra, in essence, regulates the basic life force. Athletes, for example, usually have very healthy first chakras and a lot of physical *chi.*

The second chakra, below the navel, runs in an orange frequency spectrum and feeds energy to the bladder, intestines and uterus. It also contains the feelings and emotions pertaining to one's self and drives our passions. "Your emotional inventory is set in utero by your mother," says Bruyere. "Gestation occurs right behind the mother's second chakra." She calls it the "primary center for attracting patterns. . . . You pull the people in that keep you the same."

If you're holding bitterness or resentment, Bruyere notes, the chakra turns from orange to amber. If the energy doesn't move at all, the chakra may turn the color of dried blood. The holding of second chakra energy, according to Bruyere, is "one reason osteoporosis is so prevalent in the best-fed nation in the world. It's also the basis for sugar addictions of all kinds. People eat emotionally, not biologically."

One school of thought believes the second chakra controls sexuality; another group of esoteric scholars believe the first chakra controls sexuality. Both schools of thought may be accurate. Because

The Chakra System

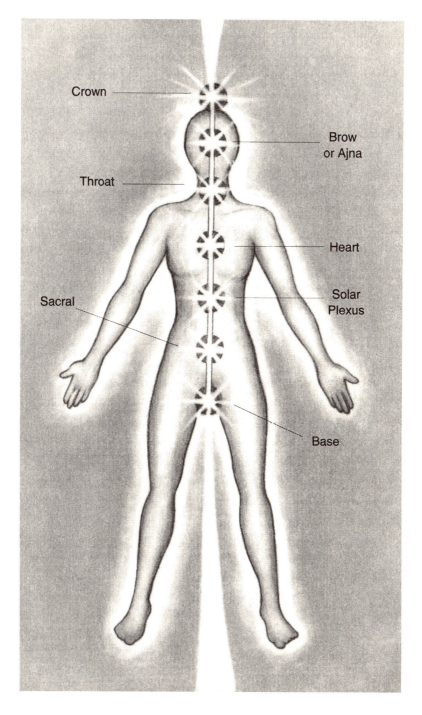

the first chakra is between the legs and faces down, it shares a *nadi* point (highway intersection) with the second chakra.

The third chakra, located at the solar plexus, feeds the pancreas, stomach, liver, and kidneys, according to Rosalyn Bruyere. It is the seat of the intellect and ego, and runs frequencies that are harmonics of yellow. We are connected in most of our relationships, including those with our parents and children, through lines of energy from the third chakra, according to Brennan and Bruyere. When these cords (and the relationships) have distortions or tears in them, it affects the chakra and the organs that it feeds.

Most people in the West suppress their first and second chakras, according to Bruyere and other healers. They overuse their third chakras. Bruyere says that many people walk around with little yellow fields. "Running yellow makes you dull," she warns her students repeatedly. The amplitude of yellow also has the smallest wave form of the seven primary colors, she notes, adding, "If you want to be smaller, be an intellectual. It's literal."

When all the chakras run yellow, Bruyere adds, "The body isn't being developed, the emotions aren't being developed, and compassion isn't being developed . . . and the spirit gets shoved up, or maybe out." A person running yellow throughout the aura "is not going to have visions. God is going to talk, and they're not going to hear."

The fourth chakra is located at the heart and feeds the heart, lungs, and thymus. It processes the pondered emotions that have been filtered through the third chakra. These emotions involve self and other, romantic love, judgment, trust, courage, honor, and acceptance. Judging, controlling, and manipulating constrict the heart, while surrender, courage, appreciation, and gratitude expand it. "The problem with protecting your heart, is pretty soon it's empty," says Bruyere. "You're not supposed to live a life where you are never hurt again." Spiritually, the heart is the great transducer between the personal and the universal, between the self and Christ consciousness. The heart chakra, which runs in harmonics of green, is a doorway to transformation and mystical union.

The fifth chakra, located at the throat, feeds energy into the thyroid, which in turn affects metabolism and issues of timing. It regulates our ability to speak the truth. It also regulates receiving, in

The Chakras: Linking Body, Mind, and Soul

Chakras	Color	Body	Gland	Involves
7	White	Ketheric	Pituitary	Surrender
6	Purple	Celestial	Pineal	Insight
5	Blue	Etheric	Thyroid	Expression Manifestation
4	Green	Astral	Thymus	Relationships Love/Compassion
3	Yellow	Mental	Adrenal	Opinions/Intellect
2	Orange	Emotional	Peyer's patches or Lymphatic	Emotions
1	Red	Physical	Gonads	Basic Vitality/Kundalini

Courtesy of Rosalyn Bruyere

general, and our ability to manifest and create what we want. A closed fifth chakra involves deprivation and lack. Bruyere and Brennan describe sound (including voice) as the physical aspect of spirit.

To make her point, I have seen Bruyere ask her students to chant "Aummmmmm. . . . Can you feel the vibration?" she asks. "Every sound has a physical effect on your body. Sound is very important. It's the physical part of the spiritual. Being your own word. Keeping your word is very valued in our culture. Your gift is what you say. It's how people receive your love. It's not just what your parents say, but also what they don't say." The color of the chakra is blue.

The sixth chakra, also known as the "third eye," energizes the pineal gland, according to one school of thought. (The other group teaches that the sixth chakra is connected to the pituitary gland. Both views may be right: The sixth and seventh chakras share a common *nadi* or root in the brain's third ventricle. It looks like a highway intersection.) The pineal gland registers the day-night cycle, secretes melatonin, serotonin, and dopamine, and also has been shown in recent research to be sensitive to the daily cycles of the Earth's magnetic field. Thus it processes electromagnetic information from the environment, according to researcher Dr. Robert Becker in *Cross Currents*.

Located in the middle of the forehead, slightly above the eyes, the sixth chakra is the center of clairvoyant vision and spiritual insight. (The vortex spins in harmonics of purple. It is also the location of the "third eye" of many primitive vertebrates, an organ used to measure the intensity of natural light.) Creative people, including Steven Spielberg and George Lucas, run "a lot of purple," notes Bruyere.

The seventh chakra, at the crown of the head, is associated with Divine Mind. To someone with clairvoyant vision, it is a vortex of white light. It is directly linked to the pituitary gland, according to one esoteric set of teachings. (Other clairvoyants believe this chakra feeds the pineal gland.) The pituitary is often called the master gland, because it produces hormones that control most other endocrine glands.

One of the personality functions of the crown chakra is directness, according to Bruyere. If someone's head is injured and the chakra is knocked off center, Bruyere says, a malaise or depression can set in. "They aren't getting guidance," she explains. "They're treated for depression. But they should be shoved back into place."

The chakras give a healer instant information about a person's overall physical, mental, emotional, and spiritual well-being. On the simplest level, if a person has a thyroid problem or trouble speaking up, it will be reflected in the spin of his or her fifth chakra. Alternatively, a healer looking at someone's field and seeing a weak fifth chakra will understand some of that person's emotional, physical, and spiritual issues.

The chakras are not separate from each other any more than water stirred by overlapping whirlpools would be separate, or two laser beams that intersect would be totally separate. In fact, the less interactive they are, the less integrated a person will be physically, emotionally, mentally, and spiritually. (In Bruyere's experience, multiple personality disorder is a condition that occurs when a person's chakras aren't "speaking" to each other. All of us, until all our chakras are fully open, have fragments of consciousness of which we are not aware. It is just a matter of degree.)

"The anatomy of the aura is as complex as human anatomy," says Bruyere. "When you play the note C and then you play A and then you play A and C together, it is much more complex than either A or C. And the same is true in healing."

When people feel that no one cares about them (second chakra), they may also have a parallel belief that God either does not exist or does not care (seventh chakra). And what is in the heart will also be in the voice. Bruyere illustrates by saying "I'm fine" in a completely flat and unconvincing tone. And, she adds, "If a man's voice breaks, then you know you're talking to a [man who was] wounded [as a] teenager."

The second, fourth, and sixth chakras process different aspects of emotion. Unresolved feelings of self-worth (second chakra) color how you receive others (fourth chakra) and how clearly you can see others (sixth chakra). For example, if you've been abused (second chakra), you may be abusive (fourth chakra) and you may not see your behavior or the behavior of other abusive people clearly (sixth chakra). Any emotional issue you do not see or see clearly will cause distortion in the sixth chakra, the seat of inner vision.

The first, third, fifth, and seventh chakras deal with more structured energies and create the structure of the auric field. The first level is a web of fine blue lines (visualize Spiderman) on which the cells of the physical body grow. When we have a physical trauma these lines get cut or tangled. If they are repaired, wounds heal more quickly, and in some cases, immediately. The third level is a gridwork for the mental body. When the lines are in order, we have intellectual clarity. The fifth level is the spiritual matrix of the physical body, a cobalt blue gridwork that usually retains its perfection. Bruyere notes, "You can heal someone's connection to it."

The chakras are also in intimate relationship with the physical anatomy they help to create. Bone marrow vibrates red, carrying the energy of pure life force. The bone itself vibrates orange, the color of emotional energy, which is why, Bruyere claims, we say someone "cut me to the bone," if our feelings are hurt. The periosteum, the skin of the bone, vibrates in harmonics of yellow. Yellow, in turn is a downward harmonic of gold, which runs through the nervous system. The skeletal muscles, like the heart, vibrate green, the skin violet, and white light should flow from every pore.

Each of the major organs have seven miniature chakras within them, according to Bruyere. For instance, the first cervical vertebrae vibrates red, the second, orange, the third, yellow, and so on.

The specific damage in an organ reflects a specific auric field distortion. And every cell in the body is bathed in vibrations from every chakra. "The entire body is a resonating device," says Bruyere.

Information that comes through the chakras also gets stored in the body. The liver, for instance, often holds our unresolved anger; the kidneys, our fear; the pancreas, our ability to digest sweetness in life, and so on. "The auric field is the hard drive," says Bruyere. "A lot of stuff is stored in the disc, which is your body."

Ultimately, healers find that the root causes of illness are not in a chakra or an organ, but in relationships that create loneliness, beliefs of unworthiness, and a lack of love for one's self or others. Narcissism, abandonment, rage, jealousy—these are the precipitating factors of disease. Healers believe even infectious disease occurs when our energy systems are weakened, creating a vibration that is attractive to various germs. Environmental, social and political issues also influence our circumstances, because we are all connected in the holomovement, the implicate or spiritual domain. Beyond all such human issues lies our deep sense of separation from God, Source, the "All That Is." At bottom, we get sick, according to spiritual healers, because we have separated ourselves from awareness of our own infinite consciousness and the creative force of the universe.

"There's always the heart involved, not just toward us, but toward others, and toward God," says Gerda Swearengen, a graduate of Brennan's program. "I always work on the first and fourth chakras: connecting a person to the Earth, to the heart of the universe, and the heart of God."

Five

Intimate Holy Contact

"How did God create the world?" asks Alan Hayes, a Kabbalistic healer and former senior class teacher at Brennan's school. "With intention."

On one level, we all understand intention. Take the person who has an idea to create a new product, a beverage for instance. With a strong enough intent, he or she can create, manufacture, and market this new product, and then, depending on a million variables, a Snapple or Nantucket Nectar appears on the grocery store shelves. A thing emerges from the level of mind, guided by intention. Step by step it becomes increasingly manifest. The same thing occurs in healing: the client and the healer have the same idea—the client's spiritual and physical wholeness—and depending on countless variables, that idea, guided by intention, might become a reality. We all use intent. All the time. If we move our arm, we must first intend to move our arm.

Intention, healers insist, underlies our experiences and guides both energy and consciousness in healing. "A lot of healing has to do with intent," says Hayes. "The energy can run if you just broadcast it in a general way. If you focus it with intent, it will have more impact. If a bone is broken and you focus your intent and know the body's process and how the bone is structured, you can speed up the body's process. In an altered state, intent is set much more."

But intention is a mysterious force. "Why did you incarnate?" asks Hayes, when I ask for a definition. "Did you have an intention? Is it a feeling? Is it a frequency? I wouldn't restrict it to a frequency."

"Personally, I think intention shapes our lives," Hayes continues. "The problem we run into frequently is our intention is not clear. . . . When we set our intention, we don't know the unconscious piece. . . . I can have a clear intent to be in Barbara [Brennan's] school and learn everything she has to teach. But if Barbara changes the schedule in the middle of the day and I had an unpredictable mother—which I did—I'll just rail. It will make me totally unable to have clear intent."

Healers say holding an intent for the client's highest good is the most important element of setting the stage for healing. "You walk in with the intent to cause or make a difference," says Marcella Thompson, an elder in the Healing Light Center Church. "Your intent is to give energy for that person's soul to do with it as it will." And often, a healer must also work with focusing or refocusing the client's intention, too, as Bruyere did with the seminary student.

Is the intention to be a great healer helpful in healing? I asked another healer. "That's ego," replied Traci Slatton, a graduate of the Brennan school. "The intention to heal your foot is what heals your foot."

Surrender is also essential, say most healers. A common refrain from a healer is: "I don't do anything. I hold the space for healing to happen." Explains Bruyere, "We're actually doing something. It's high tech. The surrender is an active state. I'm in two places at once."

No matter how much a healer would like to keep a person alive, or in one piece, it is not up to them, they say. "If I go in with: It's spirit, God, do as you will, something may happen," explains David Grady, an actuary and healer and former class dean at the Brennan school. "If I go in thinking, 'I've got to do this,' nothing happens. Part of healing has to do with the coming together of two or more beings so there is support for the one who is healing."

Nancy Needham, an elder in the Healing Light Center Church, elaborates. "To make something happen, you just absolutely have to be a servant of the universe. For seventeen years I've been at this. I'd probably have more success if I decided to be a rocket scientist or a brain surgeon. You get your degree. But every day, I have to go in empty. If I go in with any theories, I'm already off center. You have to learn to do two things at once. Everything you know has to be present. And everything you don't know has to be present. This healing is not about you."

Such surrender requires a constant giving over of one's self to God or the Divine light. "If a healer is doing his job well, he creates a space. We're in a state of acceptance, really seeing the client through the eyes of God. Seeing their stuff, which they thought was so terrible," explains Dr. Dan Kinderlehrer, a holistic physician and healer in Massachusetts. "The Kabbalah says that man was created to receive God's love. As Rabbi Moshe Chayim Luzzatto says, 'This is all that God desires of man. And it is the entire purpose of his creation.'"

"If we believed God loved us exactly as we are, we'd know we're totally forgiven," continues Dr. Kinderlehrer. "God sees our soul and our innate pureness. The rest is just stuff." At the center of surrender, he says, is love and God's grace.

"I believe there's a space within all of us, a channel of light within us, where the Divine lives, where we are in essence what God is made of," adds Dr. Nancy Reuben, a healer and physician in Connecticut. "Healing is a return to us knowing that. When we get to that place, then our inner intelligence takes over and knows exactly what to do for us to heal on all levels. Gaining access to that space is what it's all about. It's what meditation is about. It's what healing is about."

Love is also essential. Love without judgment, without narcissism, without self-interest or personal desire. Healers can reach very high states by calling in light and being in surrender. "There is a loving state that healers make, have and do. It isn't to be confused with romantic love," says Bruyere. "It's peaceful and it's about contentment. That generosity is terribly important to well-being."

One more ingredient is essential. Resonance is how that love and light gets transmitted and received. As a session begins, a healer perceives via resonance a client's existing emotions, thoughts, feelings, illnesses, and beliefs as certain vibrations or frequencies of energy. A healer will have clarity on the client's issues only to the degree to which the healer has self-awareness.

As the session proceeds, the healer induces change in the client's energy bodies by resonating higher order or more divinely aligned frequencies and intentions. The resonance works in the same way it does in crystal glasses and tuning forks: if one is struck or energized, a similar one nearby may begin to vibrate, too.

The connection and love a healer feels for a client during a session can be so intimate that Jason Shulman, the founder of Integrated Kabbalistic Healing, calls it "intimate holy contact." Says Susan Weiley, a Kabbalistic healer and a former teacher at the Brennan school, "I go into such an altered state. It can't be described. Even to try tamps down the energy. Bliss, wonder. I am in it. The client is in it. We're in it together. There's no longer a subject-object relationship." Maria Bartolotta, a healer who studied with Bruyere, puts it succinctly. "I merge with my clients," she says.

In this union, both healer and client are transformed. "Once a healer starts to transmit energy, it doesn't just change the patient," explains Bruyere. "It changes the healer. When your aura touches another aura, it temporarily becomes one aura. The Greeks had a word—*temenos*—holy space."

After I had been following healers for several years, I had an especially vivid experience of what healers mean when they speak of this union. In November 1997 I observed a practicum Rosalyn Bruyere held for her most advanced students in Los Angeles. At first, I followed Bruyere as she moved from table to table, overseeing the healing teams treating people with metastatic cancer, chronic fatigue, and irreversible muscle degeneration. (More than any other teacher, Bruyere trains her students by focusing teaching sessions on people who have an illness or injury.) Eventually, she asked me to join one of the teams.

Soon, a woman who was in an advanced stage of metastatic breast cancer arrived for a treatment. She was in her forties, but she was so fragile she needed a walker to support herself. In a voice that was barely above a whisper, she told us the cancer had taken up residence in her bones; she was in constant pain. She was not complaining. She did not have the strength. In fact, she did not even have enough energy to get on the table. We worked on her as she sat in a chair.

I could see this woman was suffering. Anyone could. But nothing she described about her situation prepared me for what happened when I laid my hands on her. I could feel the cancer running up and down her bones like mice scampering in the floorboards. Her bones were screaming in pain, but the rest of her body was deadly silent, as if most of her essence had already left. Laying hands on her, I merged with her, her pain, and her cancer. We became one.

Guided by the designated leader of the healing team, five of us held the same "red" energy of vitality. Another five healers held a focus of energy and healing intent around us. The woman got a tremendous blast of life force. And my understanding of cancer was forever transformed. Anyone who can live with so much pain is now a hero in my eyes.

Four days later this same woman walked in for her last treatment without her walker and wearing lipstick. Everyone was overjoyed for her. The healings certainly hadn't cured her, but they were nevertheless a success. Subtle energy had given her something powerful painkillers, chemotherapy, and radiation had not: vitality, and an ability to take some small pleasure in being alive. At a very deep level, she had resonated with the healthy energy of the healing team.

I could not help but wonder what the world would be like if we all perceived each other so intimately and without judgment. I also wondered what the practice of medicine would be like if all physicians made such contact with their patients.

Dr. Steven Fahrion, formerly of the Menninger Clinic, has actually measured the deep sense of oneness healers describe. During healing sessions, rest periods, and meditation periods, he recorded the brain waves of healer Mietek Wirkus and a thirty-nine-year-old woman who had been suffering from polycystic kidney disease for twenty-three years, as he described in *Subtle Energies*.

He found that at all times Wirkus's alpha rhythms had an extraordinarily high amplitude, a pattern previously found only in experienced meditators and yogis. But one particular high amplitude, high frequency pattern of alpha and beta brain waves in the right occipital, an area associated with visualization, occurred only during healing sessions. At those times, the patient's brain waves became more internally synchronous and more synchronous with Wirkus.

The shifts that Dr. Fahrion found in the patient's EEG patterns were highly unusual. But perhaps it is not unusual during healing: A Japanese research team found similar brain wave synchronicity between healers and clients.

Meanwhile, when Wirkus scanned the patient with his hands, he described feeling a change in the vibrations of the same organs within himself. The clincher for Fahrion came when his equipment measured the resonance that Wirkus claimed to experience. "At one point he reported intense pain traveling up his arm, which produced neck and shoulder muscle tension that was visible in the EEG recording," Dr. Fahrion reported.

Following the healing sessions, the patient's restless legs syndrome, a condition involving uncomfortable sensations and spontaneous uncontrollable leg movements just before falling asleep, improved during the next four months. The syndrome had been unsuccessfully treated for two years with medication. The patient's abdominal pain (from adhesions caused by surgery) diminished for nearly a year (until the time the report was submitted for publication). The patient's eighteen-month-long biofeedback training had not produced the same magnitude of relief.

"We only wish to indicate through report of the clinical data that the healing process had face validity," Dr. Fahrion and the patient concluded. "Thus there is a preliminary indication that the observed EEG changes were associated with an actual 'healing process.'"

Dr. Fahrion has also had healings and has personally experienced that resonance. "Those of us who have experienced improved health through clinical practice of energy medicine . . . usually feel gratitude for the encounter," he has written. "Energy medicine treatment often provides an experience of participating in connectedness to humanity and to the meaning of life that is commonly missing in other forms of treatment."

The physiology of healing also appears to involve the heart. For instance, a study by Drs. Gary Schwartz and Linda Russek of the University of Arizona suggests that resonance occurs between people at all times and love may facilitate it. In the forty-two-year follow-up of a famous study of Harvard graduates and their ability to handle stress, Drs. Russek and Schwartz hooked up the subjects, then in their sixties, to equipment that recorded their brain waves (EEGs) and heart frequencies (ECGs). Russek was also wired up. They found that Russek's cardiac energy pattern appeared in the EEG recordings of the subjects. In other words, her heart rhythm affected the consciousness of the other person. Intriguingly, the men who felt their parents were loving resonated to Russek's heart beat more quickly and more strongly than those who did not. Schwartz and Russek also found that Russek's heart and subjects hearts became entrained, beating in the same rhythm. But this occured much more frequently in subjects who had had loving parents.

Seven years earlier, in a study of the same group of men, Drs. Schwartz and Russek found that being loved as a child was highly correlated to good health later in life. The men who had described their parents as loving when they were in college were far more likely to be healthy in middle age then those who rated their parents as not very loving. (Only 25 percent of men in the first group were sick, compared to 87 percent in the second group.)

Drs. Schwartz and Russek believe the heart may be a unique engine, as healers suggest. Their findings also suggest that heart frequencies may modulate states of consciousness and states of consciousness may also modulate the heart. "Is it possible that . . . non-contact therapeutic touch may be correlated with, if not mediated by, cardiac energy/information communication?" they asked in their report, published in *Subtle Energies*.

During the Copper Wall studies, Menninger Clinic biophysicist Elmer Green also found a radiating electromagnetic frequency from healers during healing sessions. They showed up as anomalous voltage shifts on the copper panels four feet from the healers. Research associate Peter Parks says these electrical shifts in the panels were all timed to the healers' heart beats. "What it would suggest is a radiating effect of the human electrical system on the environment," says

Heart-Brain Wave Synchronicity Between People
Men Who Experienced Their Parents as High in Caring

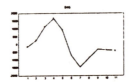

Experimenter's Heartbeat
(EKG "R" spike, averaged)

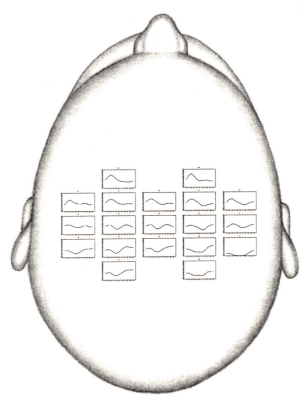

Brain Waves of Eleven Subjects, Averaged
Subjects were three feet from experimenter
Courtesy of Schwartz and Russek (Subtle Energies. Vol. 6. No. 3)

Heart-Brain Wave Synchronicity Between People
Men Who Experienced Their Parents as Low in Caring

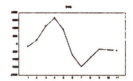

Experimenter's Heartbeat
(EKG "R" spike, averaged)

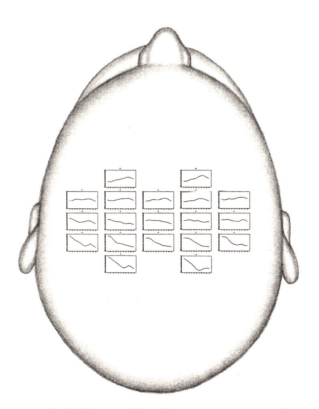

Brain Waves of Nine Subjects, Averaged
Subjects were three feet from experimenter
Courtesy of Schwartz and Russek (Subtle Energies. Vol. 6. No. 3)

Parks. The phenomenon, he says, "suggests a field is moving in the room, modulated with every beat of the heart."

"From a physics point of view," Parks continues, "it's not that difficult to think about. If you have a motor or a generator you can pick up perturbations at a distance. We just don't usually think of the body as an electrical generator."

Rollin McCraty, director of research at the Institute of HeartMath, a nonprofit research organization in Boulder Creek, California, and William Tiller, Ph.D., a professor of materials science at Stanford University, also found in a series of studies that the heart generates frequencies that are intimately related to emotions and physical health.

In studies published in the *American Journal of Cardiology* and *Alternative Therapies*, McCraty and Dr. Tiller found that as people focused on feelings of appreciation and love, heart rate variability (a measure of the beat-to-beat fluctuations in rhythm) became ordered and coherent—a perfect sine wave. In some cases the breathing rate, blood pressure, and brain waves also synchronized with the heart, creating a state of entrainment. The systems then work at maximum efficiency. People in such a state also experienced increased mental clarity, buoyancy, and "inner peace," according to McCraty.

In a follow-up study in the *Journal of Advancement in Medicine*, they found that subjects who focused on appreciation and love for just five minutes increased levels of Secretory IgA, a component of the immune system, for six hours. Conversely a five-minute session in which individuals focused on anger, which created more chaotic heart vibrations, inhibited production of Secretory IgA for one to five hours.

In another study, McCraty found that thirty adults who focused on positive feelings for a month had a 100 percent increase in the level of DHEA, the "antiaging" hormone and a 23 percent reduction in cortisol, which stimulates the "fight or flight" syndrome. A control group of fifteen adults showed no significant changes. In additional studies, still pending publication, McCraty found that coherent heart rhythms inhibited the growth of tumor cells in vitro, while they boosted growth in healthy cells.

"What we feel creates a real pattern or frequency of activity," asserts McCraty. "And that affects the level of hormones. . . . I'm not saying we've measured the frequencies of love. But when we feel love, it causes real changes in our body that we can measure."

These electromagnetic resonances that occur between people at all times and in healings may be far more significant than is generally understood, according to these researchers. Doctors are trained to think of the body primarily as a series of biochemical interactions. But our bodies are veritable symphonies of electromagnetic frequencies. These frequencies are essential to biological function.

Open a basic college physics text book, and the electrical charges that hold DNA strands together are used to illustrate electrical forces. All the actions of proteins, enzymes, and antibodies also involve electrical forces. Every cell membrane has an electrical charge.

"We are an electromagnetic cloud, if you want to think of it that way," says biophysicist Elmer Green, who has studied the electrophysiology of Hindu yogis, ordinary people, meditators, and healers in his laboratory at the Menninger Clinic. "All of matter is electromagnetic and electric in nature."

The most powerful electromagnetic frequencies—from the heart and the brain—are already understood to be intimately related to health. Brain waves, for instance, reflect and create our state of consciousness. During meditation a person's alpha (8–13 hertz) and Theta (4–8 hertz) frequencies increase, while beta waves (over 13 hertz) predominate in most people during normal waking consciousness. Delta waves (3 hertz and under) occur during deep sleep. Consciousness affects not just our minds, but also has a direct influence on our physical health. Several researchers, including Jon Kabat-Zinn, Ph.D., founder of the University of Massachusetts Stress Reduction Clinic, have found that chronically ill people who meditate, that is, shift their brain wave frequencies, often experience less pain, and sometimes fewer medical symptoms and lowered blood pressure.

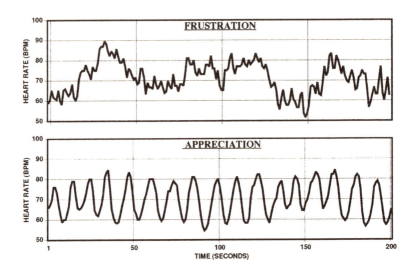

The heart rate variability pattern shown in the top graph, character-ized by its random, jerky form, is typical of anger or frustration. Sincere positive feeling states like appreciation (bottom) can result in highly or-dered and coherent heart rate variability patterns, generally associated with enhanced cardiovascular function. (Institute of HeartMath)

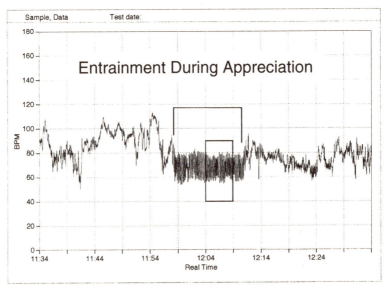

During feelings of love and appreciation, the autonomic nervous system can come into balance, causing entrainment. (Institute of HeartMath)

78

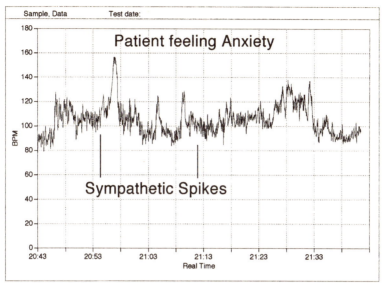

Example from a 33-year-old man experiencing anxiety. The prominent spikes are due to pulses of activity in the sympathetic nervous system. (Institute of HeartMath)

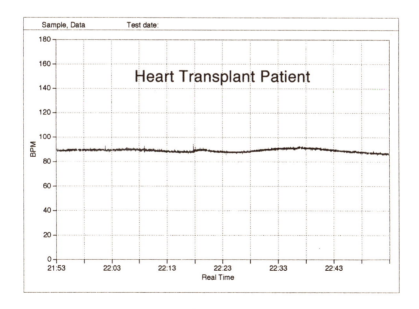

Example from a heart transplant recipient. Note the lack of variability in heart rate, due to the loss of autonomic nervous system input to the heart. (Institute of HeartMath)

Researchers have also found that monks and yogis who make meditation a focus of their lives can use their minds to control their physiology to an extraordinary degree. For example, Dr. Herbert Benson, associate professor of Medicine at Harvard Medical School, found that Tibetan monks could dry wet sheets on their naked bodies in temperatures of 40 degress Fahrenheit, as he recounted in *Timeless Healing*. He found that another group of monks could meditate through the night, covered only by thin wool shawls and wearing sandals, in subzero temperatures.

Doctors also recognize that electromagnetic frequencies of the heart are directly correlated to states of health. For instance, a highly irregular heart beat (arrhythmia) is a medical condition. In addition, doctors have found that low heart-rate variability (without coherence) is associated with everything from migraine and depression to hypertension and diabetes. And a new non-invasive test uses heart-rate variability to determine which people with congestive heart failure are at the highest risk of dying, so they can be treated quickly and aggressively.

Recent studies show that electromagnetic frequencies can have the same kind of effect on biological systems as drugs. For instance, a recent study published in *Bioelectromagnetics* found that a 20 Hz electromagnetic field had a similar influence on human osteoblastic (bone) cells as two human growth factors. And in another experiment, doctors at the U.S. Naval Medical Research Center exposed rats to a field that resonated with the lithium ion, as Dr. Robert Becker notes in *Cross Currents*. Lithium, which is naturally present in the brain in small amounts, is used to medicate manic depressives. The exposed rats were more passive and submissive than the controls, a result equivalent to what would be obtained if the animals were given large doses of lithium.

Electromagnetic frequencies elsewhere in the body also are indicators of health. For instance, cancerous cells have different electrical potentials than normal cells do. In fact, Swedish radiologist Björn Nordenström, M.D., of the Karolinska Institute and Hospital in Stockholm, originally developed the biopsy technique to study the electrical potential of tumors, not tissue changes per se. "An electrodode, moved repeatedly from surrounding lung into the

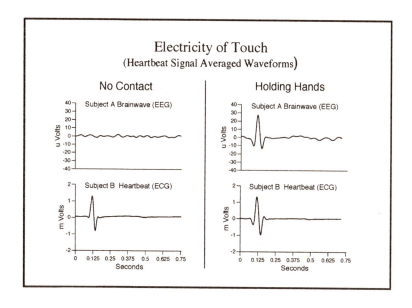

Heartbeat signal averaged waveforms showing a transference of the electrical energy generated by one subject's heart which can be detected in the other subject's EEG (brainwaves) when they hold hands. (Institute of HeartMath)

tumor and out, will disclose an injury potential, which is initially electropositve and later electronegative," Dr. Nordenström noted in the *European Journal of Surgery* in 1994.

In a series of experiments on frogs, salamanders, rodents, and human bone fractures, Dr. Becker, an orthopedist and researcher who was twice nominated for a Nobel Prize, found that all rapidly growing tissues are negative in polarity. "Cancers in animals or humans always showed the highest negativity," he noted in *Cross Currents*.

Dr. Becker also found that "vanishingly" small amounts of current could also stimulate regeneration in salamanders, frogs, and even some bone regeneration in rats. (Doctors now use electrical stimulation to heal bone fractures that won't mend on their own.) "Even a little more electricity simply did not work," he noted. Although it had little power, the more subtle current somehow conveyed more information.

Percentage of Subjects Sick at 42-Year Follow-up in Groups Who Experienced their Parents as High and Low in Caring

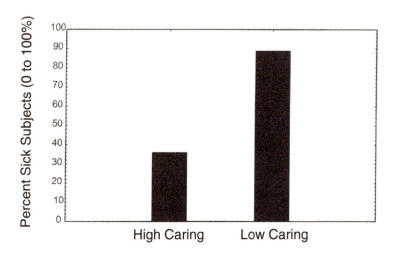

In some not yet fully understood way, the overall electrical field of salamanders and other organisms even seems to play a role in the organism's ability to organize itself and to heal. Dr. Becker found that when a salamander limb was amputated, a blastema or embryonic cluster of cells, grew at the site, with a high negative potential. If the blastema was transplanted before the tenth day to a location near an intact hind leg, it would grow a hind leg. If it was moved next to a tail, it would grow into a tail. After the tenth day, the foreleg blastema always became a foreleg, no matter where it was transplanted.

Dr. Becker, a pioneer in the study of bioelectrical effects, does not believe chemical messages are capable of conveying so much

Scientific Evidence of the Cancer "Signature?"
Frequencies of Human Breast Tissue
Using Laser Scattering by Raman Spectroscopy

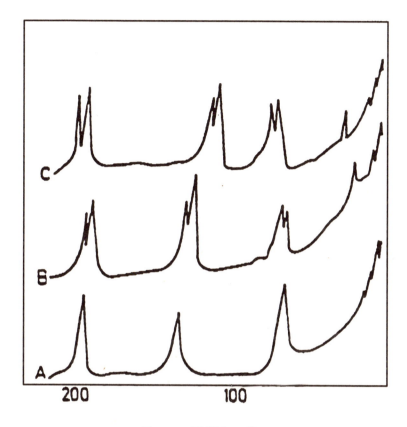

Raman Shift [cm⁻¹]

A. Normal human breast tissue
B. "Normal" human breast tissue from cancer
   patient (right side)
C. Malignant human breast tissue (left side)

Chart shows Raman Effect: scattering due to variations in the "index of refraction" of molecules. Cells that traditional analysis show as normal here have a signal that expresses cancerous cells elsewhere in the body. (S. J. Webb, "Laser-Raman Spectroscopy of Living Cells," *Physics Reports*, 60, No.4, 1980.)

complex organizational information. "The electrical currents in organisms . . . appear to be the control signals that start and regulate growth and healing," he concluded. "This revolution," he further added, "does not replace the chemical machinery that so fascinated the mechanists; rather it simply shows us what the switch is that turns the machinery on."

In this symphony of electromagnetic vibrations the heart's electromagnetic signal are especially powerful by biological standards. "The olfactory cells in the nose can detect single molecules," notes Dr. Schwartz. "The cells in the human retina can detect a single photon. The body is extremely sensitive. The electromagnetic signal from the heart is huge by comparison. The body is composed of some 60 trillion cells. The body is like a huge orchestra. The brain is more like the score. And the heart is more like the conductor."

"If sound is an energy," Dr. Schwartz continues, "then the 'lubdub' of the heart is a sound and every cell is getting massaged by the sound of the heart. Cells are being vibrated by the heart."

He notes that it is not only our own cells that get the message, but the entire universe. "What happens after it reaches the skin?" he asks. "Does it stop? After a moment's reflection you realize, of course it continues. We're not encased in electromagnetic shields. That [heart] signal leaves at close to [the] speed of light. Imagine: one second after heart beats—it's 186,000 miles into space. It's going to be infinitesimally tiny. But it's going to be there." And, he adds, when the frequencies all become coherent, they become far more focused. In addition, the energy signals are also occurring at the quantum level. "If we take what quantum physics is saying serious, everything is ultimately quantum," he explains.

"All of astrophysics is based on the idea that energy is fanning out into space and keeps going. Long after a star dies, its energy and information continues into space. Once out there, there is no way to erase it. . . . When you really get the idea of energy, the connection of energy and spirit is so obvious," he says.

In a 1997 issue of the *Journal for Scientific Exploration*, Princeton aerospace engineer Robert Jahn and coresearcher Brenda Dunne called resonance "one of the most proliferate and dramatic modes of interaction in all objective science." In everything from electromagnetic to quantum to biological systems, they noted, resonance "can produce extraordinary physical effects and responses." And, they added, resonance can facilitate experiences "such as trust, hope, and affection." Based on their research into consciousness, they concluded that resonance served to link the subjective (consciousness) and objective (physical) worlds.

All in all, these researchers suggest that when healers speak about love, connection, resonance, and health, they may not be speaking so metaphorically, after all.

But the biggest questions still remain: Why do we get sick? Why do we suffer?

Healers believe that very little happens by accident. This theory of course, can't be measured by scientists. Nevertheless, it is the world view that separates mere energy healing from spiritual healing.

Basically, healers perceive earth as a school for the soul. Everything that happens is a learning for our souls and a reflection of our spiritual nature. Healers believe that we even choose our parents, so that they can wound us and bring us to the level of our previous life. "It's not like you choose by thinking about it," explains Catherine Vajda, a Kabbalistic healer who studies at the Karin Kabbalah Center in Atlanta. "It's a whole vibrational process. It's magnetic. It's not like you're sitting on the sofa in heaven and going, 'I'll pick that one.'"

"[Your parents] are limited in exactly the way you were in your last incarnation," says Bruyere, elaborating. "Our chakras are pre-matrixed at birth. They reflect all you have accomplished in your previous lifetimes. Getting to where you were before is relatively easy. Getting beyond it—that's the work of a lifetime. We all have a set point, just as with weight loss."

Getting sick is just one form of intensive teaching. It is not a punishment, any more than a rigorous exam in a college history class is designed to be punishment. Nor does it mean that others do not have similar lessons to learn. It is just that not everyone takes the same class at the same time.

When we have a dis-ease (and that refers literally to any

frustration or unhappiness), it is nothing more than the path our soul chooses for growth. Often our lessons serve in some way to help others, as well. In fact, healers believe that many dis-eases are connected to beliefs that are held by large groups of people, and even to environmental and political issues. So, if one person heals, it helps shift the entire collective, even if subtly. (A relatively simple example is how a few early feminists helped change the possibilities for everyone.)

"We are manifesting things that our souls have to work out, but also things the Earth has to work out, and things the All That Is has to work out," explains Dr. Nancy Reuben, a Flow Alignment and Connection practitioner. "On some level you are always working on some aspect of your soul." And, she adds, "There are dimensions even further than the soul."

According to healers, dis-eases that look painful or unfair to us often look very different from a higher spiritual perspective. Deb Schnitta, R.N., a healer who studied with Bruyere and who also is a Flow Alignment practitioner recalls watching a little boy who had Down's syndrome. "He was so full of life, sitting between his parents, playing with Skittles. He was experiencing the joy of the colors of the candy, squealing in absolute delight. His mother was mortified. God forbid, people would see she had a less-than-perfect child."

Schnitta said she asked for a deeper understanding and was told by her spiritual guides that "Children with Down's syndrome have an ability to experience more joy than other people on Earth. If they had an intact nervous system, it would be too much for them. They would also experience pain. . . . It really gave me a much broader understanding. This child had a capacity to experience more joy than I was capable of. He was actually helping to anchor more joy onto the Earth. That's a really great example of a soul lesson."

Even at the personality level, diseases usually work on many levels. In part, healers believe, they serve to draw our attention and love to parts of self that we have abandoned. Dis-ease may also illuminate us by teaching us compassion, forgiveness, love, and joy. "Suffering's function is to get you to go inside," explains Bruyere. "There are some things you learn when you're sick that you can't learn any other way—like to stop whining—and to enjoy what you have. Pain," she adds, "is the final test."

Yet she notes, "Pain is greatly overrated as a teacher. I don't learn very well with a headache. Do you? . . . You don't want to keep a disease to go on learning. You want to move on and find better teachers."

At the same time, healers note it is important to keep in mind that no one totally escapes dis-ease on the Earth plane. "Illness is going to happen no matter how purified you are," says Jason Shulman, the founder of Integrated Kabbalistic Healing. "Every awakened being who I admire is dead."

Shulman believes that pain is built into the creation of the physical universe. "You would want separate beings if you were introducing a universe that was interested in experiencing everything, including healing," he says. "And for healing, something has to be broken. For us to return, we have to be absent. For us to discover individuation, we have to be separate.

"The initial separateness that was created is also responsible for the creation of evil," he adds. "But on the other side, there is the return to our true nature. Existential problems come from this journey. There's no way to do this journey otherwise. And it's tough."

Often our suffering works by the law of similars. If we need to open our hearts, we will very likely encounter people who don't have open hearts. If we put all of our self-worth in our career, the only cure may be the loss of that career. And if we are bitter, we will attract to us others who are bitter, even if we crave and need unconditional love. "If you are never betrayed, you can never develop trust," says Bruyere. "Everything is compost. And you are obliged to grow flowers."

Ultimately, spiritual healers believe healing our physical and emotional wounds is just the first step in an evolutionary process. "Once the wound is healed a lot of people just stop," says Amy Skezas, the founder of Flow Alignment and Connection. "But evolution is this process of continual expansion of consciousness. It's about a refinement and elevation of consciousness, and a penetration of consciousness into matter."

"We're all here to learn," adds Thomas Ayers, Ed.D., a graduate of the Barbara Brennan School, a Flow Alignment and Connection practitioner, a practitioner of *Kriya* yoga, and a retired Army

Reserve colonel. "And the thing we're here to learn is how our thoughts, emotions, and beliefs create reality."

In spiritual healing, the goal is not necessarily a physical cure, which may not be in the soul's highest interest, but a higher level of consciousness, a greater connection with God (or the All That Is or the unified field), and a different perspective on reality. "I define 'well' as being full of light. It's about bringing in joy, having higher energy to bring in joy," says Bruyere.

Even when a situation cannot be changed on the physical level, healers claim suffering can be transmuted by awareness of the soul's higher purpose, as well as by experiencing the interconnectedness of all things. "When you start to open up to your eternal nature, and it's not something that's just a philosophy, but that it's you, everything slowly starts to shift," explains Ken Kafka, M.D., an internist affiliated with New York Hospital-Cornell Medical Center in New York City and a spiritual healer.

"Once you can do that, the grip of fear that keeps us all so contracted starts to loosen," says Dr. Kafka, whose personal experience of his eternal nature is what led him to become a spiritual healer. "It's going to affect the [patient's] immune system, their ability to heal themselves, and to deal with what's on their plate. And they'll know they're going to be okay whether they get cured or not. It's a winwin. Your heart's desire is true. God [collective unity] really does exist."

At times, the most important thing a healer can do is help someone prepare for the transition into death. For a healer who perceives life in energetic, instead of biochemical, terms, death is merely a transition into energy states that do not include the frequencies of the physical body. It is a phase change, like that of a caterpillar turning into a butterfly, or of water turning into vapor. Whatever has been learned during the lifetime is carried forward. Consciousness is eternal.

"I can 'see' a person after they leave their physical body at death," says Barbara Brennan in *Light Emerging*. "The lower three levels [of energy frequencies in the aura] that hold the physical body in place, dissolve in the dying process. . . . It is a great change. It is a rebirth into another plane of reality. . . . These things may sound outrageous, but to stand by my reality, I must say them. It is real for me," Brennan continues. "If it is not your reality, then do not try to force my experience into your reality."

Six

Seeing

"When does the soul enter an unborn baby?" I asked Barbara Brennan. It was early January 1995 and I had just interviewed Brennan for the first time in her East Hampton office. She was riding with me to Manhattan. We were on the Long Island Expressway and twilight was descending.

I wanted an answer to the question. Yet I didn't think one existed. Although I was intrigued by Brennan's claims about the spiritual realms, I was sure there had to be a hole in her theory, somewhere. Brennan, however, didn't skip a beat.

"Before conception," she said.

"Before conception? How can that be?"

Brennan laughed gently. "It's an agreement between the mother, the father, and the child," she explained. At the soul level, she added, time doesn't exist as it does for us in physical reality.

"I have a personal reason for asking," I confessed. I didn't elaborate. It didn't matter. It was as if Brennan was inside my mind. I could almost feel her there. "I know," she said. "I see your daughter. She is still very close to you. She's a lovely little girl. But you did the right thing. The father did not want the child, and you didn't need to bring rejection on yourself or your child."

I was stunned. Just two weeks earlier, I had terminated a ten-day-long pregnancy. It was probably easy for Brennan to guess as much from my question. But during my pregnancy, I couldn't shake the feeling that I was carrying a girl. How could Brennan have known? And how could she guess with such confidence that although I had desperately wanted the baby, my boyfriend just as desperately did not? I had decided I could not bring this child into the world on my own. Because of a genetic disorder from which the father suffered, the child might have serious congenital problems. I did not think I could be a full-time caretaker, single mother and sole wage earner. It was one of the hardest decisions I had ever made. Ever since, I had been racked by grief. At moments, I even feared I would burn in hell. The fear had no logic to it: I did not even know whether or not I believed in God.

"Now you have to ask yourself," Brennan continued, "why would you choose a man like that?" The question took me by surprise. Yes, I was involved with this man and thought I loved him, but surely not because he behaved the way he did. Brennan was implying otherwise.

She began speaking in a stilted, slower cadence. She said she was channeling Heyoan, her spiritual guide. "The child is fine," she said in her strange lilt. "She may even incarnate as your child again, with a different father. It will be the same soul, with different genetic ties."

This sounded like hokum to me, I said. She retreated. "That's just one probable reality," Brennan said, still speaking in the odd cadence.

Strangely, whether Brennan's vision was accurate or not, it almost didn't matter. I felt better. My anguish lifted for the first time. Brennan did not lay hands on me. But it felt as if she had *seen* into my soul. And she had helped me *see* myself and my situation in a new light.

Here is another early encounter I had with the inner vision that so many healers develop. I was talking on the telephone with Gerda Swearengen, a healer in Virginia. Suddenly she asked: "What's that black thing on your wall." There was no black thing on my wall, I assured her. She wouldn't be put off. Finally, I admitted, "There is a moth on the ceiling." I had been watching it during most of the phone conversation. It was just a few inches in from the wall, which had recently been damaged from a water leak. But it was not on the wall. "Oh, that's it!" she said. "Just a minute. I'm going to clear it."

I waited, feeling pretty smug. I knew no matter how hard she concentrated, she couldn't affect anything in my apartment. But all of a sudden, a tiny light appeared around the moth, like a spotlight. I closed my eyes, sure I was hallucinating. When I opened my eyes, the light was still there. A minute later the light faded. "Okay," Swearengen said. She was done.

Still on the phone, I grabbed a little glass jar from the kitchen, cupped it over the moth (it didn't even react), carried it to the window, and released it. What that whole episode was about, I still don't know. Swearengen said the moth was the symbol of some "dark energy" and that she had "transmuted" it.

Later on, it still shocked me when someone could *see* in a way that was a revelation for me. This time, I was having lunch with Susan Weiley, a Kabbalistic healer, a one-time student of Rosalyn Bruyere's, and a former senior teacher at the Brennan school. It was late in December, 1996. I was eating everything on my plate, but one of my signature headaches was already setting in. These headaches descended on me when I got tense and my blood sugar dropped. They often lasted for three or four grim days and made me nauseous. But I didn't say anything to Weiley. Instead, she said to me: "You're not feeling too well, are you?"

"No," I admitted. "How do you know?"

"Your pancreas is wavering," she replied. "I can *see* it."

Now that she had my attention, she told me that my blood sugar problem wasn't really truly located in my pancreas. I was overworking my adrenal glands. The adrenals stimulate the pancreas, she explained. My adrenals were being stressed because I was wound up, a syndrome that frequently plagued me.

I had been researching healing for two years. Until that moment, it had never occurred to me that the headaches I got with some regularity had an underlying cause. (We all have our blocks in consciousness.) I basically treated my headaches as isolated occurrences. When I was in pain, I was grateful if a healer worked on me. Only three healers could get the tension in me to release immediately. (Each had worked on me long distance.) With other healers I could feel the headache unwinding, and I always felt fine by the next morning. But no one had directly suggested to me that the head-aches were a symptom, and the cause could be healed.

As we sat at lunch that day, Weiley assured me energy work that focused on the underlying emotional issues, combined with a high-protein diet, could change the whole dynamic.

Later, another healer, Don Van Vleet, who focuses deep into the organs and bones, showed me yet another form of *seeing*. During a session, he put his fingers just below my rib cage and a stab of ago-nizing pain shot through me. I had a knot in my body that I never knew existed. "That is the location of your original neurosis," he said. Every time he worked on that area—a knot between my stom-ach and liver—I developed one of my headaches, along with nau-sea, a few days later. It was a sign that the energy of that knot (which stimulated my adrenal glands) was getting released. (In energy heal-ing, symptoms are sometimes temporarily magnified as the energy trapped in them dissolves. The phenomenon is so common it is known as "a healing crisis.")

One day, after about a dozen sessions over the course of a year, Van Vleet said to me: "I'm going to rewire your nervous system. We've been working on it all along. But after today, you are going to find a place of calmness you couldn't access before."

My attitude, as always, was: when I see it, I'll believe it. I doubted anyone could reset my nerves. But I laid down on his mas-sage table.

The session was tough. Van Vleet seemed to find every knot that had ever existed in my body. He even ran energy inside my mouth until I gagged. A few days later, I got very sick. But this time I saw the underlying energy—a dark roiling storm—before it settled into my body. The headache and vomiting mercifully lasted only a few intense hours.

Now, six months later, it is safe to say I still get an occasional headache. But, except for exceptional circumstances, it lasts only a few hours. And I no longer get headaches like clockwork once a month or more. I thought the debilitating headaches were a natu-ral part of my inner landscape. It turns out they are not, at least not anymore.

Seeing is a fundamental part of healing: It is much easier for a healer (or anyone) to address the things he or she can perceive. At first the process of *seeing* mystified me. "How do you *see?*" I asked all the healers I interviewed. "Why are you asking me?" responded Richard Dobson, a former student at the Brennan school. "How do you *see?*"

Other healers, too, kept insisting that I could *see*. In particular, Gerda Swearengen, then a student at the Brennan school, made a point of asking me what I *saw*, whenever I asked her to describe the energy behind something. At first, I thought I was imagining whatever I described. I had to sink down to a level below my thoughts, where there was a stillness, and allow the information or light to emerge in my "inner mind screen." When Swearengen and other healers continually confirmed my perceptions, I eventually accepted that I could *see*. With that acceptance, my *seeing* expanded exponentially. I began to *see* through my regular eyes, as well as with my inner eye. I also realized I had been *seeing* emotional patterns in and between people since before I could walk.

The truth is everyone *sees*. In fact, Kabbalistic healer Jason Shulman considers this psychic openness a "birthright." And, he adds, "It takes a lot to remove a person's birthright." Scientists are now beginning to document this extraordinary and innate human ability.

"Rocks; with uneven holes; also smoothness . . . a lighthouse?—tall structure—round with conical roof . . . or larger structure similar to a castle . . . old, unused feeling; fallen apart? . . ."

The speaker was a remote viewer at the Princeton Engineering Anomalies Research (PEAR) Lab at Princeton University in New Jersey. The experiment required the viewer to describe his or her impressions of a distant scene, without having any information about what or where it was. The remote scan could occur before, during or after a second person, the agent, visited the scene. The viewer had no special talent or training. Nor did the agent. The viewer was merely asked to give his psychic impressions.

In this particular trial, the remote viewer gave his description twenty-three and a half hours before the agent arrived at the ruins of

Urquardt Castle, Loch Ness, Scotland—3,500 miles from the viewer's location. Yet when tallied empirically and analyzed by a computer, the details of the remote description closely matched the site. Altogether PEAR conducted 334 remote perception trials; more than 62 percent of the individual trials scored above a chance outcome. And the probability that the data from all 334 trials was mere chance was 18 in a billion.

PEAR researchers Robert Jahn and Brenda Dunne found that clairvoyance transcends time and space. They termed the results of their studies "starkly inconsistent" with how most physicists currently understand reality. They know from personal experience, too, just how shocking the findings are.

Brenda Dunne, the manager of the PEAR lab, did her first study on remote viewing in the early 1970s, when a college professor pointed out studies in the area. She did her first informal test, she says, because the results of published studies "bothered me a lot." One Sunday afternoon around 3 P.M. she decided to predict where a friend would be at 5 P.M. "No sooner than the thought had popped in my head, I had this very clear impression of her walking in the woods," she recalls. "It was just there. It was not a logical thing." It was not even the kind of thing this friend liked to do.

An hour and a half later, Dunne's friend arrived on her doorstep. "She said, 'You know, I've been going absolutely stir crazy. I thought it might be nice to go for a walk in the woods. Would you like to come?' I just stood there," says Dunne. "It was very clear to me the idea of transmission is wrong. It's a sharing of information."

Other laboratories have obtained similar results, even in studies where no agent visited the remote site. (The sharing then is between the consciousness of the viewer and the consciousness of the site.) Many of these studies were conducted between 1972 and 1986 by the Stanford Research Institute for the United States Department of Defense and other government agencies and were declassified in 1995. The subjects did remote viewing of everything from Soviet weapons factories to churches in Palo Alto to lost airplanes.

"We never found anyone who could not learn to perceive scenes and people, even those at great distances, and blocked from ordinary perception," says physicist Russell Targ, who ran the study with physicist Harold Puthoff, Ph.D. They found that accuracy and reliability was unaffected by distance, size, or electromagnetic shielding. Yet people were more successful when the task was more exciting or demanding. The government spent more than $20 million on classified remote viewing studies.

Targ believes the answer to the seeming mystery lies in the nonlocality described in quantum physics. "We misunderstand the nature of the separation," he says. "We live in a nonlocal space. There's some kind of contiguity between all things. I think we've got a lot to learn. I don't think it's magical."

Targ predicts that the new science will inevitably be embraced. When it is, "The world view will change," he asserts. "In Christian terms we'll recognize we're all children of God—that our awareness extends beyond our physical bodies. And that there's a connection among all of us. That we live in a community of spirit. That's what's going to happen."

In July 1997 Steven Amoils, M.D., a family physician affiliated with the Health Alliance Group of Cincinnati, conducted a pilot study in which he tested Rosalyn Bruyere's ability to *see* the medical problems of four patients. She scanned each one by hand, looked at their auras, and then drew anatomical diagrams of the problems they had. Then he compared her drawings to MRI pictures that had been taken of the patients and compared those to Bruyere's drawings.

"There was a very high correlation," says Dr. Amoils, the medical director of the Alliance Integrative Medical Center, which is in the planning stages. "In addition, there was information the MRI couldn't give about the patients' personalities, their past, and future health-related issues." Altogether, Bruyere's clairvoyant sight, says Dr. Amoils, yielded more information than the MRI pictures.

For instance, one patient was a young man with damage in a lumbar disc in his spinal column. Bruyere depicted the anatomical injury accurately. But she also noted that he had gotten the injury just after breaking up with his girlfriend, and that he was feeling depressed and unstable. When they checked with the referring physician, the information turned out to be precise. "He felt he lost the love of his life," says Bruyere. "Now he feels not fit to find a new love. That's the kind of information an MRI can't pick up. Some of the pain someone suffers is emotional."

Amoils cautions that such a small study does not have statistical validity. But he presented the findings to fifty physician colleagues, who, he says, were intrigued. In the meantime, Bruyere attributes her four hits out of four trials to "a good day." "I didn't do that on my own," she says.

In a slightly larger follow-up study, a physician referred a series of patients. First the patients were asked to make drawings of their pain. Then Bruyere and another clairvoyant were asked to make drawings of the patients' pain. Dr. Amoils says the anatomical data from the healers was not as precise this time, but the qualitative information was eerily precise. "If the patients drew their pain in boxes, the healers drew their problem in a box," he says. "When they circled their problem, then the healers drew circles."

How does a healer, or anyone else, *see* at all?

"Rub your hands together," says Rosalyn Bruyere, rubbing her hands to demonstrate and smiling as if she is going to share a big secret. It is a Saturday morning in February 1997, the first day of a weekend workshop on the chakras at a hotel in Los Angeles. A few students have flown in from as far away as Hawaii and Ohio, and a local Catholic archbishop and three sisters in full habit are also in the class.

"Now shake them out. Do you feel your hands? This is what I call 'not numb.' Can you control the tingling? Now, rub your hands and then separate them and bring them together," she says, pulling her hands slightly apart and then slowly bringing them together. "Feel where there's resistance, where the field [from one hand] starts to touch [the field from the other hand.] Now cut that space in half. Your hands start to suck in together."

"It's the same with hugging," she says. "There's a hump at the edge. But once you're past that, you're drawn together."

Bruyere assigns her students homework. "Scan everything—furniture, lamps, flowers, walls, cats, dogs, and people," she says. "Everything has a field."

The lecture could be called "Subtle Energy 101." It is taught at most of the healing schools and at complementary care centers. The exercise is designed to help beginners learn to feel the aura, and the energy running through the collagen and the *nadis*, or subtle channels, including the meridians used in acupuncture. The energy is considered subtle for good reason: To feel anything can take months of practice. Gerda Swearengen, a graduate of Brennan's four-year school, whose high sense perception is now quite keen, recalls that it took months before she sensed anything. "When you keep with it, it feels like taffy," she says. "If you don't feel anything, you haven't done it enough."

To run energy Bruyere tells her students to imagine letting water flow through a hose as they pull energy up from the earth and down their arms. Usually, at first, she says, students can send barely a trickle (except for a retired firefighter who was apparently inspired by the imagery). Brennan breaks the process of running energy down into steps: connecting, pushing, allowing, pulling, stopping, and disconnecting. It all starts with the intention. Slowly students begin to perceive the subtle energy that goes with the intention.

Bruyere, Brennan, and other teachers of auric healing also teach their students to connect to each chakra and to become familiar with the subtle vibrations specific to each one. You don't have to see or feel your chakras—but intend to connect to them and amplify their spin. The easiest way is to feel yourself awash in tomato red as you intend the first chakra to spin, and to become the color of each chakra in turn. Red is heavy and dense. White, at the other end of the rainbow, is much finer and lighter. In this way, students become proficient at sensing their chakras and those of others. At Brennan's school, students routinely spin their chakras in unison, time and again, over the four years, much the way music students practice scales.

A healer who can embody a specific frequency can also use that frequency during healings. Red, for instance, can be used to stimulate bone regeneration. Orange, the color of emotion, can melt emotions that have stopped flowing. Blue and green can be channeled to freeze something like bacteria out of the body. Purple and white bring in the light of a person's soul.

Spinning the chakras expands a person's field and consciousness. The chakras become more coherent. The coherent light of the chakras works in the same way that the coherent light of a laser works. "The same light becomes arranged so every peak and valley of the wave occurs at the same place," explains healer Alan Hayes. When the waves of light all become coherent, they have much more force. Using the same amount of energy that it takes to light a room, a laser beam can burn through steel. "If you can make all the chakras coherent," Hayes says, "and the waves of light coherent, instead of putting hands on someone and broadcasting various energies, you can really impact that person."

Different teachers emphasize different vibrations. Bruyere tells her students it is much more important to hold a higher state such as grace, courage, or Divine love than to embody a chakra color. Conversely, Brennan spends three years of her four-year program getting students to regulate their chakras with the precision that the military uses in getting soldiers to march. Only then does she introduce concepts like holding a state of joy.

Many clues about a person's energy system are also closely linked to the physical body. Students gradually learn to shift from perceiving physical information to subtle information. At the School for Enlightenment and Healing in North Carolina, Michael Mamas, D.V.M., a former student and teacher at the Brennan school, asks beginning students to put their hand on the next student's thigh and sink in with their *intention*. A few minutes later, students do the same exercise with a second classmate's thigh.

The contrast between one thigh and another is remarkable. When I tried this exercise, I was amazed at how different the thighs of two different people can feel. One can feel dense, another jellylike. One can feel sad, another springy. It is also possible, with *intention*, to distinguish between the skin, the muscle, the nerve and the bones. It literally was as if the frequency of each of these layers had a different resonance. If you touch a thousand different thighs, you develop an inventory of touch information. (Doctors do this naturally.)

A healer can also see where a person's energy is blocked just by looking at the body. If someone has excess padding at the hips disproportionate to the rest of his body, for instance, there may be congestion, a blockage of energy, in that region. If a person complains of pain in the neck, or in the back, there is typically some energy disturbance. "Look at the way a person's chest looks," explains Mamas. "If a person's shoulders are concave, he will have a partially collapsed fourth (heart) chakra."

But subtle energy involves much more than the flow of chi through *nadis* and chakras. Our thoughts, emotions, beliefs, and spiritual essence are also subtle energies. They don't just flow through meridians, but spread out into space. In fact, many healers don't ever see chakras. Rather, they *see* directly at this deeper level. In fact, a healer once told me, "You're going to be so disappointed when you finally see the aura. It's just wisps of color. You still have to interpret it."

"One person in tune with another," adds Kabbalistic healer Jason Shulman, "simply says the right thing, the insightful thing, and it is not the product of behavior, but simply happens. And both people are surprised and enlightened by it, because no one owns it. It is no one's product. It's like a sunrise or a running stream. It gives pleasure with no self-consciousness, with no keeping up of the little self."

Seeing of any kind typically starts with noticing the *seeing* you already do. "You have a place in you that sees," explains Joan Luly, a Brennan-trained healer who teaches at a Swiss healing school founded by another Brennan graduate. "It's a matter of removing the veil." The first layer is easy, she and other healers say. Walk into a neighborhood bar. Then step inside a church. Do they feel different? That sense of a place is a form of subtle sense perception.

Most of us also resonate with the feelings of others. We know when someone is angry or sad or happy or frustrated, even if they deny it, because we can *feel* it. We resonate with their emotions. Someone else's anger often evokes our anger. (This is one reason fights escalate so easily.) A happy person may brighten our own mood. A depressed person can bring us down. We are not as tightly confined to our own skins as we have been led to believe.

We all use extra sensory perception in daily life, notes Bruyere. The best doctors often intuitively *know* whether a stomach pain is cancer or an ulcer or an infected appendix. A truck driver may have a "sixth sense" about highway radar. Stockbrokers may use that "sixth sense" to navigate their investments. I even know a reporter who sometimes hears a little tune in her head as she is interviewing someone. If she hears, "What's the rap, man," she says she knows the person is lying.

One way to develop *seeing* is to first notice when it is occurring. "Feel it in your body," Luly told me one afternoon, while we were talking in her garden in San Diego. "It's a real fine-tuning process. That's why people get discouraged. They get into a feeling of not being able to do it. And it doesn't happen in an instant. . . . When the feeling gets consistent, it's because you've strung each little pearl [of perception] together."

"Your body will be your marker point," Luly continued. "No one else is exactly the same. That's why the more you know yourself, the more you can do this work."

At the same time, it is very helpful to get feedback from those whose *seeing* has already been tested. *Seeing* can be taught. "Ninety percent or more of the time, people are looking at what's there," says Luly. "It's trusting in yourself."

Barbara Brennan calls the ability to perceive subtle energy *high sense perception* (HSP). Our normal five senses of sight, touch, taste, smell, and hearing slowly expand to take in more and more subtle information at a broader range of frequencies. *Seeing*, in her view, is best translated as perceiving. "I *see*" is often used in the colloquial way, meaning, "I understand."

The best known form of *HSP* is clairvoyance, which varies from person to person. One healer may *see* congested arteries, knots in organs and muscles, and structural defects, while another person will *see* barbed wire around someone's heart. Some healers *see* colors in the aura, others *see* visions which unfold like a brief movie, often on the inner "mind screen." Some healers have vision on many levels, and tune into what is most appropriate. "Rosalyn doesn't *see* the aura when she's doing a healing," explains one of her students. "You want to see the cancer and the cells. The aura gets in the way."

For many people *HSP* is kinesthetic. When they touch another person, they may feel organs, or the emotions of that person, usually through a resonance in their own bodies. Some clairvoyants actually receive information kinesthetically first, and then translate it into vision. "First I feel [what's in a person's body] and then I ask: what is it? And then I get a picture," explains Deborah Scott, a former computer industry executive who has studied with several healing teachers.

Some people also develop heightened taste and smell. They automatically perceive the vibrations of chemotherapy, hormones, body chemistry, and drugs as their characteristic tastes and smells, what Bruyere calls "smell-a-vision." For Bruyere, a room full of healers working on chemotherapy patients can taste fairly toxic by the end of the day. In the increased energy, healers and clients alike go through a process of what Bruyere calls "chemicalization," whereby the metabolism of emotional and physical toxins accelerates.

With clairaudience, or subtle hearing, a person *hears* spirit guides and sometimes the thoughts or feelings of another person. Channeling is a clairaudient skill. Instead of *seeing* information, a healer might literally hear "cancer" or "put your hands on her heart." The information from the "higher" order or spiritual guide comes in the form of an inner voice. "Almost everyone can tell when they have their own mind chatter, and it will sound like them. And they'll also have inspired ideas, where they know it's something more than them," explains Bruyere. "That distinction is the first one. . . . And the slower you do it, the greater the chance that you maintain your sanity and don't get delusional and don't get megalomaniacal."

All in all, "natural knowing is the best," says David Grady, a former class dean at the Brennan school and an actuary. With direct knowing there is no need to make interpretations, which are inevitably colored by the healer's own history.

People perceive subtle energies, according to Brennan, because they are frequencies, just as light and sound are electromagnetic frequencies that we perceive. When we look at a flower our eyes don't see colors. They see frequencies that we interpret as specific colors. When we hear music, our ears are taking in frequencies, which our brain processes as sound. Likewise, subtle energy is all around us, all the time.

HSP opens naturally with increased consciousness. In the Hindu tradition it is well known that people who meditate develop *siddhis*, or powers. The more conscious one becomes, the more open all the chakras are, and the more information comes in. "There are seals within the chakras," explains Brennan. "Energy has to get through to get information in. It's just like light that can't go through a dirty window."

Clairvoyance is very complex, as I learned through personal experience. Even people who are highly clairvoyant do not see everything. For instance, I watched Barbara Brennan do a healing demonstration on a senior student in November 1996. Brennan focused on the central alignment of this woman, which had been displaced in a car injury. Less than two years later, the woman had a recurrence of a cancer she had been treated for in 1991.

The subtle energy disturbance that led to the cancer may have been in the woman's field at the time of the *hara* healing. But it is simply not possible for any human to address or even see every issue in just one session. And sometimes issues won't "pop" or become visible because the person is not yet ready to deal with the issue—or the timing is not right from the soul level.

People can also be extremely clairvoyant without having an especially open heart. It becomes another skill, just like musical ability. The possibility then exists that someone's *seeing* might be distorted by their own issues. A person may also use clairvoyance to gain power over people instead of empowering people. I found that most of the healing teachers I encountered were still resolving basic personality issues, whether it was a concern with their status, a need to have control, or some other issue.

In the end, clairvoyance is not a measure of enlightenment. The openness of one's heart is far more significant. This is not a momentary altered state. It takes years, even lifetimes, to burn away the personality desires that obscure the Divine love that is our true essence.

"What doctors do is very literal," explains Bruyere, who embodies her teachings in a very deep way. "What healers do is different. It requires a different form of consciousness that takes time to develop. It takes four to six years to train a healer. It's 50 percent technique and 50 percent personal development, clearing [emotional issues and distorted beliefs], and reaching altered states."

"Imagine a friend of yours who is not taking care of herself," Kabbalistic healer Jason Shulman suggested to me one afternoon. "Her husband calls you up and says she's eating wrong; she's drinking. She's doing this and that. And you think about it on a day when you're not very connected [to your self]. And you say, 'Oh my God, Nancy is . . . she could die. I've got to get on her case.' You panic. And there's fear in you. You know what I'm saying? And you go and you say, 'Nancy, you can't do this. What's the matter with you?'

"And it has an effect or it doesn't have an effect. Then you go do it on another day, when you are connected, and you know we are all held in God's hands. And you say: 'Nancy could die. Could I let her die? It's her life. I don't want her to die. But could I let her die?' 'Yeah,' Shulman whispers. 'I could.'

"You could only say something like that if you'd gotten through [your own fears] and truly trusted the universe. Then, you might meet Nancy and say, 'Nancy . . . I want to say I care for you, and I've always loved you and I continue to love you, even though you have these difficulties.'

"That might have a different effect on a person. Maybe it won't. But it's going to go in in a different place than if you say"—his voice turns angry and frightening now: "'Nancy, you're being so bad. How come you're not thinking about your kids? How come you're doing this?'

"But one way can't take place without a certain amount of inner development. You can't just do that from a technique. You have to have gone through some things in your own inner self to be able to say that. . . . A person who doesn't understand loneliness, doesn't understand being ill, doesn't understand fear, can't help a person heal loneliness, illness, or fear," Shulman explains.

To open the space for someone else to heal at a deep level, a healer must do his or her own inner work. Medical students have to study what drugs to use for what illness. But for a true healer, many dark nights of the soul are the required course work. "You're never finished as a healer," explains Bruyere. "You're never cooked. You're going to learn techniques. Mostly, you're going to learn about yourself. Three thousand years ago, the temple dedicated to Isis had a sign at the entrance: 'Know yourself.' What you find is, you don't know yourself the way God does. Get yourself ready to meet the Divine."

The process, when done deeply and in surrender, is transformative. Living in this way, everything that is painful is an opportunity and a gift. It is the same journey that a skilled healer helps a patient make. "I learned how my defense systems operate and keep me from connecting to myself and to others," explains Dr. Dan Kinderlehrer, a healer and holistic physician in Massachusetts. He says that, as a result, he sees at a deeper level. To illustrate, he recalls a patient who came to him complaining of chronic fatigue, chronic muscle aches, chronic gastrointestinal problems, "and about twenty other chronic complaints."

He put her on a food elimination diet for a month to test for allergies. A month later, he recalls, "She is as mad as hell. She can't believe how depriving this diet was," he recalls. "And I made her do it. And she's not any better. She's almost screaming at me."

Dr. Kinderlehrer noticed her rage, but didn't react. He went down a list of her complaints. "It turned out she was much better. She couldn't own it. I said, 'Feeling deprived really triggered you and made you angry.'" Then she told him that as a child she had been locked in the basement for weeks at a time and deprived of food. "Before I studied with Barabara Brennan, I could never have been present to do that," he says. "I would have been defending myself."

"You need to feel your anger," he told the patient. When her psychotherapist objected, Dr. Kinderlehrer referred the woman to a healer. The patient has been transformed, he says. When she comes for an office visit, she almost always brings a gift. Most important, "At this point, she's virtually asymptomatic and eating most foods." Even so, it was not a complete cure. "She's still quite sensitive to chemicals," he explains.

Recently, while studying Kabbalistic healing, Kinderlehrer's own process intensified. "I went through a meltdown," he says. First, he got sick with Lyme disease. Then the husband of a patient who died of melanoma complained to the medical board that Dr.

Kinderlehrer was giving unconventional medical advice, which could threaten his licensing. The patient had lived three years longer than her oncologist had predicted. But this did nothing to quell the husband's fury.

When her husband filed the complaint, "My anxiety hit the roof," says Dr. Kinderlehrer. "I went into despair. Some of it could be tied to my external life. But I knew it wasn't. At the same time, I knew it was for my greatest good. It shattered patterns I knew I had to let go of—ego patterns. I thought I was this person who knew what he was doing, who was in control, who could help people, who was smart. I had strong attachments to knowing and doing," says Dr. Kinderlehrer.

"Suddenly, I felt I didn't know a thing. And I couldn't do anything either because I was so wiped out from Lyme disease and sleep disorder. Suddenly, my identity structures were gone."

The medical board summarily dismissed the husband's complaint: Kinderlehrer had done the healings at home, not in his medical office, and had encouraged the patient to continue her conventional treatment, which she had done. He considered the board's decision a victory for spiritual healing. But when Dr. Kinderlehrer went to a therapist to help with his feeling of dissolution, she told him, "You know what? Healers go through this."

Dr. Kinderlehrer says the Lyme disease and medical board complaint were just teachings. "It was my soul's longing to let go of a pattern of living that wasn't serving me. . . . I was always controlling my life, my next day, my next week. . . . I had built a palace and it had become a prison. My life has dramatically changed. I no longer live my life motivated by unconscious fear. I didn't know before that I had fear. But when I looked at it, I recognized it had always been there, every moment of my life. I had avoided it by doing.

"That's the difference between healing—going the next step in your evolution—and taking some drug to move you away from embracing what is," he says. "The fear, of course, is that nothing is there. . . . It's letting go of the illusion of control. You know the old joke. If you want to make God laugh, tell him your plans.

"If we surrender the personal will, egocentric will, we can get in touch with our own essence. And our essence is to be at one with the Divine. And then we become cocreators. True will is surrendering to the Divine will."

In the old mystery schools, the process that Dr. Kinderlehrer describes was called initiation. Many healers believe all serious illness is a form of initiation. The illness literally serves to burn away karma—unconscious patterning. Slowly a deep transformation occurs, whether the sick person is aware of the spiritual purification or not.

When I first heard the concept of initiation, I assumed wonderful mysteries would be revealed. I learned initiation is no party after a healer told me, as he worked on my energy bodies, that he felt as if he was preparing me for initiation. "I feel like we're back in Egypt," he said, as he claimed to open channels from the bottom of my feet all the way through my third eye. I assumed he was taking poetic license.

I subsequently had one of the worst weeks of my life: one of my earliest and most continuous fears seemed to become my total reality. A few days after the session, I got so sick that I couldn't get out of bed. I thought my life was ruined. Every muscle in my body tightened up in fear, as if I had descended into a kind of rigor mortis. When I tried to eat, I threw up. Another healer ran some energy to calm me down and release the tension that was causing a headache. During the session, she performed last rites over me. "A part of you is dying," she announced. "You're in fear. But you'll be okay. It's a good thing."

In an initiation, something has to die before you can be reborn. No one warned me about that. (It is one reason spiritual evolution is so difficult. One has to constantly give one's self away.) Eventually, I was able to unravel a major warp in my psyche. Part of the initiation required me to make peace with a person whom I perceived (symbolically) as both sibling and enemy. It felt like the hardest thing I ever had to do: to take this person into my heart. I resisted for several days, even though I could not move forward at any level during that time. Finally, I embraced this person. Immediately I knew I had passed some kind of test. For the first time, I saw a fear and belief that had been running me since early childhood was, and always had been, an illusion. It made a subtle, but significant, difference in my life. The immediate consequence was renewed energy to do my work, and a broadening of my perspective.

Bruyere describes the process quite well. "How do you know if you're in some sort of initiation?" she asked her students during an intensive session in New Mexico. "You say to yourself, 'God, I hope this is an initiation, because it if isn't, it's a nervous breakdown.'"

According to Bruyere, the outward signs include: "What you used to like, you don't like any more. It can be food, people, phrases. They become boring. Or toxic. Then," she adds, "things around you start to fall apart, break down, dissolve themselves." Energy is always holographic, so it affects your life as well as your psyche and your body. "If the plumbing in your house goes, it's a second chakra issue," she said. "If it's your computer, it's your sixth chakra. Each chakra falls apart in an initiation.

"Next," she said, "people start telling you extraordinary things in extraordinary places. Messengers come." Also, she added, "You experience the loss of a lover or a job, or you need to move.

"The normal way you get somewhere breaks down," she continued. "With acts of God, you can tell you're in an initiation. For instance, an earthquake knocks out a major highway for nine months. Am I saying everyone in Los Angeles went through an initiation because we had a quake? Yes, I am. Most people don't realize it.

"Initiation," she concluded, "comes from a 'Big Bang.' You have a profound need to change. You're expanding."

Bruyere spoke from experience. Her life has been a series of initiations. In the process, she has gathered experiences that enable her to bring, in a systematic fashion, the ancient mysteries into modern times. Now, thanks to her and a few others, there is a pathway anyone can follow. Healing is now being taught to hundreds of people at a time. It's a first in recent history. "When I began," says Bruyere, "There was no one to train me."

Part Three

Seven

High Priestess of the Ancient Mysteries

In 1969 Rosalyn Bruyere seemed like the last person you would select as someone destined for the international lecture circuit. She was an unhappily married twenty-three-year-old mother of two toddlers and a college dropout living in Van Nuys, a blue-collar suburb of pastel stucco tract houses in the San Fernando Valley. To keep the family afloat, she was working as a checker in a local Safeway.

The daughter of a factory worker and phone company employee, Bruyere was born out of wedlock when her mother was just sixteen. Declared stillborn by the delivering physician, she was rescued from oblivion by a nun who heard her cry a few hours later. Although her parents eventually married and had two more children before divorcing, Bruyere was raised by her grandparents in the San Gabriel Valley and the Monterey Peninsula. It was an ordinary childhood, except for the turmoil in her parents' lives. (Bruyere's mother ultimately married six times, and her father four times.) When she was little, however, her great grandmother, "Nana," taught her to see the lights around plants. (Second sight, she later learned, was a family gift.) After "Nana" was given shock therapy to cure her habit of conversing with her deceased husband, Bruyere, just seven, shut down even the memory of seeing auras.

111

As a teenager, Bruyere raced motorcycles, and painted her nails to match her bike. She planned to become an electrical engineer. Yet after just three semesters at Monterey Junior College, she got married and dropped out. Practically before she blinked, she gave birth to two boys, Mark and Joe, barely a year apart. By then she already knew her marriage to Joe Winsky, Sr., a sometime Hollywood sound engineer, was not meant to last.

To make matters worse, the kids started talking about fuzzy colors around people almost as soon as they could talk. Soon Bruyere saw the same colors too and thought she was going crazy, until one day the kids pointed out an orange light around Bruyere's mother's stomach. That night her mother was taken to the hospital with a bleeding ulcer. By the time Bruyere went to visit her mother the following day, the bleeding had stopped and the orange light had turned a sickly blue. By now Bruyere knew she needed help.

"Nobody gets up in the morning and says, 'I think for the rest of my life, I'd like to be a weirdo,'" she says, looking back. A neighbor explained that she was seeing auras and sent her to see a medium connected to the Universal Church of the Master, a spiritualist church in West Hollywood, who became her first teacher, followed by spiritualists in The Church of Antioch in nearby Santa Ana. The spiritualist church, part of the Dutch reform movement, teaches that "death is simply life in another dimension," as they advertise on their web page nowadays.

"It's a branch of Christianity that believes in communicating with the 'dear departed' 'across the veil,'" says Bruyere, laughing affectionately. "Spiritualism is the Christian religion that uses the same language as the funeral industry. So nobody is dead. They are 'across the veil.'" Despite its unusual teachings, or perhaps because of them, the church in the past attracted such luminaries as Sir Arthur Conan Doyle, and even Abraham and Mary Lincoln, who participated in seances at the White House.

The spiritualists trained Bruyere to do psychic readings of jewelry and other objects; to scroll back and "read" the akashic records, where, according to legend, everything that has ever happened or will happen is recorded; and to channel spirits. To this day, when people around her recite The Lord's Prayer, she claims she can leave her body, and make room for a spirit, usually Master Chang, the 4,000 year old Bonpo abbot, whom Bruyere considers one of her most important teachers and guides. She channels only for her students, late at night during intensive retreats, and now for the Tibetan Bonpo, the indigenous people of Tibet who have influenced, and also adopted, much of Tibetan Buddhism.

The spiritualists also taught Bruyere about the aura, or spiritual light, around every human being. The teaching was perfunctory. But in Bruyere's hands, touch had uncanny results. Early in her education, she touched the hands of a classmate who suffered from arthritis. The next day the woman claimed her arthritis was better. "The woman started calling everyone under the sun and telling them," says Nancy Needham, an elder at the Healing Light Center Church. "I had what is classically known as beginner's luck," says Bruyere. "It means you've done it before in a previous life."

Almost completely untrained, Bruyere says she was soon ministering to twenty-two people a day and sometimes to twice as many. "I would scan the aura, find holes, put my hands there and pump them up," she says. She learned by doing. She used no colors, no patterns, and in the early days knew nothing about the chakras. "If I saw a flaring maroon coming out of the joint, I'd know [the person] was in pain and that there was a congestion that was both biological and energetic. And I would run energy through it until it would lighten up. When it got to pink or blue, I would stop. And then it would be like—now what do I do?" When she laid hands on, "Pain left," she says. "And sometimes major disease left." Her own crippling arthritis all but disappeared except in one hip.

At night Bruyere pored over anatomy charts, Merck manuals, medical books, and the literature from various foundations dedicated to specific illnesses, such as multiple sclerosis. In her spare time, she studied old esoteric texts to soak up whatever information she could about chakras and different methods of healing. "Books would fall on my head," she says. "And every time I picked up a book and tried something, it worked."

The people who came to Bruyere often had illnesses doctors couldn't cure, whether it was arthritis, whiplash, or cancer. "They were desperate," says Bruyere. "They weren't new age people necessarily."

Eetla Soracco, then a twenty-eight-year-old housewife and mother of three children, was one of those people. She had a tumor on her pituitary gland, which was shutting down her entire glandular system; the doctors, unable to operate, had sent her home to die. A friend bundled Soracco up to hear Bruyere speak in a neighborhood church. Soracco, an Estonian-born woman who had served as a nurse on the Russian front during World War II, had been seared by the devastation she had seen during and after the war. Hearing Bruyere speak, she recalls, "I thought: What nonsense." But her friend insisted on taking Soracco for a healing. "My friend was very persistent," recalls Soracco. "To me, [Bruyere] was nothing special.

"When she first saw me, she said, 'I feel you are a natural healer. Why don't you come work with me,'" says Soracco, who eventually did become a healer, specializing in AIDS patients. She went to Bruyere's office every day. "I always got lost. I couldn't see or drive a car very well. I didn't know what made me do it," she says. At first she still wanted to die. But soon she began to feel differently. "Her work gave me so much energy, I was able to drive. I was not getting better, but I was not dying," she says.

Eventually, Soracco says violent anger and self-hatred buried deep inside came to the surface. "After you have a healing, you sometimes feel like you become worse," explains Soracco. As she dealt with these feelings, her desire to die changed to a desire to live. "Something opened up. I took responsibility," she says. Over the years, the tumor disappeared. "Later, one of the doctors saw me in the supermarket," she recalls. "He almost fainted. He had to come over and touch me. 'Are you really Mrs. Soracco?' he said."

One of the techniques Bruyere developed in those early days is chelation, which charges all the chakras. In chelation (not to be confused with the intravenous treatment for atherosclerosis) the healer begins at the feet and slowly moves up the legs, joint by joint with his or her hands, and then along the torso up to the heart, and down the arms. It gives a healer a sense of exactly how the energy is running through the system and where the energy field is at is weakest.

"When someone brings me four diseases in one body, which is common, I do chelation so I know what to do first," Bruyere explained to me when I met with her in her office for the first time. "I do that as part of my overall approach. It's something that puts them together in one piece."

Chelation has become a kind of MS-DOS for healers, a basic, universal operating system. A modified form of chelation is the fundamental technique at the Barbara Brennan School of Healing as well as at many of the other major healing schools. By now, healers all over the United States and Europe and even as far away as Tokyo and South Africa use the basic chelation technique.

Besides charging the energy field of any client it is used on, Bruyere says it has specific applications in serious illness, although these claims have not been studied by scientists. "It's a lifesaver," she claims. "Take for instance someone who is in heart failure. Because the technique will cause capillary dilation, you've now relieved maybe 25 percent of the pressure on the heart of someone who's in congestive heart failure. They'll live long enough to recover. It's a big deal."

Or she continues, "Take someone who had a drug overdose. It will keep their brain from absorbing too much of the drug, it will flush the drug through their system, and they'll recover instead of dying of a drug overdose." Many healers also use chelation to clear the field of excess radiation or chemotherapy.

Chelation can also be used after traumatic injury. "There's a lot of energy around the crisis," Bruyere explains. "For about forty-eight hours after a trauma, there is a huge amount of extra energy all around the body. If the healer organizes that, you can get a more thorough healing more quickly."

When I asked how Bruyere developed this technique, she hesitated. "Who is this for?" she asked. It turns out Bruyere believes she was taught the technique by a spirit guide, Dr. Johnson. Dr. Johnson had actually lived. He died in 1887, according to Bruyere. She stumbled on his grave, she says, when she accompanied her first husband on a film shoot to some of the old mining towns. "He was an old country doctor in northern California in a mining town, and he actually knew my great great grandfather."

Bruyere researched Dr. Johnson's life after she realized he was an historical person. "He was in the merchant marine. He was stuck one time in Shanghai, and he stayed there long enough to study medicine."

The interesting thing about Dr. Johnson is that he gets around. I talked with healers who had never met Rosalyn Bruyere who spoke of Dr. Johnson as if he were an old friend, and a great "person" to have helping out in healing sessions.

Bruyere was ordained as a spiritualist minister in 1971. Her education as a healer, however, was just getting started. One of her first mentors outside the spiritualist circle was Bill Gray, a huge bear of a man who weighed 325 pounds when he died—after he had lost 100 pounds from abdominal cancer. When they met, he was already in the advanced stages of the disease.

Gray, the subject of a book, *Born to Heal*, was somewhat of a celebrity in esoteric circles. While Bruyere did healings on him, he instructed her. At one point, she says, he put his hand on her abdomen as she was working on him. "I felt like I had been plugged into a 220-volt socket," she says. Then, he had her try to do the same thing to him.

After he died, she says, there was a flurry in esoteric circles that he had passed his gift on to her. "Five years later, I realized he had," she says. "Bill passed sound waves on to me. The electrical current sensation in my hands came from him. Prior to that time, I was 'allowing' energy. I learned to 'push' energy."

This is an energy Bruyere demonstrated on me, without any warning. At the end of my first face-to-face meeting with her, after we had spent four hours talking about healing and her own development, she told me she wanted to show me something. She patted her healing table, motioning to me to jump on it. I was surprised that she was offering a demonstration. Bruyere was not one to show off, make claims, or even talk about healings she had done. Quite the opposite.

I laid down and instinctively closed my eyes. Bruyere put a hand on my belly. All of a sudden my flesh was vibrating, as if my belly was a lake and a motor was running on it. "Open your eyes," Bruyere instructed. "Look at my hand." Her hand was completely still on my body. Yet the vibration was stronger than any vibration from motel "Magic Fingers." I have never felt such a physically palpable energy from any other healer. Bruyere was smiling, clearly amused.

The vibration stopped. "Now, I'm moving into a higher frequency," she said. "You won't feel as much." She was right. Whatever energy she was running was not easily discernible. After a minute, she stopped. "You're going to be very high," she said.

I laughed. I didn't think a five-minute demonstration of subtle energy frequencies was going to have much effect. It was only when I started driving back to my hotel that I realized Bruyere had not been exaggerating. I felt drunk, but without that cloudy feeling. I had become hyperlucid and very happy. Nevertheless, I was still under the illusion that Bruyere had just given me a five-minute lesson on how different frequencies feel. A week later, I realized otherwise.

Quite suddenly, or so it seemed, I saw the behavior of a man who had been buzzing about me, half-friend, half-suitor, half-there, half-not, for what it was. Just as suddenly, I had had enough. It was like the air had gone out of a balloon. I have rarely acted so decisively. I *knew* then that Bruyere had done something. But what? I had a chance to ask her a few months later. She smiled, a twinkle in her eye. "I just grounded you." "No," I replied, "you did much more than that." She knew what I meant. "Someone was playing with your second chakra," she explained. The second chakra involves emotions and sexuality. This man had definitely been toying with me. She said no more.

These were the sound waves that Bill Gray had bequeathed to her. Gray also taught Bruyere about male-female polarity. Sometimes, Bruyere says, the only thing a healer needs to do to help a woman get pregnant is reverse the charge on the ovaries. It is a technique originally taught by Bruyere that is now in common circulation, and, according to a number of healers, is often (but certainly not always) effective. "You pick up a vibration and reverse the charge from right to left," says Bruyere, who has helped several doctors' wives become pregnant, among others. "You just feel the current and then reverse the charge. . . . With a whole group of people trying to get pregnant, sometimes this is the problem."

Bruyere's second teacher, Grandfather David Monongya, a Hopi elder, also came to Bruyere for healings. He had cataracts. Bruyere claims healing cataracts is not complicated. "You make a little tiny laser light come out of the finger that goes into the lens itself and helps the cells reform themselves." There is no way to verify her claim, but she says she has healed "not more than 200 or 300 of them. I've had thirty years." Sometimes, she adds, it can take ten or more energy sessions before the eye "unclouds even a little bit."

Grandfather David doesn't fall into those statistics. "I didn't do very much for his eyes," she admits. "He wouldn't let me do much. I'd heal him for two seconds, and he'd say, 'That's nice. Now sit down. I have something to tell you.'" Among other things, he gave her the sacred Hopi prophecy, passing over the younger generation of his own nation. The reason for his decision "was very hard for me to take in," she says. "There wasn't any one among his people he could teach. Not after five generations of fetal alcohol syndrome."

The prophecy was a revelation for Bruyere that forever changed her understanding of reality. "There are certain assumptions in white culture," she says. "And one is that the Bible is sacrosanct. You can't fight it." But in the Hopi prophecy, eerily similar to the apocalypse, mankind has a choice for survival that is not described in the Bible. More than a thousand years ago, the Hopi prophesied that an opportunity for change would come when "the sons of white men wore their hair long" and "the eagle landed on the moon." At that time, the Hopis foretold, "The secret mysteries of the People, shall be known," as Bruyere explained in her book, *Wheels of Light*. "It meant that the basic assumptions of Western thought were up for grabs," she says. "Once you can grasp that, your life as a practitioner changes dramatically."

Grandfather David was like the father she had never had. "Because of my background and personal life, I didn't have strong permission from father figures," she says. "Legitimacy is an issue in my life." Grandfather David gave her the legitimacy that her own father had failed to provide. By giving her the sacred Native American teachings, he "literally entrusted me with our children," she says.

Bruyere now had a truly rare gift: the freedom to think outside the standard box. Around that time, she became transfixed by the theories of Albert Einstein. "From the metaphysical, the teaching is that God is all there is," she says. "From the physics, energy is all there is." The theory of relativity seemed to her to be the key to what she was doing. The metaphysical community used the word energy all the time; but people thought it was metaphoric. Bruyere began to look at it literally. Einstein had proved that matter was a form of energy. Perhaps medical doctors and everyone else were missing the point: "If energy is all there is, why can't you change tissue?" she wondered. The question gave her tremendous freedom. Energy flowed. It was far more malleable than matter.

Hyemeyohsts Storm, a Cree ceremonial healer and medicine man and another mentor, also came to see Bruyere for help with cataracts, and in what seems like a pattern, she lists him, too, as "one of my great healing failures." He wouldn't sit long enough to let her do very much, she claims. Something else, namely her continued training, was the real agenda. "He was able in ways no one else had been able to, to make me listen to myself so I could hear what I was doing and know when I was making mistakes," she says. "My association with him was formative. And transformative."

Once, she says, she went to visit him, and he told her a story about her. "I hadn't asked for it. But he thought it was time." He named her Sun Bear, because if someone poked their head in a dark place, Bruyere would say, "Let me see" and stick her head in. "What are you talking about?" she would then ask. "It's not dark in here." It wouldn't be dark because she had illuminated the place, Storm told her, adding, "You're like a little tiny bear with a sun for a head."

To others Storm seemed a little crazy. "You can't get out of Storm the same thing he gave me," she says. "I got more. . . . I believe he seeded [teachings] in me." Adds Jeanne Farrens, a long-time student of Bruyere's and the editor of her book *Wheels of Light*, "He gave her initiations and information she's never revealed to anyone. She was welcomed into the tribe."

Bruyere also apprenticed to elders in the Apache, Sioux, and Shumash tribes. "The primary cultures still have ruthless teachers," she says. "They don't care if they ruin your life, if they'll save your soul. They'll test you. They'll put demons in your dreams. They'll manifest things in your living room." Her teachers never tried to control what she learned, she says. "My native teachers knew if you put in information, it would grow in its time. What's going to happen is life is going to go on, but with a couple of tools no one else has." Now, she says, of her and those she's trained, "It's our job to give these tools to everyone else."

In many ways, Bruyere is the Godmother of modern spiritual healing. Delores Krieger, who learned some basics of spiritual healing from theosophist Dora Kunz in the early 1970s, introduced the concept of subtle energy to far greater numbers via Therapeutic Touch—tens of thousands of nurses and others, making a tremendously important contribution to the shift now taking place. In the very beginning, she talked about *prana*. But she soon dropped any references to mystical teachings in an effort to make the technique palatable to doctors and nurses. And she certainly did not emphasize spiritual anatomy.

Conversely, Bruyere has spent her life gathering the fragments of esoteric knowledge that have scattered through the centuries and transmitting the teachings to a new generation. In her teachings, she weaves together Egyptian, Native American, Chinese, Tibetan Bonpo, and Christian spiritual energy practices, which she sees as aspects of the One.

"The tragedy of Christ," she says, "is that most of the healing techniques of Jesus were lost." But she believes some of that lost knowledge lies in the Egyptian tradition. Her historical view, after decades of study, is that Jesus went through a series of initiations in the healing temples of Isis in Egypt, the last of which closed only in 423 A.D. "My sense about Egypt is that's where Jesus was changed," she says. "It's a long way to India from Israel with that particular travel of the day. And it's a very short trip to Egypt, which had, at that point, a full chakra system."

"The hymns of Isis often reveal things that are in the Parables, Bruyere asserts. Mary in Christianity becomes the Isis figure. Christ is the redeemer. The Egyptians call Horus the Redeemer. That's as clear an overlap with Christianity as you can possibly imagine."

Many of the esoteric teachings, she adds, are right there in the Bible. "If you really know what auras are and you already know where the chakras are, you can read the gospels and see references to light. You can piece it together. In the West, most people think these references are a metaphor. Yet you find, when you study this, it's not a metaphor at all. St. Paul writes about it by saying, 'The many will see what the many will see, the few will see what the few will see.'"

In fact, she believes the Bible is much more literal than people realize—even the reference to the Valley of the Shadow of Death. "It's the burial grounds outside the old city. When you're standing there in late afternoon, a shadow falls because of the altitude of the plateau." Likewise, she feels many archaeologists have missed the point of various illustrations of Egyptian temple processions. "Some of them are really chakra drawings," she says. "People think in terms of 'either or.' I've gotten smart by [using] 'and.' I can never let myself see just one layer. I never have been able to do that."

Bruyere is the first modern healer to emphatically assert that healing is scientific and spiritual, and to codify the practices that have served for thousands of years. From the beginning, her guiding vision has been that the entire body of spiritual knowledge can, and must, be taught to as many people as possible and returned to the population at large. "I have done everything I can to build in my own competition," says Bruyere. "That's a moral stand. They can't all do what I do with thirty years of practice. But when they have ten years, they can probably do more than I could do after ten years."

Before Bruyere, great healers carefully guarded their secrets, as do many *chi gong* masters and shamans even today. "I can't tell you the secrets of *chi gong*," Master Hong Liu, a *chi gong* healer from China, told me when I interviewed him at his Los Angeles home. And the most famous healer of the previous generation, Olga Worrell, openly asserted that healing couldn't be taught; it was a gift. Other well-known healers, like Edgar Cayce, worked entirely through trance; to know what he had taught, he had to listen to the tapes others had made of his channelings.

Bruyere came of age as a healer at an extraordinary moment. "There was an opening of the generalized consciousness," she explains. "There was the beginning of a process of questioning conventional wisdom." The human potential movement was under way. Biofeedback researchers were documenting how much the mind could influence the body. And below the visible level of activity, healing was gathering its first momentum as a mass movement. In 1961 Bernard Grad, Ph.D., a researcher at McGill University, published the first study measuring a spiritual healer's ability to affect tumors in an animal.

The spread of Eastern spiritual teachings helped lay a foundation. In 1959 the Dalai Lama left Tibet because of the Chinese invasion, taking the teachings and practices of Tibetan Buddhism to the West. After the Beatles made the Maharishi Mahesh Yogi famous, he imported Transcendental Meditation to the West, making meditation almost as popular as rock n' roll. And in 1970 Swami Muktananda, a Hindu yogi, introduced *Siddha* yoga, giving tens of thousands of people *shaktipat*, a sacred initiation of the kundalini energy which had been reserved in previous generations for a few devoted disciples at a time. These Hindu teachers in the West built on the base begun by Paramhansa Yogananda, a teacher of *Kriya* yoga and the founder of the Self-Realization Fellowship a generation earlier and on the theosophists in the previous century.

Many other Hindu, Buddhist, and Chinese teachers also moved to the United States, teaching everything from meditation to tai chi to martial arts and eventually acupuncture, all of which got the subtle energy moving and focused. Meanwhile, Carlos Castaneda described his initiations into the shamanic world in book after book, sharing experiences that were so other-worldly that many dismissed them as drug-induced fantasies.

Thousands of Westerners began meditating, learning to change their state of consciousness at will, or using martial arts exercises to get in touch with their subtle energy bodies. Others were at least exposed to the idea that reality was more complex than previously understood.

Then, in 1972 *New York Times* correspondent James Reston made acupuncture famous when he wrote about his emergency surgery for appendicitis from his hospital bed in China. He was part of the elite press corps accompanying President Richard Nixon on his historic visit that helped open China to the West. His successful experience with acupuncture to prevent post-surgical pain made the front-page headline of the *Times*.

All of these events were subtly changing the Western consciousness. Some of the leading voices in integrative medicine today began meditation practices that ultimately revolutionized their approach to medicine: Deepak Chopra, M.D., advocate of meditation and author of *Ageless Body, Timeless Mind*; cardiologist Dr. Dean Ornish, author of *Eat More, Weigh Less* and an expert on reversing heart disease through diet, yoga, and meditation; and Dr. Jon Kabat-Zinn, founder and director of the Stress Reduction Clinic at the University of Massachusetts. They found that the calmness and self-knowledge gained through meditation may have its own biology.

On a parallel track, Dr. Andrew Weil, director of the Program for Integrative Medicine at the University of Arizona, went the shamanic route, traveling to South America after graduating from Harvard Medical School in the late 1960s in search of a teacher. He, too, came away with an understanding that the body can heal itself, and that natural herbs, the basis of most modern medicine, can be very potent. These experiences would influence the general public, but they would do so only decades later.

In 1994 Christiane Northrup, M.D. became the first mainstream doctor to write about energy anatomy in her best-selling *Women's Bodies, Women's Wisdom*.

In 1974 Bruyere got a call from Richard Grossman, M.D., a plastic surgeon at Sherman Oaks Medical Center in Los Angeles. He had run into one of his patients and had noticed that her ears, which he had surgically fixed were finally healing nicely. It turned out the patient had also been treated by Bruyere. The patient insisted that he should check her out. Somewhat ahead of the times, Dr. Grossman invited Bruyere to treat some of his burn patients.

Over three or four months, she treated several patients at the hospital before the little experiment came to an inconclusive end. Dr. Grossman "began taking a lot of heat from the other doctors about the wacko he had in the burn ward," recalls Bruyere, who says that, besides being outspoken, she was more than 100 pounds overweight at that point—and was hard not to notice. But, she claims, there was another issue: "At the point at which you heal a patient underneath the skin graft and the skin graft falls off, you've now made the plastic surgeon obsolete, haven't you?" she says. "He didn't want to continue a project to study the effects of healing on burns."

Dr. Grossman remembered the experiment, too, but could not recall either positive or negative effects. "He tried it and that was about it," his nurse reported. "He didn't see anything special." In fact, she added, "He made a joke about it. He said, 'I also wore a headband back then.'"

Bruyere had better luck at the University of California in Los Angeles, where Valerie Hunt, Ph.D., an eccentric professor of kinesthesiology, wanted to study the physiological effects of Rolfing with electronic equipment—and the input of an aura reader. Bruyere's name came up as the best aura reader in Los Angeles.

For Bruyere it was a chance to put the ancient wisdom to the laboratory test. She knew from experience that each chakra had its own set of frequencies, which created a series of frequencies in the energy field. Ancient texts also spoke of a specific mathematical relationship between the frequencies of each chakra, known as "the multiple." And the frequencies increased as the energy moved up each chakra. But no one in modern times had ever conducted experiments to document this. Bruyere became a key figure in the first team to experiment with these concepts.

While a Rolfer worked on a subject who was attached by electrodes to an oscilloscope, Bruyere described what she saw. Bruyere's descriptions matched frequency readings recorded by the oscilloscope. When she saw red, the oscilloscope always showed the same frequency pattern. It was not the same frequency as the "red" in visible light spectrum, but it was a distinct frequency. The same was true with the other colors. Hunt hypothesized that the oscilloscope was recording electromagnetic harmonics of subtle energy. What the ancient texts claimed appeared to be true in a lab.

In another experiment, Hunt discovered that in the areas where the chakras are said to be located, the body gave off electrical charges with frequencies of 100 to 1,800 cycles per second. The normal frequency for electrical activity in the brain is 0 to 100 cycles per second. Muscle activity tops out at 225 cycles per second. The heart generally registers 225 cycles per second.

Both experiments suggested that the chakras emitted some kind of electromagnetic radiation. The chakras were either electromagnetic in nature or were coupled to the electromagnetic spectrum. This was significant. Bruyere already knew each chakra was responsible for a different state of consciousness. These experiments meant that, as the ancient texts stated, states of consciousness were directly related to frequencies of energy. But while the Rolf Institute has a copy of the Rolf study, Hunt never published her studies in a scientific journal, thereby diminishing their value. Nor have her studies ever been repeated in any other lab.

Nevertheless, as word of the UCLA experiments got around, Bruyere's reputation grew. The spiritualists, uncomfortable with the spotlight, invited Bruyere to go her own way. At the same time, Bruyere filed for divorce. It was a new beginning and a dying of the old. "My initiations always have to do with coming to a new reality," she explains. "I would have to say the theme is always taking me away from the narrow focus of the person and family I was born to be in, and moving me into a global focus."

Bruyere left her marriage and her job as a grocery checker. She began to charge for healings to support herself and her two sons, and she founded the Healing Light Center Church (HLCC). (As a minister, Bruyere could lay hands on people without risking arrest for practicing medicine without a license.) She ran the Healing Light Center as a ministry, a clinic, and a school. "This is before the zoo started out in the world," says Alisha White, a professional singer who visited the center for help with migraine headaches in 1976 and ultimately became a healer. "This is before you could pick up new age magazines with pages and pages of ads of people doing this and that, when people really didn't know what a healer was. Rosalyn pioneered there."

The center had its headquarters in the basement of the Maryland Hotel in Glendale. It was a dismal place. "It was not earthquake prepared," recalls Jeanne Farrens, a student in those days. "It leaked. Every time it rained, we would have to use buckets. There was no privacy between rooms. You could hear people during the sessions. The carpet was threadbare. You're not supposed to have this healthy soul and be homeless. But that's where I trained."

For a while Bruyere also did outreach in Englewood, a predominantly black neighborhood. "Glendale was considered John Birch Society," explains Marcella Thompson, who was working for an answering service when she first heard Bruyere speak in Engelwood. As a black person, "you wouldn't be caught there after sundown. But [Rosalyn's] attitude [about Englewood] was: 'We need to get into that community. These people are not being served.'" Thompson, who ultimately became an ordained minister, now answers the phones at the Healing Light Center Church, acting as the first screen for those trying to reach Bruyere.

Bruyere gave lectures three nights a week on healing, creating the first completely open forum on healing in modern times, which she dubbed "The Crucible Program." From the line of people outside her own office door, she felt the demand for healing couldn't be met fast enough. "I saw medicine's disasters," she explains, "the people [doctors] couldn't help or even give any solace to."

Classes cost $5, and eventually $10, and students got more than their money's worth. Bruyere would spend three months lecturing on heart disease, move on to cancer, and then devote several months to diseases of the female reproductive system. "We'd start at six and usually go until after midnight," recalls Farrens.

Bruyere downloaded both practical and esoteric information. But much of the time she taught the way she had learned. The unsaid, the implied, the metaphoric, and the power of her own energy field to resonate and awaken her students was at least as important as the literal information she conveyed. "Twenty years ago, when we studied with Rosalyn, she was as she is now," says Maria Bartolotta, then a high school teacher, and now a Los Angeles healer who was in The Crucible's first graduating class. "She's very circuitous. But after twenty years, I still learn new things from her."

"What goes on is not contained just in the words," adds Nancy Needham. "It's the energy. What's different at the end of a week with her is not the things you've learned, but the cells in your body that grew during that week."

Needham recalls a workshop called "Inner Worlds." "I don't think she said hardly anything worth remembering." Needham left the workshop wondering if Bruyere had been bored. It was only weeks later that she realized the purpose of the workshop. "I realized after, that in the inner worlds, it's important to make space. All Rosalyn did was make [psychological] space. Most people are trying to make *things*. She was making creation."

On Saturdays and Sundays, Bruyere and her students ran a healing clinic where the sick donated what they could in exchange for treatment. It appears to be the first, and so far only, clinic run by a team of spiritual healers. To date, it is probably the best practical training that has ever been devised. Bruyere's students laid hands on people who were sick and who were suffering from a myriad of conditions. Bruyere insisted her healers do a session in a half hour. "It pushed them to a higher level of efficiency," she says. "I didn't know initially that I was pushing them beyond the normal limits of human interaction."

During the week, the HLCC's staff of healers saw paying clients, keeping careful charts of patients, just as in a regular medical clinic. Five years into her grand experiment, Bruyere graduated her first twenty-one students in 1979. Most of them did not take up full-time healing practices.

In her own life, Bruyere continued to face her personal challenges. "We age just like everyone else," she says of herself and other healers. "We have problems in our love lives, just like anyone else."

Bruyere had married her second husband, a carpenter, on a trip down the Nile in 1978. When that marriage ended after less than a decade, she took stock. Looking at her relationships with men, she says, "I realized people weren't there. I sort of made someone up." She began walking up the mountain behind her house daily and shed 100 pounds. It was a time of deep transformation. "When you go on a diet, the emphasis is on d-i-e," she says. "The diet resurrects information. There's more to fat than fat." She met her present partner, Ken Weintraub, a sixth degree black belt karate master and former rabbinical student at the dojo where she went to train and further develop her *chi*.

Bruyere closed the Healing Light Center's Glendale headquarters and moved to Sierra Madre in 1992. The free clinic came to an end. Bruyere began to travel to Germany to teach and to focus more on workshops around the United States, especially in Cleveland, the Northeast, Arizona, and Chicago. In January 1994 she stopped teaching weekly classes.

To this day, Bruyere treats healing as a ministry with a higher purpose, much as medicine was originally a ministry. She still teaches, but her Crucible Program has little structure and students in workshops don't get much hands-on practice time. (She encourages new students to apprentice to more advanced students.) Bruyere, who is running the Healing Light Center as a nonprofit church, charges less for workshops than most other healers, in the belief it will be available to more people. She also sponsors weeklong pro bono healing clinics at Native American reservations, with as many as a dozen of her ministers also volunteering their time, and does many other healing programs as an act of service.

Some people go to one of Bruyere's lectures and hear her tell stories about her partner or her latest trip to Germany and decide she is coming from her ego. But after following her closely over several years, I found that she has one of the most open hearts. It's not something she wears on her sleeve. While she is talking to someone, I have noticed her address that person's situation—whether it's a broken heart or a broken psyche—energetically without ever mentioning it. Almost nothing that goes on in a classroom escapes her attention or her compassion. Sometimes, even as she is saying hello, she places a hands just so, for instance, right at the point of a spinal cord injury. And I have never seen her pull rank on another person or act holier than thou.

That does not mean she is without solid boundaries. Once I focused in on Bruyere during a lecture she was giving, not realizing that I might be invading her. (At that time I still thought of my mind as being strictly inside my head.) She sent me right out of her field and gave me a stern look, without ever breaking the rhythm of her speech. It was quite a performance—and a lesson for me about the nature of consciousness. The whole thing was almost a physical experience. I realized then that psychic etiquette is something everyone should learn.

Her teaching style, however, is not for everyone. She says she plants seeds. She does not care if they grow in a minute, a week, or a few lifetimes. "She carries a lot of information in her field," explains Marcella Thompson, a minister in the Healing Light Center Church. "She passes it field to field. Some of it happens in dream time."

Even when I interviewed her I found that our conversations worked in this way. Occasionally something we discussed would take on a new meaning days or weeks later, floating to the surface as an epiphany. I would know it had come through her energy field rather than her words because of the quality of revelation. Once, for instance, I asked if she thought a spiritual awakening might be taking place in the world.

"The problem with these vast spiritual awakenings is they are not spiritual awakenings once they become a scientific fact," she said. The comment didn't strike me as particularly insightful. But a few weeks later, while talking to a psychiatrist who was an avowed atheist and who was strikingly hostile to the concept of subtle energy, I had an epiphany. I saw that this psychiatrist's future counterpart would be using subtle energy as part of standard medical practice. And he might very well still be an atheist. When subtle energy becomes a scientific fact, it will not be proof of the existence of God. That debate will probably be eternal. Some people see God in natural phenomena, others do not. While making this observation, the conversation with Bruyere was in my thoughts, as if in another dimension the insight and Bruyere's comment shared the same space.

Bruyere always works on several levels at once. A beginner and an advanced healer might be sitting side by side yet hear almost two entirely different lectures. Likewise, Bruyere gathers to her some very fine healers, and some very wounded souls. She sees her job is to heal, not to judge. She does not spend an excessive amount of time pushing or cajoling or reprimanding or policing. Although she elucidates spiritual law, she doesn't give students a set of rules. Her ultimate goal is to help her students connect to source directly, for it is source that heals.

"This is not a trade school," she says. "A lot of people go to schools with a curriculum where they think they know what they're going to get. I don't let my students have such illusions."

She is as likely to teach students to pray as to run *chi*. "Praying is the legitimate way to open the channel [to spirit]," she tells them. "And poetry is what you pray." But, she adds, "Prayer will not work unless you pray for something." Prayer, she advises, should include praise, thanksgiving, and asking. Not a workshop goes by where she doesn't bless a baby or a union or do an ordination or an anointment. When Bruyere conducts ceremony, it goes beyond mere gesture. "If a healer is blessed," she explains, "Healing becomes a blessing. And if a blessing is real, it should become a healing."

Bruyere dispenses knowledge freely. Once, in the early stages of my research, I said I wished she could just download even part of what she knew. "I wish I could, too," she said. "I would like to plug it into half the healers on the earth—and all the psychotherapists."

She seems to have a technique for almost any situation, whether it's resetting the heart rhythm or jump-starting failing kidneys or cleaning out someone's lungs or breaking up an astrocytoma brain tumor or embodying the good mother. Yet she understands that techniques are merely a conduit for spiritual essence. "You don't just pass energy," she tells her students. "The energy is alive. You're also passing your experience."

In her own mind, she attributes her power as a healer to her inner alignment. "It's probably because of who I am religiously," she says. "I'm a very unconventional Christian woman. And my Christianity early on took a turn where I decided that I would serve God by doing the best I could on behalf of my fellow humans without judgment."

"Rosalyn is running the only authentic mystery school in the country," adds Healing Light Center minister Needham, half-jokingly. "It's a mystery how to find it. It's a mystery how to get into it. And it's a mystery how to get out of it." Adds Jeanne Sande, another Healing Light Center minister, "The paradox and the irrational and the symbolic—that's where Rosalyn is teaching."

Bruyere estimates she has taught between 5,000 and 10,000 people the basics of energy healing. A few of the doctors who have studied with her are now bringing healing into integrative centers at leading hospitals, and Bruyere now teaches doctors and other medical personnel about energy anatomy. But she has only formally graduated 158 healers.

People often study with her for a decade before graduating or being ordained. Bruyere and her students quietly help many in need. But the center, in many ways, is so focused on spirit, it lives in the Shambala mists. It does not even publish a list of healers who trained there. It runs on a tiny budget with a very small staff. It often seems to work outside, rather than inside, this world.

But someone Bruyere briefly trained would do things differently. Just as Bruyere was graduating her first students, a blonde, former NASA physicist showed up at some of Bruyere's classes. Bruyere did not exactly pass the baton. But the energy had its own path. After an initiation at one of those workshops by one of Bruyere's students, Barbara Brennan would take healing in a new direction, laying out basic techniques in a step-by-step format and opening the world's first "Healing Science" trade school.

Eight

A Physicist Maps the Subtle Realms

"The speed with which your guides can work is related to the power you have and the communion you have with them," Barbara Brennan said, opening a lecture on "fifth-level" surgery on a November morning in 1996. The Barbara Brennan School of Healing was convening at the Seasons Hotel in McAfee, a tiny resort town in central New Jersey, as it now does five weeks a year. With its dark corridors, rambling institutional architecture and frequent sales conventions, the hotel seemed like an unlikely place to discuss metaphysics. That did not stop the teachers and students who spread out over the "campus," least of all Brennan.

In fifth-level surgery a healer can improve the body's functioning by repairing the connection to an etheric organ, explained Brennan to the 150 students in her junior class, including several doctors. The actual organ may have been damaged or even surgically removed. At the level of the fifth template, however the vitality and wisdom of the organ still exists.

The "trick" to fifth-level surgery, however, is that the healer does not actually do it. All the healer has to do is hold the frequencies of the fifth level. The spirit guides who exist at that energy state then come in through the healer's body and do the actual work. "The more you can stay connected, the faster the work will be from a linear perspective," Brennan explained. With her slender figure

132

and her hair curling gently about her face, Brennan, a former home-coming queen, looked much younger than her then fifty-seven years.

The students listened in rapt attention. For many healers, working with spirit guides is a given. The Brennan curriculum, how-ever, is designed to take students slowly from three-dimensional re-ality into spiritual reality, all the while keeping a linear framework. Students spend the first three years of the four-year program study-ing the basic structure of the energy field. During this time, they slowly make the transition from understanding the body strictly in biochemical terms, where everybody is separate, to perceiving life as a system of energy structures, where all things are interrelated through resonance.

Once the fundamental structure of life is understood to be en-ergetic, the idea of spirit guides is no longer so unfathomable. They are simply beings with a different set of frequencies than humans or other physical life forms. Brennan does not quite say this, but in the end, the implication is that spirit guides are really no more bizarre than microbes. It is simply a matter of scale. With microbes, the scale is one of physical size. With spirit guides, it is one of frequencies.

As the students absorbed what Brennan was saying, a hand went up. "Why do the guides need us?" the student asked.

Brennan looked pleased. The student was addressing one of the biggest philosophical questions posed by the claims of spiritual heal-ing. If spirit guides exist, why would they need the interventions of an earthly healer?

"It's the same as cooperation between parts of yourself that are conscious and the parts that are not awake and aware," Brennan an-swered. "We're all one. We are tapped into the collective conscious. Guides are tapped into it as well. They just don't have physical bod-ies. So, as they work through you, there's a utilization of your body and your field and the lower levels of the energy field. They don't have these lower levels."

Now it was time for the students to connect to these spirit guides. Junior class teacher Peter Faust, a healer and an acupunc-turist, took over, as seventy-five students laid down on the massage tables set up in orderly rows. The other half stood by the tables as healers, and Faust addressed them. "Hold your first level," he called out from the stage, as if he was giving directions for a twenty-second-century aerobics class. The students focused on spinning their first chakras. Then Faust moved them to the second chakra, then to the third. The room was totally silent, as the students concentrated on charging their energy fields and raising their frequencies.

"Bring your consciousness to the fourth level," Faust instructed. "Breathe deeply. With each breath you charge your field. Now move to the fifth level. Continue to charge. To do this work, you have to hold this level the entire time.

"Everyone put your hand on the client's third chakra, simply making contact," Faust said. He paused to feel the energy in the room. "I'd like to hear everyone breathing," he said. "Don't be afraid. It's life force."

"The guides cannot come into your field unless you have enough power," Brennan interjected. "The guides are coming in now through your right shoulder. I am watching the guides come in now to your hand, through your right shoulder."

The room had the hushed feeling of a church during silent prayer. But try as I might, I did not see any spirits. Neither did all of the students. Some of them felt the guides in their bodies; others heard them; still others just trusted. Around me, some student healers were deeply connected with their clients, others less so. Teachers walked through the aisles, observing and giving instruction, where needed.

A few minutes later, Brennan and Faust called the experiment to an end. The students would do healings on each other, teamed with the guides, after lunch. I could not quite visualize seventy-five or more spirit guides flowing lockstep into a New Jersey resort hotel for a drill. "Why do the guides come?" I asked a junior class teacher, Joanna Seere, who was chaperoning my visit. "Because they have an agreement with the school," Seere answered.

Around us the students streamed out for lunch. For them it was just another day of classes at the Barbara Brennan School of Healing.

"From a spiritual perspective, my life task is to dissolve the imaginary veil between the spiritual and material world. Or to help,"

Barbara Brennan told me the first time we met, in her office in East Hampton, Long Island. It was a cold winter day in January 1995. Bright sunlight streamed through the tall windows, illuminating Brennan, who wore white pants and a white sweater. Books on healing, physics, metaphysics, and psychology lined one wall of the former living room, which had become Brennan's private sanctum. A photo of a young Hindu woman, Mother Meera, a spiritual leader viewed by seekers around the world as a living incarnation of the Divine Mother, rested on the mantel over the fireplace. A cot, for meditating, stretched out next to her desk.

Brennan, M.S., a former atmospheric physicist for NASA, helped to make healing a serious topic in certain circles around the world. Her two books, *Hands of Light* and *Light Emerging*, have sold more than three quarters of a million copies around the world, giving her an international reputation. She founded her school in 1982 with just a handful of students shortly after she had launched her own spiritual healing practice. She now oversees classes for more than 700 students a year, and seeks to keep her classes big. As of June 1998 she had graduated 629 healers, including 15 doctors, 43 psychotherapists, 54 nurses, and 16 physical therapists from her four-year, part-time program.

In the grand scheme of things, the numbers are relatively small, but the school now graduates 100-150 healers a year. Many graduates do not become full-time practitioners. Nor are Brennan graduates uniformly talented. Nevertheless, Brennan has increased the number of professional-caliber healers in a short amount of time. In the process, spiritual healing is gaining glamour and cachet. Students come from as far away as Europe, Japan, New Zealand, and Australia, and from all around the United States, as well as Mexico, Canada, the West Indies, Puerto Rico, and the Bahamas. Other programs have also grown more popular in the reflected glory.

The commitment of these aspiring healers is anything but frivolous. Students paid $5,200 for a year's tuition as of October 1998. Then add on the expense of required anatomy classes and biweekly therapy sessions, plus airfare and room and board for the five week-long sessions each year. A diploma from Brennan's school represents a minimum $30,000 investment, and many students end up shelling out more than $50,000 over four years. This is not counting the disruption of the student's normal professional life—as a doctor, nurse, banker, lawyer or mother—during those four years. All for a certificate from an unaccredited program, in an area in which there is no career track. As in all programs, some graduates are fully booked and others struggle to put a practice together.

What makes Brennan's school so popular is her unique ability to put energy healing into a Western framework. In vivid, easy-to-read language, she links spiritual anatomy, psychology, and physical and emotional illness and suggests it is all related to physics. The ideas, for the most part, are not exactly new, but she packages the ideas in new and alluring ways. Her illustrations of healers working in a blaze of light, surrounded by spirit guides, are the icing on the cake.

Like Rosalyn Bruyere and Delores Krieger, Brennan is evangelical about bringing healing into the mainstream. Healers making a bid for scientific veracity generally have not discussed things like channeling and spirit guides in print. But Brennan pulls out all the stops. She speaks unabashedly about spirit guides, channeling, past lives, etheric chord connections between people, hexes, and astral entities—as scientific phenomena. Even better, in her books she promises readers that they too can channel guides, see auras, and get to know their own souls.

For Brennan spirituality is a science. The whole purpose of living on Earth is about "learning and creating greater aspects of the self," she told me. "The great plan of salvation is the realization of more divinity." Or, she added on another occasion, "God is all there is—but God is always becoming more. The act of creation is a continuing act."

Brennan believes spiritual phenomena and spiritual realms are a matter of ever more subtle frequencies and higher states of consciousness. "The light itself, I think, is at a very high frequency. The aura has infrared in it, too, which is lower," she said. But, she added, "This is really an issue for highly trained physicists. Most of the aura is outside of our measuring capability at this time. . . . So all of the concepts we have to describe this phenomena are religious."

Brennan took healing out of the church. The decision to do so was simple, she says. All kinds of healing systems, from physical healing to psychotherapy, are taught using an academic model. Why not "healing science?"

"The choice was to train professional healers to work in the health-care profession or to work in the charismatic religious movement," she explains. "I was very interested in the educational realm. A church meant having services. And that's not what I wanted to do." Besides being an academic institution, Brennan's school is also a lucrative business.

By all accounts, Brennan is a driven and demanding leader. Many students can go through four years without direct personal contact with her. But Brennan makes sure the teachers she employs grade students on skills such as holding specific auric frequencies, being able to do past life healings, spinal cleanings, chelations, and brain balancing—basic auric techniques, most of which are taught in one form or another in other programs. Brennan rounds out the curriculum with two more healings in the senior year that she claims she channeled through from her spirit guide, Heyoan.

In addition, students are graded on their facility with *HSP* and on their understanding of psychological and energetic character structures as perceived in Core Energetics. This branch of psychology is based on the theories of onetime Freud disciple Wilhelm Reich, M.D., who both sensed and described what he called "orgone energy" in and around the body.

Juniors and seniors are even graded on their ability to surrender, described in a student manual as: "To willingly deliver up or give over to a higher imperative." God or spirit is never directly mentioned. In the student manual this surrender is directly tied to the student's willingness to loosen their psychological defenses, which prohibit the student from living directly from pure essence.

Students must also complete regular homework and reading assignments. They must write up the healings they conduct outside of class (preferably on another student). To graduate, seniors are required to write a thesis and present a case in which they have conducted at least ten healings with a single client. In the case report, the students are expected to analyze the client's and their own transference—both psychological and energetic.

Along with the academic work, the school is a four-year program in personal process. According to spiritual philosophy, once the inner light is awakened, it then slowly burns away the personality attachments. But here teachers make sure students face their own emotional wounding. In fact, the school sends warning letters to students who do not face their own negative intent and anger. As in most other programs, self-awareness is considered more important to being a healer than is being highly clairvoyant. "What the school is great for is it gets you to look at your personal stuff," says Gerda Swearengen, a recent graduate.

"From the time someone's going into the school, and the time they're coming out in their senior year, they are very different people," adds Susan Weiley, a former senior teacher at the school. "It's not the techniques. That's not what it's really about. It's about clearing enough of the personal material so you are a clear channel [for energy]. I say to students, 'Barbara could teach these techniques in four months, but it takes four years to do the personal process work. Teaching the techniques keeps your attention, so you can do the processing and deepen into yourself.'"

Students are constantly encouraged to view all life experiences as being related to their soul's purpose. At the same time, the curriculum is highly technical, based on rational knowledge and empirical experience. Some graduates say the emphasis is more on techniques than on reaching the highest states of spiritual essence. Brennan herself once joked with me that she was teaching "aural mechanics."

Some graduates believe more emphasis is put on rooting out the "lower self" rather than on reinforcing the light of the soul. "It makes those issues stronger in the unconscious," explains Catherine Vajda, a former teacher. The character structures focus on what's wrong. "How is someone supposed to heal if you keep focusing on the negative? All the ancient teachings tell you to focus on the higher aspects."

No school can satisfy everyone completely, but Brennan has developed a system for teaching basic energy healing and one model of psychodynamics in a step-by-step way to hundreds of people at once—a first in the West. "One of her greatest gifts is she codified the information," says Weiley. "And there's the codification in her school."

"People are critical that the student body is so large," adds Weiley, who was an art journalist and the photography book editor for the Museum of Modern Art in New York before she became a healer. "My personal opinion is we need as much light on this planet as we can have. Every person who studies with her affects so many people around them. Just from that school, we can raise the vibration [consciousness] of the planet. One student can have such a profound effect. And there's such a rippling effect."

Brennan's ambitions for subtle energy healing are grand. She predicts scientists will eventually build instruments to measure the human energy field. "The field shows all the precursors to any illness you'll get," she says. "We'll learn much earlier detection. Now we don't detect things until there are physiological parameters."

"Not only can we diagnose with an instrument," she continues. "We'll develop instruments to feed energy into the field." She says she even envisions a day when feedback monitors will instantly give people the frequencies missing from their field—the energy version of one-a-day vitamins. "We are shifting to consciousness-based reality," she asserts. "What we're doing is bringing in a miraculous way of living. Or, rather," she corrects herself, "what we call miraculous is becoming a way of life."

It is as a teacher that her ambitions are the most grand. "My vision for the school is to train healers all over the world and to bring healing into a recognized profession in the Western societies," she says. Brennan is pushing to make healing a trade like farming or music or art or investment banking, all things that come from the Divine for those who believe in the Divine.

She hopes that one day her school will be accredited, but she asks students not to disseminate any materials from the school. Teachers sign a contract promising not to teach the esoteric wisdom as Brennan teaches it, except at the Brennan school. It is not the way medicine is taught at Harvard or history at Yale. Normally people, whether they pay for their education or not, are free to apply it as they wish. Non-competition clauses and proprietary information are more common in the business world than in academia.

Brennan has in the past even sent graduates letters warning them not to teach her work. In 1995 the school threatened legal action against the Institute of Core Energetics, which was sponsoring a lecture series on the human energy field by a graduate of the Brennan school and the institute. The school claimed that the material was too similar to what Brennan taught. The institute, run by Brennan's key mentor, John Pierrakos, M.D., cancelled the course, citing "possible pirating . . . as well as plagiarism" in a mailing to its faculty and students. The Brennan school graduate sued Brennan, the institute, and related parties for defamation. Brennan and the others named deny any wrongdoing. The case is pending.

More recently, Brennan has also filed service mark claims with the federal patent and trademark office to protect her core star and hara healings. She says she has done this to preserve the integrity of these healings specifically as she teaches them, a way to codify her teachings. "There are freshman who say: 'Oh, I just did a *hara* healing.' And they don't even know what it really is," explains Brennan.

In addition she has filed service mark claims on the "*hara* line" (Brennan's name for a central column of intention and grounding that goes through the *hara* or *tan tien* point, described in martial arts, hatha yoga, and Japanese and Chinese healing arts) and the "Core Star" (Brennan's name for divine essence). In doing so, Brennan says, she was just following the suggestion of one of her employees. Trademarks on Brennan's name and the name of the school have already been granted. (A service or trademark protects the "brand" name, not the underlying concept. For instance, Kleenex is not the only company to manufacture tissues. In addition, a service mark is not granted when it is merely descriptive: "apple" can't be registered as a name for apples.)

Graduates, many of whom revere Brennan, have mixed reactions to some of these efforts. Some believe that Brennan is only claiming what is hers. Others are disappointed, noting that Brennan's work is based on a very long tradition that is in the public domain. "If your whole goal is to bring consciousness to the world, then you just want the material to get out, à la Rosalyn Bruyere," says one former teacher. "You can copyright what you write," adds another former teacher, Catherine Vajda, "But it's all taken from a single universal energy field." Besides, graduates note, people who want to learn healing through the Barbara Brennan teaching method are always going to seek out Barbara Brennan.

Brennan's drive has made her a wealthy woman. The Brennan school grosses $4 million a year. Two former senior employees estimated that Brennan nets more than $1 million a year, not an extraordinary sum for a top administrator in business, but paradigm shifting in the world of healing. Brennan declined to comment.

Brennan is unapologetic about reaping the financial benefits of her efforts or about encouraging her graduates to do the same—at least in their practices. If healing is a profession, she notes, then people should be paid. "What is this idea that many people have, this myth, that healers shouldn't get paid for what they do?" asks Brennan. "Why should I need to work for eight hours a day at a regular job, then take care of my family, and then, if there's time left over, squeeze in healing? Healing is needed all over the world. This is crazy."

Brennan *sees* differently than the average twentieth century American. Unlike many others with similar talent, she is not afraid to talk about it. When she went to a Catskills, New York ashram and knelt at the feet of Swami Gurumayi Chidvilasananda, the successor to *Siddha* yoga master Swami Muktananda, she says she saw "a beautiful lotus" in her heart. When she went before Mother Meera, a Hindu woman who lives in Thalheim, Germany, and who many believe to be an incarnation of the Divine Mother, she said her field was completely clear. "You know what white light is?" she asks. "It was beyond that." Both of these teachers, she says, "in meditation had the clearest fields I've ever seen. I haven't seen Sai Baba [another Hindu guru believed by devotees to be an enlightened master]."

When I asked her if DNA has a melody, as Paul Pearsall, a Harvard-trained psychologist claims in *Sexual Healing*, she cocked her ear and, laughing with delight, told me my genetic code sounds "like Mozart, only not so fast." When I brought up a friend's health problems in our first meeting, I could feel her looking over my shoulder, as if she could see him there. I was very conscious of how

Brennan easily moved back and forth between dimensions. Her clairvoyance is one of her strong suits, like her ability to articulate her psychic experiences.

She talks openly about Heyoan, the guide she claims to channel. Heyoan is a spirit who has "finished his incarnations," she said. But he is also, in Heyoan's words, "What Barbara is becoming." She also channels energy that she calls "the Goddess" for a schoolwide assembly on Saturday mornings.

At the same time she speaks as a scientist quantifying phenomena. When she channels, she said, she expands her energy field to incorporate higher and higher frequencies. With Heyoan, she said, her field has a radius of about fifteen feet. "When I channel Heyoan, I feel much bigger. I can answer all the questions. I know a lot more." When she is in the Goddess state, she said, her field is much larger than when she channels Heyoan and "I experience myself as limitless," she claimed. "There are many different ways to look at the phenomena of guides.

"The broader I can expand my definition of self, the clearer the picture of the universe becomes," she continued. She says this is true for everyone. "Your soul is so huge," she explained. "You who are incarnated right now is an itsy bitsy, teenie part of who you are. You come here in this form to learn."

Brennan told me on another occasion that when she channels at the school, "We go into all these deep states. I'm purposely not using terms like *shaktipat* [awakening of the *shakti*, or spiritual energy, by the intention of the guru] and initiation. It creates transference issues that puts the leader in a superhuman state." Nevertheless, she makes some pretty strong claims: "What happens in the Goddess is just as powerful as any guru *shaktipat* as I have ever seen because of the mystical body that is being grown in the school."

While appreciative of her gifts, graduates do not describe their experience of Brennan or the school in quite such lofty terms. Brennan has certainly helped her students awaken to their spiritual natures. But a true *shaktipat* guru, or enlightened master, no longer has personal attachments, and embodies unconditional love and compassion at all times, and awakens that state in others, through pure intention. Brennan, by her own admission, still does her share of emotional processing. Like most of us, she has ordinary concerns. The Goddess sessions do, however, bring a higher level of energy into the school and are a highlight for many students.

Brennan's learning curve has been steep. The second of three children born to a laborer father and supermarket cashier mother, she was raised on a Wisconsin farm with no central heating or indoor plumbing, in what she describes as difficult circumstances. "My father used physical punishment," she says. And money was so tight, "we used Sears catalogs for toilet paper. It wasn't just financial poverty. There was not a lot of emotional expression."

Through the eighth grade, Brennan attended a one-room school. At home, there were no books in the house but the Bible; to amuse herself she spent hours playing alone in the woods. There, she says, she began to notice that everything was connected by energy fields. Assuming that these types of experiences were normal, she soon forgot them.

While in grade school, at a camp sponsored by the Evangelical United Brethern Church, her counselors asked if anyone wanted to come to the altar and give their life to God. "I went up and did that," she says. But science came to mesmerize her. Her high school yearning was to be an astronaut; the yearbook refers to her as a "the girl with the atomic giggle." Thinking she had found her life's passion, Brennan went on to the University of Wisconsin, where she earned a bachelor's in physics and a master's in atmospheric physics. Her mentor, Verner Suomi, developed some of the first infrared instruments for weather satellites.

In 1965 Brennan, then newly married to her college sweetheart, left Wisconsin for Washington, D.C., to become one of the first female scientists at NASA, where she developed light-sensitive detectors that were used from satellites to measure the ultraviolet and infrared spectra. In 1971, caught up in the restless, antiestablishment spirit of the times, Brennan divorced, married NASA scientist Jack Conaway, and left the space agency with her new husband.

"We were going to go to British Honduras, build a boat, and sail around the world, while having a baby." She laughs. They had the baby and settled for a house in the Yucatan. Says Brennan, "There I was, barefoot, pregnant, nauseated." She painted pictures of a girl with red hair and brown eyes, and "before Celia [her daughter] was born I knew she had red hair. . . . I didn't understand all of this then."

After her daughter's birth, Brennan suffered from recurring symptoms that turned out to be Typhoid fever. She says she was also facing stresses in her marriage. She began meditating daily. A few months later, Brennan and her husband moved back to Washington, where they trained to become counselors in bioenergetics, a form of therapy developed by Alexander Lowen, M.D., based on the work of Dr. Wilhelm Reich, with an experimental group, The Community of the Whole Person. A therapist who was there at the same time recalls that Brennan, while psychically gifted, was not emotionally integrated.

According to bioenergetics theory, the body's structure mirrors the character structure and is shaped by the original psychological wounds. Therapists are trained to understand someone's early childhood experiences merely by looking at the physical body. As Brennan began to counsel people, she saw light around her clients. Eventually, she began to make basic correlations between colors in the aura and emotional states: dark red, for example, indicated anger; bright red signaled passion.

Opening psychically was grueling at times. After Bud, a client at the community, committed suicide, the group held a meditation with his ashes in the center. Brennan recalls going up to the box. "Where are you, Bud?" she asked. "I felt all this wild energy." Shortly after, her training counselor told her she had been invaded by a dark entity and helped her "send it to the light." A year later, she says, she realized the entity had been Bud. "I called to him and he was clinging to me because I was the only one who saw him. He was stuck in the lower astral realm."

Much later she became attuned to higher frequency realms. "I remember seeing angels and guides," she claims.

"And what does an angel look like?"

"They have wings. They do."

"And are they white?"

"Yes. They look like the angels you see in paintings. They have wings. They wear robes. They have a lot of golden-white light."

In 1975 Brennan moved to the Pathwork Center in Phoenicia, New York, a small spiritual community in the Catskill Mountains that has since closed down. There she found two teachers: psychiatrist John Pierrakos, who had studied with Dr. Reich, and Pierrakos's wife, Eva, a trance channel. Together, they had created the Pathwork, which focused on psychological purification as a path to God.

Many of Brennan's ideas about psychology and spirituality originate from her Pathwork training. The Pathwork was based on the idea that if you did not clear up your "lower self" and your "mask," all the meditating in the world would not be enough. "We felt that psychology and spirituality are closely linked," explains Judith Saly, a longtime Pathwork member. "You can meditate and have very beautiful experiences and it's not enough for the rest of your personality."

It was a community in which everyone was expected to be excruciatingly honest and to strive to be in the "higher self." Brennan and others now see much of the old Pathwork model as too focused on the lower, ego-motivated self. In addition, they say the system was sometimes used in an abusive manner. Yet when the Pathwork began, the idea of incorporating the soul into a psychotherapy model was novel. And it was the crucible in which Brennan was shaped.

Eva Pierrakos soon asked Brennan to shut down her channel and focus on her unresolved personal issues. "It was quite a challenge," says Brennan. "I was in a tough marriage. It was much easier to talk to angels." The former NASA scientist washed dishes in the communal kitchen. "I knew I had to work on humility," she says. "There are a lot of tests to see if you will follow God's will. And this was the hardest."

"There was a lot of volatility and intensity to her process," recalls Judy Bachrach, a singer and songwriter who later became one of Brennan's first healing clients. Life was far from luxurious at the Pathwork Center, which was basically a summer camp for adults.

Brennan, her husband, their daughter, and his son lived in two rooms. "They lived lousy," says a friend from that time. "On weekends, when everyone came up [from the city], the kids slept under the [bunk] bed." And, Brennan recalls, the ceiling leaked. "We had buckets on the bed and the kids under the bed."

All the while, she worked on her marriage. A friend recalls, "She was willing to be told everything was her fault." Adds Sue Thesenga, head of the Seven Oaks Pathwork Center in Virginia, "She was such a gifted psychic, but people didn't take her gift seriously enough. She did need to work on the personality levels."

During this period Brennan studied core energetics with Dr. Pierrakos and ran a counseling and massage practice in Manhattan. Core energetics is a form of psychotherapy that combines bioenergetics with spiritual teachings from "The Guide" that Eva Pierrakos channeled. Dr. Pierrakos taught Brennan about the chakras and how to measure their spin using a pendulum. He also related chakra functioning to character structure.

Altogether, Wilhelm Reich described five basic character structures: the schizoid (who was rejected before or soon after birth); the oral (who was emotionally abandoned as an infant); the psychopath (who was seduced or betrayed by the parent); the masochist (who was overly controlled by the parent); and the rigid (whose sexuality was denied by the parent). (This is only one model of psychology.)

Brennan added her own piece to the puzzle. She saw that character structures were also auric-field configurations. A person in hysteria had an aura marked by "flares of off-shooting energy," as she puts it in *Hands of Light*. A prickly person would have prickly energy points coming from the aura. A schizoid's energy bodies might fly up and out of the physical body at the first hint of danger. The "rigid" personality had a tightly bound aura; the "oral" personality had tendrils to pull in energy from others. She, like Dr. Pierrakos, linked psychotherapy into the more all-encompassing paradigm of subtle energy.

On a trip to Findhorn, Scotland, five years after moving to the Pathwork, she says she stood on a power point in the earth and asked for her channel to reopen. A few weeks later, she says, it did—stronger than ever. Afterward she had regular healing sessions with a Columbian healer living in Manhattan. Then she heard about Rosalyn Bruyere and the scientific research Bruyere had done at UCLA.

For the next eighteen months, Brennan estimates that she made between four and six trips to Los Angeles, each time spending a week or so at a time studying with Bruyere. "I learned all about energy," Brennan recalls. For a time, she and Bruyere became close, according to a friend of Brennan's. "She was so happy to have met Rosalyn," says this friend from the Pathwork days. "She said, 'You don't know how lonely I've been.' They were good friends." Once, at Brennan's invitation Bruyere visited the Pathwork Center and gave a workshop.

During one trip to Los Angeles, one of Bruyere's students did a series of healings on Brennan. In one week, Brennan says, "I went through fifteen past lives, doing fifteen different things that were unhealthy. I was married for fifteen years to this person. And in all the past fifteen lives, I died from the unhealthy things. It was amazing."

Brennan now calls such a conglomerate of issues that holographically thread through a person's life, "a psychic nuclear point" because when such an energy block gets released it causes a cascade of changes. As for "past" lives, it is not necessary to take that literally, she says. "Past" life is a misnomer, she claims, although a useful one. In reality, she believes, everything is happening at once; from the perspective of the higher dimensions, time is an illusion. We just do not yet understand the nature of time and space.

Brennan says her Pathwork teachers were more influential in her development than Bruyere was. But she came home a changed person. "It's the first time she got what her interests and passions were," recalls Judy Bachrach. "Rosalyn made it possible for Barbara to be a healer," adds Susan Weiley, a former senior teacher at the Brennan school who also studied with Bruyere. "She'd been a therapist. She learned enough to make it possible. Where else could Barbara have gone for that?"

At first, everything in Brennan's life dissolved. "I went into terror," she recalls. Her marriage ended. But three months after her initiation, she had fifty new clients in her New York City practice.

Previously, she had offered Pathwork counseling, massage, and bioenergetics therapy. The new clients came for healings.

The following year, in 1982, she met her present husband, Eli Wilner, the owner of a successful framing business handling top-end artwork, a man twelve years her junior. Brennan, who now lives in a sprawling East Hampton house she designed herself, says Wilner helped dissolve her poverty consciousness. (As with everything in the spiritual realm, money itself is neither good nor bad. If the intent is to provide a service to help people, then the money that flows from it is pure. If someone's underlying intent is to make money or have ego-based power, the service will be subtly distorted. This is true in every field, not just healing.)

"When I was a healer, I used to figure out the least amount I could charge to live," Brennan recalls. "I would add up how many hours I could work in a year and divide the amount of money I needed, and from that I would get my hourly rate. I did it that way for years."

The Barbara Brennan School of Healing began in 1982 as an informal study group that Brennan taught after hours at her East Side office. Brennan did not have years of experience as a hands-on energy healer. But she had a decade of training and practice as a therapist and spiritual counselor.

First, she slightly modified Bruyere's chelation technique and made it a foundation of her teaching. (To this day, although she guards the processes she developed, Brennan uses Bruyere's technique as the calling card for her school at introductory workshops.) Some people speculate that this caused friction. Both deny it, though. "She actually gave me permission to use it in my book. And I credit it to her," says Brennan. "How I feel about it, it's done exactly what Spirit wanted it to do," adds Bruyere. "It's gone around the world now. A lot of people use it, and are going to use it."

The two leading teachers of healing have very different understandings of spiritual energy, however. Brennan cautions that beginning students might actually feed cancer extra life force and make it grow, although she says she has not seen it happen. She says she reached this conclusion after watching Bruyere teach a technique to surround a tumor mass with light before "lifting" the energy of it out. "Give me a break," says Bruyere, who is just as emphatic in the opposite direction, "You can't spread cancer."

Brennan also teaches students to run energy away from the heart in someone with heart disease—because, she says, she learned it from Bruyere. But Bruyere and healers she has trained also work directly on the heart and heart chakra when treating heart patients. "These energies generally work on the health of the body, not the disease," Bruyere explains. (Of course, that assumes that the healer is holding an intention for the highest good of the client to emerge.)

Brennan's first students were primarily from the Pathwork. "The first year was very chaotic," recalls Caren Barowsky, one of the first graduates. But the classes were also highly educational. "We spent the last part of every session doing healings on each other," recalls Barowsky. "Barbara would do readings on us as we did it. 'You're losing energy here,' she'd say. Or, 'Do this. See how it affects the flow.'

"Barbara was just Barbara then," adds Barowsky. "She was not famous." Brennan was working on her first book, *Hands of Light*. The class received mimeographed pages from it and also helped Brennan refine her ideas. For instance, Brennan was confused to find that sometimes when two people looked at the same person's energy field, one would see purple while another might see green. As a scientist, this did not make any sense. If it was a real phenomenon, people should be seeing roughly the same thing.

The key, she realized, was that each chakra and each level of the energy field exhibited different frequencies just as the ancient texts described. "The key was to learn how to shift frequency bands. All the physics taught me that. If you look at the sun with certain kinds of filters, you can see solar flares. If you change the filter, you can see fairly deeply into the sun. Using another filter and blocking out the solar disc, you see a corona."

Brennan found that depending on the chakra frequency she embodied, her perception of the field changed. (The different levels of consciousness actually exist in the same physical space simultaneously. According to Brennan, the second level extends further from the body than the first level, and so on.)

Most healers work holistically on all the levels of the field at once. Rosalyn Bruyere, for instance, trains healers to work multidimensionally—in both auric and causal realms—at the same time. But working with each level of the aura became a cornerstone of Brennan's teaching.

"The levels are very good for intellectual people," explains Gerda Swearengen, a graduate of the school. "It gives them something to understand. As you progress, you don't go through all the levels individually. In school, you have to do protocol healings."

In general, Brennan put new names to things, giving phenomena in the spiritual dimensions the patina of scientific validity. Clairvoyance and other psychic senses went from being *ESP* to *HSP* (*High Sense Perception*). The aura became the human energy field, HEF for short. Working with guides in healings got taught as one specific technique, fifth-level surgery. Time and again, she spelled things out.

Instead of talking about chakras being "open" or "closed," or spinning clockwise or counterclockwise, Brennan taught her students to use a detailed, if tedious, notation system developed by her Pathwork mentor Dr. Pierrakos. "C6" meant clockwise, six inches in diameter: a healthy chakra and a highly functioning level of consciousness. "CCEL2" indicated the chakra was spinning both counterclockwise and elliptically with a two inch diameter—and a significant splitting off of consciousness was occurring.

Chakras are always changing. But Brennan's point was that chakras are real. They can be measured, just as blood pressure or sun spots or any other phenomenon could be measured. They could be put in a medical chart, like any other scientific measurement.

In *Hands of Light*, Brennan basically kept to the immediate auric field (the astral dimension in the Hindu cosmology.) When she could not find a publisher, she took the $50,000 she received in her divorce and published it herself. "She'd come out of this poverty," recalls Karin Aarons, a senior teacher at Brennan's school and a friend for nearly thirty years. "For her to put out the money to publish her own book was a big deal. She'd be: 'Can I buy this?' about everything. It was on such a deep level. 'Do I deserve this?'" It unnerved Brennan on another level, too. Here she was, a former respectable scientist writing about chakras and spirit guides. Says Aarons, "she was worried the world would think she's insane."

The first edition quickly sold out. (Bantam then snapped up the rights to it.) *Hands of Light* turned out to be one of those books that has an electrical effect. In 1988 Brennan's school had its first two graduates. That same year, inspired by *Hands of Light*, 128 students enrolled as freshmen.

Kate MacPherson, a critical care nurse for twenty-six years, says the book literally fell on the floor in front of her when she was in a bookstore. When she opened it, "there were pictures of the aura—things I'd been seeing for years. I took the book home and read it." She immediately enrolled in the school. "For twenty years, I was able to tell the doctors things," she claims. "They thought I was a witch. I was able to see what was going on. I'd say, 'This patient has to go to surgery; his bowel is turning black.' They'd say, 'We'll wait.' And I'd say, 'You can't. It'll be too late.' And sometimes it was."

Many of the people who signed on had never even been interested in occult topics. "To be honest, when I started at Barbara's I needed structure," says Alan Hayes, who went to her four-day introductory workshop merely to indulge his then-wife and who went on to study and then teach at the school. "I'm an accountant. I have a bachelor's in math and physics. . . . I could do [the work] because I still had my known world with me. Without it maybe I would never have tried to do healing again."

Even some scientists took note. "Barbara Brennan's model is a whole lot more sophisticated than we have in the scientific circles," admits a research scientist who has done preliminary controlled studies on energy healing. "I'm very interested in her work and I've been aware of it for ten years. It's an interesting model in that it contains so much structure." But, he adds, "We have no way to validate what she says through scientific methods. At least—not yet."

Brennan closed her own healing practice in 1986 to focus full time on teaching and administration. The only healings she does now are class demonstrations. Many of them are done on relatively healthy people. But every so often, she does a healing that leaves a lasting impression on her students. "On two occasions, I saw her perform very dramatic healings to unravel curses put on people who were deathly ill," recalls Susan Weiley. "They were completely changed.

"In one a woman had had a curse put on her by her boyfriend's ex-girlfriend and she was very sick. The woman was in her four-day introductory workshop. And Barbara picked her to work on. She did that twice that year. Very few people would even recognize that the curse was there. People get sicker and sicker and no one in the medical world knows why. It was really awesome. It had a profound impact on everyone there." Weiley has since treated several people in her own practice, who, she says, were also the subject of hexes.

Another time, Brennan did a past-life healing on retired home economics teacher Barbara Ann Nelson, who was diagnosed during her sophomore year in March 1993 with idiopathic macular degeneration, a disease of unknown origin in which holes develop in the macular part of the retina. Her condition was documented by photographs taken by Al DeRamus, M.D., a leading retinal surgeon in Fairbanks, Alaska. The diagnosis was confirmed by Francis L'Esperance Jr., M.D., a world-renowned Manhattan eye surgeon affiliated with Columbia Presbyterian Hospital, who urged Nelson to have surgery the very next morning. Instead, Nelson went to classes at the Brennan school.

In a two-hour healing, Brennan guided Nelson through memories of having her eyes plucked as part of ordination as a healer in an ancient time. As Nelson, who did not believe in past lives, relived the experiences, she says she came face to face with a belief that God had allowed and wanted her to be blind. She had seen something so awful—the way she was treated by those she loved—that now she unconsciously wanted to blind herself from the truth.

After Nelson got in touch with the beliefs in her psyche, Brennan restructured the energy lines around Nelson's eyes, as well as the energy lines all the way from her feet to her eyes. Many of these were tangled or entirely broken. When she repaired these lines, Nelson's eyes would have a healthy matrix on which to grow. That night, Nelson recalls, "I felt so connected to God or my core or whatever you want to call it. I knew I would be eternally grateful."

At first it seemed as if Nelson had had a "miracle" healing. Within six months, the vision in Nelson's formerly troubled left eye was 20/30, almost normal. There was no sign of macular degeneration then or a year later. "I made a diagnosis," Dr. DeRamus told me in November 1995. "It was confirmed by four specialists. When I saw her in April [1993], the condition was present in both eyes."

Nelson's sight eventually deteriorated again, despite frequent healing sessions from other healers. In the spring of 1997 she finally had surgery on her left eye. Part of the teaching, she says, is about learning to trust God instead of going into terror. Sometimes now, she adds, she can "sit and be held in the arms of God and know that I'm safe. It's that high vibration that keeps my whole system in a healing mode."

Most of Brennan's program, however, is designed to have students practice healing techniques on each other. The training serves two functions at once. Students develop several basic healing techniques, and they also go deep into their own emotional issues. Many people, even those who have already gone through psychotherapy, are surprised about how much comes up. "For the first two years, I was in emotional process every class. I had no idea what I was going to have to go through myself," recalls Connie Myslik, a psychotherapist who had been through psychotherapy. "Some of it was stuff I was aware of. I thought I had gone much further than I actually had."

In the senior year, Brennan teaches her *hara* healing. This is a subtle healing that can have a powerful effect at the level of intention. (Other healers, along with martial artists, work with the *hara* or *tan tien* points, as well, but Brennan emphasizes the importance of the *hara* more than most healers.) Brennan also developed her Core Star healing, which addresses the level of pure Divine light. Brennan says it looks like a star just above the belly button, at a level even deeper than the *hara*. In a Core Star healing, the healer literally floods the client with the light of their own divine spark. (Other healers, of course, also work directly with core essence. Some of them consider it the basis of healing, rather than a special technique.)

Brennan's goal is to take linear-minded people into the mysteries. Many of the people she has taught might never have tapped into their talent as healers without the foundation her school provided. But ironically, Brennan's biggest strength—her linear approach—has it's limitations, according to some of these same graduates.

For instance, testing skills ensures that every student really understands every technique. In the view of some, however, it is the antithesis of encouraging students to move into the highest levels of surrender. "Teachers would say, 'Set your intention to pass the skill,'" recalls Thomas Ayers, Ed.D., now a retired Army Reserve colonel. "Nothing was said about the highest and greatest good of the client. I always did it on my own."

Adds New Jersey healer David Grady, a former freshman class dean at the school, "With testing, students tend to freeze up. Healing has to be done in a relaxed meditative state. You can't be worrrying about your performance. You want to focus on the client's highest good." But, he notes of the school, "I'm happy that it existed for me." Grady now teaches healing workshops, focusing on an open heart.

Ultimately the real "magic" of healing is not in the chakras or the techniques alone, but in love and surrender. Some people feel that Brennan stresses doing more than being. Others disagree. "Barbara teaches all these things you do until you clear enough of your emotional issues that you can get to a state of grace," says Cheryl Ann Bartenberger, a recent graduate of the school. "But some people miss the whole point. They get hung up on the techniques. Or they're waiting for a lesson on holding a state of grace."

Levent Bolukbasi, a former Brennan school student and teacher who now runs the IM School of Healing Arts in Manhattan, remembers when he realized there was more to healing than chakras and the aura. He was working with his first AIDS patient in 1990. The man, a young aspiring actor who was working as a waiter, had a virus that was destroying his eyesight. He lived in constant fear and suffered from insomnia, fatigue, and depression.

"I just faced the enormity of this person's predicament," Bolukbasi says. "All of a sudden, I had this moment where everything stopped. And all I could do was align myself with the highest Divine wisdom, to be as present as I could be, and to bring that to this person, with the hope that it's going to help him."

"As I was with him, I was moved to do some things. It's like I worked with grace, and the energy of hope. It was truly recognizing this person as a Divine being, lying down here with this condition. I was appreciating the essence in him."

Levent, as he is known, claims that when the session ended, the man's eyesight had improved. The following week the man reported that a rash covering much of his body, which the man had not even mentioned, had disappeared. Levent notes that the man died of AIDS the following year.

Levent concluded that it was more important to teach healers about Divine essence than how to manipulate chakras. He quit to start his own school. A few years later, another teacher, Michael Mamas, also left to start his own program, in many ways modeled after Brennan's school, but teaching more meditation and less technique. Both men are essentially trying to offer an alternative, and competition, to the Brennan school.

The criticisms do not phase Brennan. People come to her school precisely because of the aura of academia she has created. People want rules. And she knows it. "There's a particular thing I'm supposed to do, to present healing in a more academic light," explains Brennan. "I think everyone is needed to bring this paradigm shift into the world," she adds. "God isn't so insufficient as to provide only one way."

Like people everywhere, graduates of the Brennan school have unresolved issues, even glaring blindspots. And there is always a range of talent. But I found the most talented healers from the Brennan school to be passionate about healing, God, and their own evolution. They strive to be in surrender and to keep a clear intention. More than a few also align themselves with a living realized master or with the spiritual teachings of a major religion.

Connecting with spirit is an ever unfolding process. A few Brennan graduates supplement their healing studies with classes by Rosalyn Bruyere (and vice versa). "Barbara gave me the techniques, straightforward, scientific," explains Brennan school grad Deborah Scott, a former computer programmer for a large insurance company. Before she applied to Brennan's school, she spent three years studying with Rosalyn Bruyere and continued to take classes with her even after she graduated from the Brennan school.

"Rosalyn gave me the container to hold it all, the perspective," Scott adds. Without the training at the Brennan school she says she probably would have remained more a dabbler than a healer. "Barbara was focused on technique, whereas if you blink, you could miss what Rosalyn says about technique."

Some graduates have also turned to Amy Skezas, the founder of RoseLight and the Flow Alignment and Connection methodology. That form of energy work begins in a dimension beyond the auric field. Students must first awaken their Light Bodies, energies that include higher harmonics of the chakras and the *hara* dimension in a more casual realm.

Flow sessions are always conducted in a high state of surrender and in concert with a group of high spirit guides. Without the foundation that Brennan provides, however, many would be lost in Skezas's work. She focuses largely on the spiritual realm and gives almost no intellectual or personality basis for her work. (However, she was inspired indirectly by Brennan's two books.)

Meanwhile, demand for Brennan-style training grows with each year. Former Brennan school teacher Rolf Steiner opened the first European school of healing in 1995, inspired by his onetime mentor's program and using her books as teaching texts. Although it is not a total copycat of Brennan's school, its big draw is that it is Barbara Brennan-style training, taught by Brennan graduates, and a few healers trained by Bruyere. It is a sign of just how much cachet and trademark status hands-on healing and the Barbara Brennan School of Healing has achieved.

Some of this cachet, say critics, is based in ego rather than Spirit. "It's a big machine that's making a lot of money," says Catherine Vajda, a former teacher at the school. "It's got a lot of glamour to it for the teachers and for the students."

Maybe so. But there is certainly more to the Brennan school. Brennan, like Bruyere, has become a catalyst. All the frequencies of all the different healing teachers are needed. There are many paths into the mystery. They all inform each other. And no one teacher has all the pieces.

Another Brennan protégé, Jason Shulman, also left to start his own school, A Society of Souls, taking many of his first students from among his former Brennan school students. In turning to the Kabbalah, he has become one of a few teachers who are bringing the esoteric wisdom of the Jewish tradition into the growing secular movement of hands-on and distant healing. It is yet another way into the mysteries, and another place for people to work on their lessons.

Nine

The Kabbalah Revealed

"God's grace never goes away. What kind of God would it be: 'It's Wednesday and it's time for grace?'" asked Jason Shulman, the founder of A Society of Souls, a school for healing based on the teachings of the Kabbalah, the mystical path of Judaism. "It's we who go in and out of phase with it."

On this Friday night in April 1997 at the Cathedral of St. John the Divine in New York City, before an audience of all denominations (including agnostics), Shulman was warming to his favorite subject: human suffering and its transformation.

From the stage, Shulman might have passed for a reincarnated Biblical prophet with long greying curls and an embroidered cap covering his crown. Yet Shulman, a former rock n' roll musician, Zen meditator, and auric healer, is not a rabbi. His primary interest in the Kabbalah is not historical or religious; it is in the Kabbalah's power as a finely tuned instrument for healing, something that modern Jewish scholars outside of the closed Hasidic community rarely explore. Shulman, however, has delved into the Kabbalah to extract its mysteries for healing cancer, heart disease, and the existential condition known as life.

The path to ecstasy "is not the pursuit of happiness," he told the assembly on the first evening of the weekend workshop. "What's the opposite? Unhappiness. To get to ecstasy," he said, "we have to get to the real. We have to get rid of: 'Might have been,' 'should have been,' 'wish it was,' 'thought it could be.' . . . The reason we cannot feel ecstasy is because we have denied parts of ourselves."

Asking for the group to toss out some causes of suffering, he wrote out a list—anger, pain, arrogance, boredom, fear, shame, confusion, helplessness, spite, hatred, ego, worthlessness—that are so common as to be almost another kind of shared human gene pool in addition to DNA. "What is it for you?" Shulman asked when he ran out of room on the blackboard. "Why do you hide from the light of bliss? You may not know. But there's something you cannot accept."

"Life in this universe, the Kabbalah teaches us, is based on imperfection," Shulman continued. "The job is to relate to our shortcomings in a new way—as having meaning and value.

"What do we think we're doing, giving God our perfection? It's a task we can never accomplish," he said. "For that to be the only thing worthy to give to God would be torture. What we have to give to God, often in abundance, is our imperfection.

"What will God do with our imperfections?" he asked. "I don't know. I can tell you what God will not do. He will not treat you the way your parents did around your imperfections. God will not humiliate you, yell at you, punish you. . . . What God loves in us is our real self."

This concept of the Divine being in everything, even in what pains us most, is one of the fundamental tenets of Kabbalah and many other spiritual teachings. Shulman just made it tangible. I felt people around me breathing a little more easily. For a moment, I did too.

The next day Shulman demonstrated what he calls a Healing of Immanence, based on the *Shema*, a Jewish prayer noted in rabbinic literature for its healing power. Then Shulman had everyone in the workshop try it. In the Healing of Immanence, there is no channeling of *chi*, just a witnessing of the oneness and the divinity of a person—a reflecting of the Divine light—that seems to work on a level beyond the aura. The previous year, at a different workshop, Shulman did a demonstration on a young Lutheran minister, who literally appeared to vibrate under Shulman's hands.

"If you're able to [witness the divinity], amazing things will happen," Shulman promised. "Our imperfections become a bridge to the Divine instead of an obstacle. If you don't believe in God, you have to test it out empirically. See if releasing imperfection doesn't make you feel better."

Jason Shulman is consumed by the question of relationship, especially relationship to God. He defines God as "The All That Is." Living in awareness of God, he believes, is what heals. "Heal us, Oh Lord, and we will be healed." It is the way the "Amidah," a Jewish prayer, begins.

"It means anything that heals us from a lower level is not permanent. To have the true and deepest healing, we have to go to the highest," he told me during one of our many discussions on healing. We were sitting at the rough-hewn wood dining table in his house in semirural New Jersey, where he lives with his wife Arlene and daughter Ariana. Inside, the furnishings were simple; the wood floors mostly bare. An occasional soft pastel watercolor by Shulman broke up the walls. Outside, an expansive lawn gave way to a small pond.

Shulman believes the Kabbalah teaches that the highest is also right here. "If God is just, then going into the most human is also going into the most divine," Shulman explained. "How can they be different? Otherwise, it would be a sham, right? 'I'll make you human, but that doesn't really count.' . . . Well, that makes this life a very poor thing. And God's creation very one dimensional. It makes him a stupid creator. And God's not a stupid creator."

As a Kabbalist, Shulman is a renegade. Traditionally the Kabbalah has been restricted to married Jewish men, usually rabbis, over the age of forty. Yet Shulman's three-year training program, at A Society of Souls (S.O.S), in Lebanon, N.J., like other secular programs in healing, has far more women among graduates than men, and his students come from all religious backgrounds. A few are even protestant ministers. For Shulman, a desire to be a healer—and to know God—is far more significant than religious background, age or marital status. He takes his guidance from the roots of the word Israel which include *El*, the name of God, and

Sau-rawh, to struggle or contend. Broadly then, Israelites are all those who struggle with God, or who are engaged in the struggle.

Kabbalah is essentially the study of the metaphysical underpinnings of the Torah, the Five Books of Moses which are also the first five chapters of the Old Testament. According to the late Kabbalist scholar David Sheinkin, M.D., in the hands of a illuminated person, the Torah is "an owner's manual to the universe." In essence, then, one can literally harness the forces of creation with the right understanding.

Shulman has packaged the Kabbalah into an orderly system for healing, with a specific set of rules, much the way Brennan packaged the aura and the chakras. But Jewish spiritual healing is not new. The Kabbalah itself may date back to the eighteenth century B.C. That would make it contemporary with the early Vedic tradition of India, according to the writings of the late Rabbi Aryeh Kaplan, a highly regarded modern Kabbalah scholar. Specific historical references to healing in Jewish literature date back at least as far as the second century B.C. to the Essenes. (A mystical group known for their talent as healers, the Essenes may have been responsible, in part, for training Jesus Christ, according to Rabbi Steven Fisdel, a Kabbalistic healer and Jewish scholar in San Francisco. Rabbi Fisdel believes that Jesus' parents, Mary and Joseph, were both Essenes.)

Healing had a resurgence with the birth of the Hasidic movement in the eighteenth century, according to rabbinical scholars. People often translate the name of the founder of Hasidism, the Bal Shem Tov, as "the master of the good name." But Rabbi Fisdel notes that a Bal Shem was a faith healer. A Bal Shem Tov was an exceptional faith healer. "The Bal Shems were making amulets, laying on hands, and exorcising demons," he explains.

Rabbi Fisdel believes the Hasidic rabbis today still practice healing. But like all esoteric teachings, the art of Jewish spiritual healing has been all but lost in more secular groups. No written texts on healing exist. Most modern rabbis simply view the Kabbalah in terms of historical scholarship. Yet, Rabbi Fisdel notes, guidelines for healing can be deduced from the Kabbalist literature.

The Tree of Life is basic to any understanding of the Kabbalah. It is a multidimensional grid containing ten *sefirot*, or Divine attributes. The *sefirot* are sometimes described by Kabbalists as ten windows through which God's light comes. According to the oral tradition, the world was created when "God wished to behold God." So God withdrew to create a void. Into that void, there emanated a beam of light, or Divine will, which manifested in ten distinct stages of emanation or Divine utterances: the *sefirot*.

The *sefirot* "are realities," says Michael Young, an Asheville, North Carolina, healer who studied with Shulman after graduating from the Brennan school. "They're much more than just energies. . . . When God says, 'Let us create everything in our image, not just man.' Who was God talking to? The *sefirot*."

According to the Kabbalah, a human being, too, is a container for God's light, composed in varying degrees of the ten *sefirot*. The Kabbalah (echoing quantum physics) teaches that light "vibrates at lower and lower levels and gets denser as it goes through the universes," explains Simma Kinderlehrer, another Kabbalistic healer. "We are denser light, just vibrating slower. It's all God manifesting differently." Adds Shulman, "We're in an ocean of *sefirot* because they are what makes existence. They are the intermediaries between ourselves and God."

To a healer the *sefirot* are living entities, much like grace, truth, courage and Divine love. The difference between the scholarly and experiential approach to the Tree of Life is like the difference between studying art history and being an artist. One of Shulman's gifts, according to his students, is his ability to bring the Kabbalah and the *sefirot* to life.

"I studied the Kabbalah academically for ten years, six or seven hours a weekend," says Martha Harrell, Ph.D., a Jungian psychoanalyst, and a former Freudian psychoanalyst and professor at Yale Medical School who recently graduated from A Society of Souls. "Rabbis study it from an academic point of view. It's entirely different. It's like dissecting a frog rather than getting down on the ground and watching a frog. More than anyone in [S.O.S.] I had studied academic Kabbalah. I studied these *sefirot* for years. I read *Inner Space* [a modern analysis of the Kabbalah by Rabbi Aryeh Kaplan] twenty times. But it meant nothing. I didn't understand the *sefirot* until Jason talked about them. He explained them. And, boing, I got it."

Shulman sees the underlying connections between seemingly disparate things. He reads the mystical writings of Isaac Newton for inspiration, and derives spiritual wisdom from books such as *Timeless Way of Building* and *Pattern of Language* by architect Christopher Alexander. "He's really talking about being alive, what makes something beautiful, and why do we respond to certain kinds of beauty," he explains.

Many of his students are sustained by his uninhibited talk of God. Loren Stell, a psychotherapist, ordained minister in the United Church of Christ and a poet, says that Shulman turned on the lights for him. Growing up with Calvinist theology that says every child is born with a spot of sin "permeated my thought that I am evil and that everyone I see is evil," says Stell. "Jason has helped me redefine my understanding. I feel resurrected. Jason's opening a whole world where to be alive is to be grateful."

Another graduate, Ginger Bennett, says she learned to relate to her anxiety in a completely new way. "God comes through the anxiety, too," she explains. "More than anyone I've ever been with, he is able to take experiences—in this case Divine consciousness—and articulate it in such a way with poetic use of metaphors," adds Dr. Dan Kinderlehrer. "He can reach realms, articulate them and bring people there." At the same time, Dr. Kinderlehrer notes, "He has his foibles just like the rest of us."

As a healer and a teacher of healing, Shulman does not dwell on physical shifts. Although he treats people with cancer and other ailments, many of his clients come to work out emotional issues. A physical cure is not always what is best for the soul, he says, illustrating with a parable.

"There was a great rabbi who was also a healer. A man who is ill comes to him. 'Rabbi, can you heal me?' the man asks. And the great rabbi says no, he can't. He sends him to a lesser rabbi. And that rabbi heals him. The *midrash* [rabbinical interpretation] on this is that the great rabbi saw that if he healed him, he'd only delay and maybe increase the suffering the man had to go through and he couldn't bring himself to do it. The other rabbi healed him because he couldn't see that far ahead."

There is no doubt that Shulman is passionate about the

Kabbalah and about healing. When he gives a talk he can stir people deeply, articulating pain they did not know they had, and can open space for this pain to transform. At other times, I have watched him end up in a drier terrain. When Shulman tries too hard, he can hit a note that is intellectual instead of experiential. When he intimates that his system of spiritual healing is better than others, he puts some students off, while others feel flattered to be in such a seemingly rarified club. Yet when in the service of Spirit, he can be poetic.

Shulman believes Kabbalistic healing, like all healing, follows scientific laws, just not the laws most doctors are interested in today. "[Modern] science refers to reproducible effects without personal involvement," he says. "That's what science is. Kabbalah requires the heart. Science asks us to remain the same. Spirit asks us to participate and transform." At the same time, "I would love to talk to a spiritual physicist," he says. As a foundation for Kabbalah, Shulman teaches the basics of quantum physics.

Unlike Bruyere, who seeks to bring the teachings to as wide an audience as possible and to find oneness in the diversity of traditions, Shulman seeks at times to set Kabbalistic healing apart. He shared many beautiful insights about healing. Yet he tended to circle around some fundamental aspects of his teaching. For instance, he did not want to explain how he embodied the *sefirot* so they could be used in healing. (A rabbi and one of his students explained the process to me. It takes talent and training to embody the *sefirot*, but there is no great mystery.) Shulman seemed to fear that people would somehow reduce the *sefirot*. "I can't tell you how much I've gotten from books," he explained. "But when you put something down, it becomes a method, fixed and in print. . . . It ends up creating lots of confusion. At a certain point, books become a cage."

He also insisted that the *sefirot* were not a form of subtle energy. "They're pre-energies," he explained. He prefers to have students call them 'Attributes' to distinguish them from the subtle energy of the auric dimension. The *sefirot* are, indeed, states of being similar to states such as grace, truth, and clarity and harmony that Bruyere and other teachers encourage their students to embody. Yet most healers consider such states of being to be energy. And other Kabbalistic masters do, in fact, refer to the *sefirot* as energies.

As a teacher, Shulman runs a tight ship. His first three-year class, which began in 1993, had just twenty-eight students; all but three were graduates of Brennan's school. The others were Shulman's long-time healing clients, what you might call tutorial students. Now, a Society of Souls gets about 150 applications a year for forty spots. Shulman handpicks his students, he says to create a certain level of intimacy; a Society of Souls, if you will. Many of them are graduates of the Brennan school. Others are internists, psychiatrists, psycho-therapists, or the former clients of S.O.S graduates.

This exclusivity has its price. Tuition for freshman in the 1998–99 term was $3,500 for four three-day weekends per school year. Second and third year tuition is $4,000 and the weekends are a day longer. The freshman fee, on a per diem basis, is three times what Bruyere charges for a workshop. It is also 50 percent more than tuition fees for the Brennan school. The school grosses approximately $460,000, not including weekend and graduate seminars. Shulman says he would rather keep classes small than generate bigger numbers. In addition, Shulman maintains a small private practice, and handles monthly supervision groups for his graduates.

Shulman has very decided views. He has created a diagnostic process that involves matching psychological patterns to imbalances of the *sefirot*. Without a psychotherapeutic discussion, he believes the energy healing cannot come from the highest place.

Other forms of Kabbalistic healing, while also emphasizing psychological and spiritual states, are more free form. Rabbi Fisdel, for instance, uses the *sefirot* differently in each healing, according to the client's needs, but is only just now beginning to teach classes at the Esalen Institute.

At the Karin Kabbalah Center in Atlanta, students learn about the *sefirot* and how to heal, using the central column of *sefirot*, where the energies are already in divine balance. There is no road map, except inner connection to Spirit. The idea, in fact, is to get the healer's "little self" and personality out of the way. "You're a unique being and you bring it forth," explains Catherine Vajda, who has studied with Brennan, Shulman, and also at the Karin Kabbalah Center. "Then you get a lot of creativity and that's what feeds back to God."

Shulman's way, however, has many ardent fans. Most of his students feel his program, with its emphasis on meditation and the most subtle thoughts and feelings, brings them to a much deeper level of self-awareness than they had before. And Shulman freely acknowledges he is teaching Kabbalah as refracted through his beliefs and experiences. In fact, he would not have it any other way. "You have to understand, these are all my interpretations of Kabbalah," he says. "It's not purely Judaism. I'm interested in one thing: God. And I'm interested in healing."

Becoming a healer is the last occupation that Shulman ever aspired to in his younger years. A famous musician, adored by his fans, yes. But someone who helps others? It was not, he says, on his list. The universe, however, has a strange way of guiding us, even if we go kicking and screaming.

In 1979 Shulman got sick. His joints ached. He had fevers that left him weak and clammy; one lasted for six months. He had brownouts. And he was as weak as newborn lamb. "I was unable to move," he recalls. "If I walked a block, I had to rest the entire day."

Until then, his life had been relatively uneventful. Born in 1947 in Williamsburg, Brooklyn, an ultra-Jewish neighborhood, he had spent his childhood reading Confucius, talking to butterflies and, pondering how people could make great empires of money and then be forced to leave it all when they died. Even then, he says, he wondered, "What is this about? Is it all for nothing?"

While attending Brooklyn College, he became involved in Zen Meditation. After graduating with a double major in English and art history, he tried to make a career as a musician, writing and performing lyrics for TV commercials, including a Mountain Dew ad. He also joined the Pathwork Center in Phoenicia, New York, and took the five-year training program to become a Pathwork helper, but says he had "zero interest" in helping others. Dissatisfied with his musical career, he switched his attention to music publishing.

Friends from those days recall him as "intense," "poetic," and uncompromising. Judy Bachrach, a musician and spiritual seeker, who has since become good friends with Shulman, recalls that once he criticized her songs as being emotionally sentimental. "There was a part of him that was arrogant and there was also truth in it," she says. "He was always searching for the truth, even if there was a pebble, he'd say, 'Out with the whole thing.'" At the same time, she adds, "He handed me a rose, and I could only see the thorns."

Becoming ill had not been on Shulman's agenda. He watched as the extra pounds on his once chubby frame melted and he became skeletal. "I used to sit in the bathtub—I had lost sixty pounds—and cry," he says. The doctors could not figure out what was wrong.

The illness had its positive side. Things he had longed for but could not quite manage, suddenly became possible. He finally married his longtime girlfriend, Arlene (now a psychotherapist), whom he calls one of his best teachers. In 1983 their daughter Ariana was born. He also started his own book-packaging business. He developed a "Thought of the Week" series on grief, relationships, stress, and other psychological issues and coauthored a book of quotations, *Isaac Asimov's Book of Science and Nature Quotations*, with famed science fiction author Isaac Asimov.

At the same time, Shulman was growing increasingly bitter. He would go to parties where everyone else would be eating and drinking. He would pull out a cold hamburger he had brought, one of the few foods he could eat. He felt, he says, that "life was going on around me." Finally, his Pathwork helper asked: "What are you going to do if you never get better?"

"I had to ask myself, 'If I never get better, can I live with this?' he says. He eventually realized he could not go on "like I was carrying a dead moose." He also recognized that he had a deep feeling of deprivation. The Pathwork model of psychology was not helping either, he says. "It was a spiritually materialist view, that if you could just find an answer, you'll get cured. There was a lot of forcing. There was nothing like: 'Let me just hold you.'"

Occasionally, over the years, friends had suggested that perhaps Shulman's illness was tied to a psychic gift he had not acknowledged. The idea had always terrified him. "I felt that people who claim to be psychic are weirdos—fringe characters." Now he began to keep a journal to document his thoughts, dreams, and events in his life to see how they correlated. Around the same time, Shulman began to see a naturopath, a local psychic healer, and a physician who finally made an accurate diagnosis: Lyme disease, a muscle tear that allowed wastes to enter his blood, and a systemic candiasis (yeast) infection. "The most truthful explanation," says Shulman, "is that I was suffering from a spiritual crisis. I suffered greatly in those seven years. But if someone had cured me earlier, it would have been a disaster."

After keeping his journal for a year, a psychic told him his gifts were meant to be used in healing. Shulman decided he had better find a teacher. He went to see Barbara Brennan, whom he knew casually from the Pathwork Center, in her East Side office. Brennan asked him to tune into someone psychically. He chose someone they both knew.

"He has a headache," Shulman said.

"Yes," Brennan agreed. "Now, where is he?"

"In a car."

"I think it's a train," she said. She asked him to work long distance on the man's headache as she watched. A few minutes later, she skipped Shulman out of the first year.

After graduating, Shulman began teaching. For the juniors and seniors, he conducted a class called, "It's not the map, it's the territory," that, he says, "specialized" in using confusion, fear, death, pain, sorrow, and self-hate as part of being a healer. "These people were filled with this stuff and they didn't have a chance to talk about it," he says.

He was searching for answers that he still did not have as a healer. For one thing, he did not feel that merely manipulating the chakras was getting to the very roots of illness. Every so often, Shulman would try to read one of the Kabbalistic texts, or a book interpreting the texts, but he was overwhelmed by what he calls their "abstruseness." "I read Kabbalah because it was my birth religion," he explains. "But every time I read it, it seemed like intellectual stuff, and I wanted experience."

Slowly it dawned on him that there was a complete system for healing between the lines of these complicated and deliberately obscure works. "It's very simple," he says. "Here's the system: The more we can be in union with God, the more healed we are, the more we have a possibility of truly healing others."

In his birth religion he had finally found the teaching at the root of all spiritual healing.

Shema Yisrael, Adonai Elohanu Adonai Echud. "Hear O Israel, The Lord is Our God, The Lord is One." Shulman says he decided to examine his life in the light of the *Shema*, a Jewish prayer. One day, while he had his hands on a client who had a problem with her quadracep muscle, "I had a complete reversal in my understanding of the role of a healer," he says. He realized that the pain in the quadracep muscle was God, too. It was Divine. Instead of trying to root it out, he witnessed the divinity of the pain. "It turns out that is an extremely important job," he says. In simple terms, Shulman had discovered the importance of Presence. That experience became the basis of the Healing of Immanence. (The client's quadracep muscle eventually healed.) He calls the *Shema* "the great mantra of Judaism."

"Initially, [the Healing of Immanence] allows for a psychic space to expand," explains Jim Ambrogi, a teacher at S.O.S. "If someone is feeling tremendously pressured by his shadow, even illness, by making room for that to be divine allows an innate intelligence of the soul to open. From that, almost anything can emerge."

Shulman says the healing allows for a deep level of integration, trust, and acceptance and can be applied by anyone. The first time I tried the healing, I did not notice much of anything except peace and contentment, which at the time I did not especially value. I was looking for fireworks in the early days of my research, not subtle epiphanies. Over time, however, I became increasingly able to perceive the subtle domain, and then the subtle domain no longer seemed quite so subtle.

When I tried the healing the following year, at a workshop, I paired up with a businessman in commercial real estate. First, as he requested, I witnessed the divinity of his ambition to make a lot of money. In my experience the *Shema* is about the oneness, as well as the divinity, of all things. As I entered a state of oneness with this man, I could *see* the beauty of his desire; making money was the best way he knew to express his love for his wife and children. When we talked about it in this light, something inside this man shifted and lightened; he seemed to gain a more direct connection with his own loving feelings.

Then this businessman witnessed the divinity within me. By the end, he was in tears. He had seen my soul. He was crying for himself, too; in some fundamental way our need for love was the same. I was deeply touched by the connection.

As I experimented I found that this healing technique seemed to illuminate the issue to which I applied it. When I did the healing for someone else, I felt I saw into the person's soul. Mostly, I tried these healings on myself. When I had a situation that I found challenging, I witnessed my oneness with it and the divinity of it in a meditation. It did not always solve the problem, of course. But it invariably opened up space for me to see the situation in a new way.

At the same time, the *Shema* became a doorway for me to a better understanding of all prayers and mantras. The words of God, mantras, and holy prayers in any language, all have very high vibrations. They are, if you will, well worn pathways to the Divine, much like superhighways. When one applies holy words with focused intent, they change the shape of psychic space. (This is the idea behind meditating with an established mantra.)

For Shulman the Healing of Immanence was just the first glimmer of light. His onetime mentor, Barbara Brennan, had emphasized hand techniques. Shulman now came to a world of soul qualities through the Kabbalah and his search for God. As he read the *Sefer Yitzarah*, one of the few written Kabbalistic texts, he began to understand the *sefirot* in the Tree of Life as living essences, rather than just as abstract concepts.

According to the Kabbalistic literature, the *sefirot* exist only in relationship. Therefore, Shulman realized, disease was the result of imbalances between some or more of the *sefirot* within an individual. In long meditations, he learned to embody these *sefirot*, starting with *Hesed* (loving kindness) and *Gevurah* (restraint, judgment). If *Hesed* is the ocean and boundless, *Gevurah* is the container, the structure, the boundary. They are two poles; one does not exist without the other. "Without some *Gevurah*, *Hesed* would be so overflowing everything would rot," explains one graduate.

Traditionally, the *sefirot* are embodied by chanting the names of God. (Each *sefirot* is associated with a different Hebrew name of God.) Instead, Shulman embodied the essences. With *Hesed*, for instance, one might embody the boundless ocean. To embody *Tiferet* (beauty, Christ consciousness) he tried to see another person through the eyes of God, as close as that could be conceived.

Shulman linked these *sefirot* with psychological qualities, as do other Kabbalistic teachers, such as Rabbi David Cooper of Los Angeles, author of the tape series, *The Mystical Kabbalah*, and books such as *The Heart of Stillness*. But as a healer Shulman went further, realizing that a rigid or overly strict person could be infused with more *Hesed* (loving kindness, boundlessness) in a balance of *Hesed-Gevurah*. Likewise, he understood that "someone who is all over the place needs *Gevurah*," explains Dani Antman, who teaches at A Society of Souls.

Diagnosis, as Shulman teaches it, is an art. Once, as we were talking, he described my mother's psychological patterns with an impressive precision—based on my personality. He then observed that I might be subject to skin rashes (true) and have a constant, if subtle, feeling that time presses in on me (also true). Such psychic readings, of course, are not unusual. But Shulman's perceptions were completely shaped by his understanding of the *sefirot*, instead of the chakras. (On another occasion, he gave me an analysis of my character that I felt was far less astute, probably because his personal issues got in the way.)

Shulman's system takes into account spiritual paradox, where things are not always what they seem. For instance, sometimes a person who has been overwhelmed early in life by boundless attention will seem overly rigid. In actuality the person lacks a sense of boundaries and is overcompensating. "Let's say, for instance, one had a mother who was a martyr," explains Antman. "Her attitude is: 'I'm giving to you.' But you feel smothered. You, as a daughter, become a very rigid, restrained person."

Depression, chronic fatigue, anxiety, and circulatory disease are typical reflections of an excess of *Hesed*, a lack of boundaries. Conversely, an excess of *Gevurah*—rigidity, judgment, stricture—might manifest as brittle bones, arthritis, autoimmune diseases, and emotional rigidity. Marilyn Schneider, R.N., a graduate of S.O.S. and a senior teacher at the Brennan school, recalls using *Hesed-Gevurah* with a woman in her seventies who had had both hips replaced due to arthritis. Her doctors were contemplating giving her thumb and elbow replacements.

"Everything was so held inside," recalls Schneider. "Her mother died when she was very young. Her father was in the military. She married a naval cadet who became an admiral." After working with this woman weekly for eight months, says Schneider, "The pain went away. She did not have any more surgeries."

Another technique with similar balancing properties is *Nezach-Hod. Nezach* is victory and eternity. *Hod* is splendor and submission. A healing that combines these energies allows a person to take in or see more of their own splendor without submission. "So it's about victory in yourself," says S.O.S. graduate Deborah Scott, who also studied with Brennan and Bruyere. "It's about taking in and embodying the splendor of who you are, of being who you are." Graduates of Shulman's program find that these energies are helpful in addressing issues that stem from abuse, including some issues that relate to cancer and heart disease.

Shulman recommends another pairing *Chokmah* (wisdom, point, being)-*Binah* (understanding, womb) to help resolve narcissistic wounding. According to the Kabbalistic texts, *Chokmah-Binah* is Father World and Primal Mother, so it helps to re-parent someone at a fundamental level. Relying on the natural groupings of *sefirot* identified in the Kabbalistic literature, Shulman developed fifteen healing techniques.

Shulman also explored the four universes of the Kabbalah: the physical (*Asiyyah*), the emotional (*Yitzirah*), the universe of patterns and symbols (*Beriah*) and a level beyond form of pure presence (*Azilut*). These universes are different psychic realms in which the *sefirot* operate. Once, when we were talking, Shulman briefly slipped into *Beriah*. It was as if the room became still and intense. "How do you feel?" he asked when he came out of it, perhaps a minute or two later. "I feel good," I said. Then I noticed a certain sadness, which I had not been aware of previously.

The Tree of LIfe

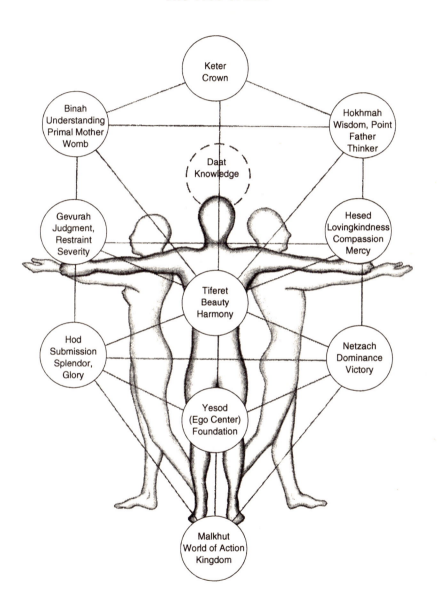

"So what I did was just to gather myself and to open up to the extent that I can to being with the Divine, as I understand it," he explained. "And I knew that would have an effect on you because we're really, truly not separate. Now it may make you feel sad. But that's because there's grief. And you need to see it. It's okay that there's grief. I have grief. And you have grief. It's all right. It's human. We need honesty, not perfection. There's joy. There's sorrow. But they have a space to come out."

Eventually, Shulman developed several healings that work in *Beriah*, where he believes the "descriptors" for physical reality exist, including one he calls a "morphic" healing. Michael Young, a graduate of A Society of Souls calls the morphic healing "a cancellation of beliefs that are received as true that are not true. In the holomorphic healing, all these distortions become clear."

Shulman believes it can take as long as six months for the client to integrate a morphic healing into his or her life. It is a healing he expects his students to use sparingly. "Here's an example," he explains. "A very overweight person comes in. If you say, I'll just do a morphic healing and change their relationship to food, well if the person has no idea why they related to food the way they do, it's magic. It's not real. You can't change someone's reality before they understand the reality they're in. . . . You can't just give someone a pill and say, 'Now you can compete in the Olympics.' They need to build their muscles first."

Manhattan healer Susan Weiley, who experimented with morphic healings on a series of long-term clients, developed a healthy respect for the process. Two clients unexpectedly filed for divorce just weeks after such healings. Another person, a senior Wall Street analyst, abruptly quit her job, quit drinking, quit an extramarital affair, and filed a sex discrimination suit. "Jason said, 'Five miles down the road, you'll be fifteen blocks to the right,'" says Weiley, who was doing distant healings on family members before she even knew what healing was. "I think it's five minutes down the road, you'll be in another country."

Spiritual healers always see illness as related to emotional, mental and spiritual patterns. The difference is that the Kabbalistic healings Shulman teaches are half in the psychotherapy model and half in the energy model, making the personality the gateway for the soul.

The Kabbalah has always been a meditative path. In teaching Kabbalistic healing, Shulman follows that tradition. Using meditations of his own devising, he spends much of the three years attuning his students to their most subtle experiences—the same thing he expects them to zero in on in clients. "A lot of inner anxiety comes up," says Alix Young, a graduate of both S.O.S. and the Brennan School of Flow Alignment and Connection. "You hold it. Jason does a lot of practice around staying in the moment where psychic space opens. . . . It brings you more and more to the present moment. And the more present you are in healing, the more validated the client is."

One of Shulman's favorite meditations, "Form Anxiety," is designed to bring students into their core wounds. Form, in this context, is emotional as much as it is physical. "Shape is a kinesthetic shape, a sensory shape, and imaginal shape," Shulman explains. "And that always changes."

The meditation takes students back to the first days of life, where Shulman believes our suffering begins. Form and feeling are "changing because one day, I hold your hand like this," he says, gently, lovingly taking my hands between his hands, as if my hands are the most precious things he has ever caressed. "Oh, my little Tattala,' he says, imitating a Jewish grandmother. "As a baby we don't have words. But we feel it.

"And another day, I'm holding you like this." His hands get very agitated and staccato from anxiety. I feel it not just in my hands, but throughout my body. I am overwhelmed by anxiety. "And I'm your life," he says, referring back to any infant and its first caretaker. "You're dependent on me, your mother."

For Shulman, these subtle experiences are the roots of all physical disease and the very essence of what can be treated in Kabbalistic healing. Many of the meditations and lectures lead to a kind of group therapy that can make the air in the room, at least when I visited the school, palpably heavy. When I sat in on a third-year class, Shulman talked about narcissism in a lecture, "The

Existential Disorders of Spirit" to provide insight on the *Abba-Aima* (mother-father) healing, using *Chokmah-Binah*.

"The parent uses the child for the parent's own needs," explained Shulman. "It happens every time there's a proud parent of a smart kid, a handsome kid, etc. Also, if you disregard the child's need, you wipe her out. 'Oh Debbie, you love me so much,'" said Shulman, imitating a cloying father who ignores a daughter's anger. "Sexual abuse is not the ultimate. I know people who have survived sexual abuse much better than emotional abuse. They're all terrible.

"What happens to the child, their needs are not met. . . . They teach the child . . . intimacy is a lonely place to be. Then the child longs for it. And can't get it." Shulman paused so the class could digest this. "The parent is using the child, so the child always feels hope. It thinks, 'I'll just work harder.'" Ultimately, Shulman added, the child "always has to watch the parent for signals of what the Self should be. And at the same time the parent is desperately trying to get [that approval] from the child. When everyone is trying to get it from the outside, no true intimacy can occur.

"All of us in this room are narcissistically wounded to some degree. . . . Some have to deal with this more. . . . It's a lonely condition," said Shulman. "The child develops an existential disappointment in the failure of relationship. . . ."

The mood in the room was thick. All of a sudden a student broke down sobbing. Tears welled up in the eyes of her classmates, who sat in a circle, and in me, too. "It's okay," said Shulman softly. "It's just pain. It has no words because it happened when you had no words."

The woman nodded, comforted.

"We were just little children," he summed up. "Our parents were just little children. No one was born wanting to hurt a little child."

Other ruminations are sweeter. In the second year, Shulman gives students an exercise to explore their shame. "Imagine you love God and you are praying to God, showing God your love, and you are in a temple, and tears begin to roll from your eyes, and you find as you say this prayer . . . you are sobbing. You think about the world and its pain and suffering. You even think about your own family and what they have gone through, and somehow, your faith in God at that moment is such that you say, 'It is good. This life you have given me with its pain and sorrow and its joy is good.'

"Now, imagine that other people begin to look at you. What do you feel? Look for the very smallest movement in your heart and feelings and body. Does anything tighten up? Why does it do that? You don't need anyone to come over to you and comfort you: God is doing that, and that is why you are crying. But you tighten up. This is the shame that must be overcome before you can know God and feel God within you; and before you can do the work God made you for, and before you can create the space in yourself for real spiritual fulfillment."

Kabbalistic healing is not as directly connected with the physical body as most auric work. A healer will sit with a client, sometimes with her hands on the client, other times just facing the client, while "cleaving" to the *sefirot*. (I have seen Bruyere, healers she has trained, some Brennan graduates, and Flow Alignment and Connection practitioners all work in analogous ways. But each system also brings with it a distinct energy quality.)

"As soon as I'm able to be with the illness and the life force within it, it's almost as if it's elated. And then it is transformed," explains New Jersey healer Maxine Lindig, who has studied with Shulman and Brennan. "Then it's almost like it's not distorted anymore."

"Kabbalistic healing is about the foundation of the building," explains Shulman, going into a beautiful rift that is also true of some other forms of spiritual healing. "If a whole house is an organic creation and you want to straighten the roofline, you don't get a ladder and fix the roof. [Kabbalah] looks at the whole structure closely and says, 'The real reason the roofline is out of whack is a foundation stone needs to be readjusted.'"

In my own experience, the Kabbalistic healings Shulman teaches are subtle. Over the course of perhaps a year, I had a series of *Hesed-Gevurah* healings. I did not notice much in the way of effects, even though around that time I spent an inordinate amount of time cleaning out my closets. A year later, I became aware that I had become more organized—something that had always eluded me. My hairstylist even commented on how "put together" I had become. When exactly that happened, I could not say. But I felt that the shift was linked to the healings. The higher level of organization I enjoyed involved more than my outward appearance.

When I received a morphic healing, I did not have the kind of dramatic results that I had heard about. The energy hit me hard. I slept about ten hours a day for more than a week. And even when I was awake, I felt almost drugged and unutterably sad. Something deep occurred, but I couldn't point to any fundamental shift in my life afterword. It is possible that the issue I was trying to resolve was one the healer was also still working out for herself. I also have come to believe that karma—patterning—is an extremely complex phenomenon. We often have more to learn by living out a particular situation than by attempting to "fix it" hastily. In fact, I believe no healing can override the soul's higher purpose. At least, I found that to be the case in my own life. Even so, I believe the healing had a beneficial effect, perhaps in helping me to accept my path.

I had many interesting and helpful healings. But over time this healer became uncomfortable when I wanted to know what healing she had done. She said such information could interfere with the effects of the healing. To me this seemed patronizing, like old-style medical doctors. Eventually, I stopped having sessions.

Some of Shulman's students are completely adoring. "They hold him in guru-like status," says one graduate, "diminishing their own authority in the process." Others note that, like everyone, he has his imperfections.

For instance, some students say, Shulman has a tendency to believe that what he teaches is The Way. At times, he almost seems to view himself as the creator of a new system of Kabbalistic healing, although in the beginning graduates say he viewed himself more as an interpreter of the ancient texts. When I mentioned a rabbi who was doing Kabbalistic healing, his first instinct was to dismiss this man's work as "magical Kabbalah" instead of inquiring about the rabbi's methods. (The rabbi, too, uses the *sefirot* to diagnose and to heal, along with prayers similar to the *shema*.) Meanwhile, at a recent graduate seminar, he told students that they were the only people in the world doing such a profound level of work. A few students were not comfortable. "I know people are doing wonderful work out there," says one.

"It's probably a flaw I have as a teacher," Shulman concedes. "I love the people I have trained. I feel they are doing the most profound work I've ever encountered." At the same time, he admits, "I have no idea about the rest of the world." He also acknowledges that, as in any program, people have a range of talents. It is not the techniques per se. It is the healer and his or her degree of alignment and the clarity of intention.

One incident illustrates this axiom of healing vividly. A Society of Souls graduate had talked to me at length about a client who had made a dramatic physical improvement. When she looked back in her notes, she realized she had not used the *sefirot*, as she had thought, but the skills she learned at the Brennan school. Her allegiance to Shulman and his work was such that, at first, she no longer wished to discuss the case.

Shulman admits a bias towards Kabbalah. Some graduates say he will ask why someone bothered to do a chelation focused on the chakras and aura. But most graduates integrate their Society of Souls training with their other studies to expand their range of frequencies and consciousness. "I find that many of the auric techniques are very effective and work immediately," explains Weiley. "Kabbalistic healings take days and even weeks to settle in and stabilize. Sometimes people don't have the time. They need help immediately.

"When I see something that needs fixing in the aura, I do that. I use the right tool for the right thing. If someone comes in and their heart chakra needs restructuring or their second chakra is blown out from cancer, I'm not going to use just Kabbalistic healing and ignore the aura. I don't know if the Kabbalistic healing will address it. I'm not going to risk it. I have the tools and I use them."

Dr. Kinderlehrer, who has graduated from both the Brennan school and A Society of Souls, has gone on to study another protocol, Guided Self Healing, which he finds to be more effective. In this system, he says, he goes directly to the root cause of the patient's problem instead of using the diagnostic process that Shulman teaches. Then, he might use the *sefirotic* energies in a healing. "Usually people are demonstrating the pattern," says Dr. Kinderlehrer. "We want to find out where it starts."

At least one graduate, Catherine Vajda, has completely stopped using Shulman's approach to Kabbalah. Studying at the Karin Kabbalah Center in Atlanta, she now links with her clients soul to soul. In this process, developed by Karin Kabbalah founder Shirley Chambers, Vajda uses the central column of the *sefirot*—where God manifests as pure alignment—and then releases the situation directly to that person's soul. "Shirley [Chambers] teaches you to work from the soul level. The intelligence of our higher self is so far beyond our intellects at this point," she explains. "Jason focuses more on equating the Tree [of Life] and the personality."

In many ways, Society of Soul graduates are on a new frontier in terms of understanding how the Kabbalistic healings work. Susan Weiley recalls giving a *Tiferet-Yesod* healing to a client who had torn a ligament from running. Through this healing, Weiley sought to ground the woman's spiritual heart into the physical plane. Weiley chose the healing not because the woman had a torn ligament, she explains, but because she had a deep longing to connect to her husband.

Much to Weiley's shock, she says, the woman "got off the table and was completely healed." And she notes, it was not just the ankle. "Very soon after there was a shift in her attitude towards the marriage. She decided to go to couples counseling." Weiley was even more surprised when a few months later, another client came in with a torn ligament. Again, she did a *Tiferet-Yesod* healing to heal a deep fracture running through the man's life, she says. She claims that he, too, got up from the table without any further pain. When she told Shulman, she says, he said he never would have predicted such a result.

"I'm still a student of Jason's," says Weiley, who graduated from A Society of Souls in 1996. "This is all new territory. And it is to Jason. We don't know what's possible with this work. There's no map." But, she says, the Kabbalistic healings help her access high realms. "In Kabbalah," she says, "people's lives and attitudes are transformed in a very profound way. . . . With new clients, if they haven't had energy work before, I don't do Kabbalah work. It's like throwing someone into the deep end of the pool. Ironically," she adds, "they can't sense the Kabbalah work at all."

Kabbalistic healings also seem to be helpful in psychological illness. Catherine Cameron, a social worker at a top private psychiatric hospital in a New York City suburb, was similarly surprised after using Kabbalistic healings in two extreme psychiatric situations. In one case, a twenty-three-year-old Hasidic woman had been severely anorexic for five years and was in the hospital being maintained on a nasal gastric tube. When her assigned therapist went on vacation, Cameron was assigned to cover. "It was so life and death," she says, "I figured I would pull out all the stops. Everything else had failed."

Altogether, in two weeks, Cameron says she did four Kabbalistic healings, starting with *Hesed-Gevurah*, and ending with a morphic healing that she says had "something to do with like, a rupture. Some kind of psychic rupture in her being. Her life energy was leaking out, or hadn't completely poured in."

By the end of the first week, the woman was admitted to a private eating disorder program "against all odds," says Cameron, describing the likelihood as being a "1 in 1,000 chance." The woman who had been pasted to her bed with a feeding tube up her nose soon perked up, got dressed, and put on makeup. "She was much more present. Much more vibrant. This is someone who had given up," says Cameron. "The last I heard, she had a complete recovery, within a year."

The second patient that Cameron conducted Kabbalistic healings with was a thirty-year-old woman who had been diagnosed with multiple personality disorder. The woman's father had been involved in a ring of pedophiles and had allowed a friend who was a political torture expert to experiment on her. "The things this man did to this woman when she was three years old, it's so heinous it's beyond anything you can imagine," says Cameron. "They experimented to see how much she could tolerate and stay alive. She saw another child murdered."

Cameron did shamanic work to retrieve lost soul parts trapped in a "hell realm." Together she and her client witnessed some of the client's original traumas. "They relive what happened at the age when it happened. . . . It's some kind of time-space travel. . . . I had to work very hard to stay grounded in the present." Cameron admits, "I started to feel the same desperation she felt." At times like that, she says, she did a Healing of Immanence. "Without exception, when I did it, she would calm down. I didn't even tell her what I was doing."

Cameron says the woman has not had to be hospitalized since. "She's continued to have a rough time," Cameron reports. Nevertheless, she says, working with these two clients in a hospital setting were "profound experiences."

Cameron started as a client of Shulman's before she became his student. After eight years of healing sessions, she did not become pregnant, as she had originally hoped, but, she says, "I essentially healed my childhood wounds. My basic psychopathology is healed." She says she would not have believed the results in these two cases "if I hadn't been on the receiving end of it for eight years myself. I still have days where I go: 'Is this really happening?'"

Shulman himself does not yet know either the limits or the full potential of Kabbalistic healing. It is still unfolding. But, he says, "I believe Kabbalistic healing has a profound, reproduceable, life-changing effect on people. . . . It doesn't mean someone's always going to get well. But it does mean the [connection to the] soul is always going to be more healed."

In the end, with all these forms of healing, the question still comes down to: How does spiritual healing affect people who have major illnesses? It is a question that doctors are just beginning to look at. In the meantime, healers and their clients already have a lot to say.

Part Four

Ten

The Heart
of the Matter

Doris Dennard, a sixty-two-year-old retired social worker with congestive heart failure, lay under a sterile cloth on an operating table at Columbia-Presbyterian Medical Center in New York City on May 22, 1996.

Dennard, the mother of two children and two stepchildren, had two defective heart valves. Mehmet Oz, M.D., director of the medical assistance device program at Columbia Presbyterian and a leading heart surgeon, estimated that without surgery Dennard had only another month or two to live. She was not in a great deal of pain. But she was terribly tired. And her legs were very swollen.

"She was going to die in the very near future," Dr. Oz told me when I spoke with him about the surgery later. "But what was making her life so miserable was the valves that were failing. If these valves fail, you'll die drowning, because the blood will go to your lungs."

Hoping to extend and improve the quality of her life, Dr. Oz replaced one valve and repaired the other. It was a fairly routine procedure, except that Dennard's condition was very advanced. What was most unusual, however, was the person in the operating room along with Dr. Oz and his surgical team. Gently holding her feet during the surgery was Phil Marden, a healer who had trained with

Bruyere and Brennan and with whom Dennard had been working on and off for nearly a decade.

After four hours, when the delicate repair on Dennard's heart was completed, Dr. Oz took her off the heart-lung machine so her own heart could resume the job of pumping her blood. Dennard's heart started beating wildly; her blood pressure plummeted to zero. She was dying on the operating table.

Dr. Oz ordered emergency drug infusions. At the same time, Marden silently communicated with Dennard's soul. "I talked to her about coming back in," he said. Dennard's physical condition stabilized.

No one will ever know what caused the dramatic turnaround. "You can't tell," said Dr. Oz. "We gave her a lot of drugs at the same time." But Dennard's husband Fred, the retired executive director of the Harlem Interfaith Counseling Service, recalled that when she woke up in the recovery room, "She said to me, 'I was dead. This is a miracle. I know something happened. I was literally dead.' She felt that she had died on the operating table."

Meanwhile, Oz believes Marden did something for his patient: She was noticeably calmer than the average patient after surgery, he said, and made a good recovery. All in all, the surgery was considered a success. Instead of the few weeks that she seemed to have left, Dennard lived another fourteen months, and had much more vitality than before the operation.

Dr. Oz, the son and son-in-law of prominent cardiothoracic surgeons, is possessed by a fierce desire to save and improve lives. A dedicated surgeon, he arrives at the hospital daily by 6:15 A.M., begins surgery less than two hours later, and often does not leave the hospital until after 9 P.M. In 1997, he treated 450 heart patients.

Even when the seconds are not matters of life and death, he tends to move, think, and speak at twice the speed of a normal human being. Dr. Oz, not yet forty, wants to get things done. One healer who briefly worked as a volunteer in the cardiac ward before political infighting drove her away claims she saw, in a vision, a flame above his head, as if he had a holy mission.

A graduate of Harvard College, the University of Pennsylvania's Medical School, and the Wharton School of Business, Dr. Oz is the first, and so far only, surgeon in the United States to openly encourage energy healing for patients before, during, and after surgery. Critics—and he has many now—accuse him of using energy healing as a marketing tactic to lure patients to Columbia Presbyterian instead of another hospital.

"Therapeutic Touch is a 5,000-year-old delusion that there's a vital life force, which doesn't exist, which nobody can measure, but which you can bend to your will," asserted one of his critics on the "Newshour with Jim Lehrer" August 1998. "Oz is a superb surgeon, but he takes customers away from other superb surgeons by saying, 'I've got therapeutic touch.' It's a big seller for him. It brings him a lot of patients he would never otherwise get. So he makes a lot of money from it."

Dr. Oz laughed. "If we spent the money—more than a quarter of a million dollars—that we spent on complementary medicine on an advertising campaign instead, we would have made a lot more money." He believes his patients come to him because they have heard he is a compassionate surgeon. Besides, he noted, a lot of patients are not even willing to pay for Therapeutic Touch in the operating room, where an eight-hour operation can rack up the bill. In addition, Oz's team had trouble measuring results in twenty-minute sessions on a patient here and there, and every so often in the operating room. But, he said, "There's a fairly uniform sense among patients that it's a comforting sensation."

Talk to Oz for just a few minutes and it is clear that his interest in alternatives is based not merely on a marketing scheme, but rather on an ambition to satisfy the Hippocratic Oath he took. He is keenly aware of the failures and unanswered questions that inevitably arise in the practice of modern Western medicine. He faces these anomalies all the time.

"For example, a patient comes to me with angina, chest pains," he explained to me very early one morning in his office before surgery. "An angiogram shows blockage in a vessel. So I need to put a bypass graft past the vessel. So I do that operation. And I find the patient's chest pain is perhaps gone. But they still have a symptoms complex that is not resolved—which theoretically, in our paradigm of body work, should be resolved.

"For instance, anxiety and depression. You say they have anxiety and depression because they have chest pains. But that doesn't go away when the chest pain goes away. The bodily discomfort, aside from the physical heart, doesn't get better all the time. You say you're anxious because your heart is sick. But perhaps your heart is sick because you're anxious."

Dr. Oz said that in his experience, the people who come in with heart problems often have other problems. Intuitively, he added, he believes it is all related. "A guy comes in and talks to you and during a conversation you learn he retired six months ago, his wife left him three months ago, and he lost all his investments a month ago. And all of a sudden, he has coronary disease. I see that a lot," he said. "There are so many examples, so many examples of that. That's not even anecdotal any more."

Dr. Oz said he now believes that even the straightforward Western model for how atherosclerosis causes heart attacks is simply not complete. "Many times, the really dangerous heart attacks are from a sudden closure in vessels that aren't that blocked. Most heart attacks aren't 99 percent blockages that suddenly close down. They are 70 percent blockages that suddenly close down. Why? A 99 percent blockage that suddenly closes down is not going to kill you, probably. If it's already 99 percent blocked, you're getting your blood supply from elsewhere." He could only conclude, he said, that atherosclerosis alone doesn't cause a heart attack.

In general, Dr. Oz added, the results of successful heart surgery are, no pun intended, not always heartening. "The biggest problem we have in heart surgery is depression," he explained. "It's endemic. One-third of all heart surgery patients are depressed post-op."

Dr. Oz suspects there are multiple causes. "Number one, obviously, you all of a sudden have to face your mortality. And that's a depressing concept, if you're not ready to deal with it," he said. "But in addition, we put people on a heart-lung machine and stop their heart. . . . If we don't deal with depression, we haven't done our job.

Heart disease is the number one killer in the United States, causing more than 954,000 deaths annually, according to the

American Heart Association. Of 258 million people, more than 60 million people have some form of it. As many as 1.5 million Americans have a heart attack each year. Yet no one knows how atherosclerosis, a leading precursor of heart attacks, begins or precisely what causes it, although theories exist. And 90-95 percent of the 50 million cases of high blood pressure are of unknown origin.

The American Heart Association lists smoking, high cholesterol, physical inactivity, and excess weight as the known risk factors. Yet dozens of medical studies support Dr. Oz's view, as HeartMath notes in its *Research Overview*. For instance, in 1995 *Circulation* magazine published the results of a study concerning recovering heart patients at the Montreal Heart Institute that was conducted by Nancy Frasure-Smith, M.D. Those who were hopeful and happy were eight times more likely to live than those who were sad and depressed. A 1997 study in the *Journal of Critical Care*, found that the emotional state of heart attack patients and the strength of their relationships was as important an indicator of survival as the severity of their disease. And a 1995 Mayo Clinic study of individuals with heart disease found that psychological distress was the strongest predictor of cardiac arrest, heart attacks, and cardiac death.

Meanwhile, a 1994 Harvard Medical study of 1,122 heart attack survivors reported in the American Heart Association's sixty-seventh sessions, found that those who tried to remain calm during emotional conflicts had half the risk of heart attacks compared to those who tended to get angry. A meta-analysis of over forty-five studies published in the *Psychological Bulletin* found that hostility was one of the most important personality variables in coronary heart disease, according to Dr. Dean Ornish in *Love & Survival*. Dr. Ornish noted even hostility is a manifestation of loneliness and isolation—a lack of love. Dr. Ornish also cited a study conducted at Yale, which found that 119 men and women who felt loved and supported had substantially less blockage in their heart arteries, based on coronary angiography tests. The effect was independent of diet, smoking, exercise, cholesterol, genetics, and other standard-risk factors.

In Dr. Ornish's controlled trials, he found that even severe heart disease often can begin healing in only a few weeks, without drugs or surgery. And, as Dr. Ornish has noted, diet and exercise are not the most significant aspects of his program. "I have found that perhaps the most powerful intervention . . . is the healing power of love and intimacy and the emotional and spiritual transformation that often result from these."

Dr. Ornish and Dr. Oz are in a different place from many of their peers. As Dr. Ornish noted in *Love & Survival*, when the *Journal of the American Medical Association* listed all the known risk factors for heart disease in May 1997, it did not even mention emotional stress, loneliness, or spiritual issues. When he searched the National Library of Medicine database from 1966 to 1997, he found that only two of more than nine million articles described the relationship of love and heart disease.

There is a myth in America today, and doctors subscribe to it too, that Western medical science has all the answers. When it comes to heart disease, the truth is far more grim. Doctors like Mehmet Oz save and prolong lives every day. But more than 500,000 people die from coronary artery disease annually, including 240,000 women. Altogether, 52 percent of Americans will die from coronary artery disease—more than from cancer or AIDS.

Meanwhile, people who live with heart trouble are not all running marathons. Doctors nationwide see more than 400,000 new cases of congestive heart failure a year. Severe heart failure that is unresponsive to even maximum medical therapy occurs in approximately 60,000 patients per year.

Even high blood pressure is not so simple. Doctors can only bring high blood pressure under control for half of the 27 million people who seek help for the condition, according to a 1998 report in the *New York Times*. Most of that control must be maintained through drug therapy. Drug companies sold about $9 billion in high blood pressure medicine in 1991. "We are struggling now with the concept that we are not doing a good job," Dr. Franz Messerli, of the hypertension department at the Ochsner Clinic in New Orleans, told the *Times*.

Even bypass surgery is not without risk. A study published in December 1996 in the *New England Journal of Medicine* found that 5 percent of 2,100 bypass patients surveyed suffered serious physical and mental impairment from strokes and other brain damage. And the mortality rate for coronary artery bypass graft is 2.5 percent for men and nearly twice as high for women.

In addition, irregular heart rates occur in 35 percent to 50 percent of patients after open heart surgery and is a major cause of prolonged hospitalization. Meanwhile, according to Dr. Ornish, up to half the bypass grafts clog up again within three to five years, and up to 50 percent of angioplastied arteries clog up again within four to six months.

Heart transplant patients face a far tougher course, taking immunosuppressants, which can cause liver and kidney dysfunction, tremors, nausea, bone loss, fluid retention, stomach ulcers and mood swings. In addition, 20 percent of recipients do not survive the first year. Another 40 percent do not make it to their ten-year anniversary.

Considering these facts, it is not surprising that Dr. Oz, like Dr. Ornish, would search for factors that might tip the scale in favor of his patients' health and happiness. He began experimenting with dietary supplements first. In 1994 he started exploring the benefits of yoga (which he himself practiced), hypnotherapy (which he had studied in medical school and which is commonly used by psychiatrists), and Robert Monroe's Hemi-Sync tapes (which produce soothing brain waves).

But when it came to energy healing, he had trouble convincing his colleagues that it was a subject worthy of study. Oz, however, was insistent. While still an undergrad at Harvard, he stumbled on the research of Dr. Björn Nordenström, chairman of radiology at the Karolinska Institute in Sweden, who believes that tumors have different "energy spheres" as Oz puts it, than normal cells. The energy concept never caught on; but the biopsy did. "Yet," says Oz, "there are little glimpses of insight you get into [Nordenström's] process, which make you think, 'Maybe the guy is on to something.'"

A recent medical study also supports the concept of these energy circuits. "If you inject radioisotopes here," he says, pointing to the soft flesh between the thumb and forefinger, "it tracks up along the energy meridian line, not the lymphatic line, like you'd normally expect it to track, which is interesting, because there's no way you'd be able to explain it. It may just be, for some reason that is completely un-energy related, that it happens to go in that direction. But it's strange."

"It raises the question that our understanding of how our body works is correct, but not the complete understanding," he continues. "There's more to it than that. If you start putting it all together, you start thinking, there's something going on here."

In the modern West, we think of the heart as a physical pump that sends our blood coursing through our veins. But the poets who write of the heart and its mysteries are not just speaking metaphorically, according to healers. They claim the heart chakra is designed both to generate and to receive love. And like mystics through the ages, they perceive the heart as a gateway to transcendence. Even today, we see examples of the power of the heart to transmute pain. Mother Teresa embodied this concept by loving even the poorest of the poor as the embodiment of Christ. And Princess Diana became beloved as she turned her suffering into compassion for others. Love is transformative. And the world responded to these two women because they reached out to others with love.

"The whole spiritual quest is about embracing all of creation," explains Rosalyn Bruyere. "And most of us don't naturally like all of creation." Bruyere raises her arms as if she is about to embrace the world. "The heart should be about the muscles doing this," she says, her arms spread wide. "I should love you by taking you in."

According to healers, our hearts get clogged by unresolved emotional issues. The feelings that belong in the second chakra, which should be filtered through the third chakra, end up being held in the heart. "The heart chakra is not meant to function on that frequency," explains Healing Light Center senior minister Nancy Needham. "So it goes awry. Plaque builds up. Blood pressure increases." The plaque "views its job as a protector," Needham adds. "And it's gotten out of control. It's layering all the vessels. Because that's the order it got a thousand times." Adds Don Van Vleet, a Manhattan healer whose gift is in focusing on the energy structures of the physical body, "The whole chest gets jammed [energetically]."

The emotional baggage is nothing esoteric. We all have some varying amount of emotional pain. But in heart patients the locus of injury settles in the heart. "I feel it has to do with disappointment that is never gotten over," says Needham. "People start at a very young age to learn to take disappointments personally. There's no perspective to recognize that on some level [emotional injuries] aren't personal at all. Look at how many times a kid or a teen says, 'I'm never going to trust anyone again.'"

Even when hereditary patterns are a factor in heart disease, Needham says, there are also usually emotional issues. She cites the example of one of Bruyere's students, a hard-driving business woman who had bypass surgery in her fifties. Both of the woman's parents had had heart disease. But the woman's problems developed twenty years earlier than her parents' diseases. "I think it's the betrayal," says Needham. "She definitely has incredible repressed anger. She's the most soft-spoken person in the world, but she walks around with a tortoise shell on her. . . . The real problem is people don't know what to do about it."

Betrayal. Anger. Rejection. Judgment. Inflexibility. Untended, these are the precursors to much heart disease, according to healers. Getting to the point where we realize that the hurts we experience typically have more to do with the unhealed areas in other people than with malicious intent can take, well, lifetimes.

That does not mean that healing is a panacea for heart disease. Far from it. Healers say that the very issues that tend to exacerbate or cause or coexist with heart disease often prevent people from seeking help. It is often hard for people who suffer from heart disease to reach out, to trust and to ask for help. And while cancer patients fear for their lives, heart patients believe everything is under control. "Doctors give the impression that Western medicine is effective. It's diet, angioplasty, a new heart valve, or bypass surgery," says Susan Weiley, who works with several heart patients. "They convince people this is where Western allopathic medicine is at its strongest."

Weiley has recently worked with three men who have heart disease. But not one of them sought out healing to work on their heart problems. Instead, she says, they came to her for help with the problems the heart disease caused in other systems. For instance, one man, a corporate lawyer, came to her because he wanted to save his eyesight. He had had six operations to correct his detached retinas. And they had all failed. But the reason his eyesight was failing is because his heart was not functioning properly. "The problem was his circulation was so bad he was going blind," says Weiley.

Another client, a retired entrepreneur in his sixties, came to her for help with optic neuropathy. The first time she worked on him she says she noticed that, "There was something very different about his heart. It turns out he has a metal valve in his heart. He didn't mention it to me. He didn't want to talk about it. 'I'm fixed,' was his attitude." His eye problems, too, stemmed from his heart disease, she says.

A third man she treated for heart disease is a psychotherapist, someone she has known for many years. He called for advice on finding a health-care practitioner who could recommend vitamins. He had complete blockage in one artery, and a 75 percent blockage in another. He was also leaving a marriage of twenty-seven years for a new romance. Weiley suggested he come in for a session. When he got off the table after the session, she claims he said, 'I didn't realize how jammed up my heart was.'"

Nevertheless, she doesn't expect him to return. Most heart patients do not want to take time out of their busy schedules. "They'll say, 'No way. I'm a busy man.'" Healing is not going to appeal, easily to a type A personality. "It's not a one-shot thing," explains Weiley. "Plus, it's not tangible. The heart patients need that. They need something quantifiable that can be measured, like angioplasty or bypass."

But some heart patients do take the plunge. Through spiritual healing they physically stabilize. More important, their lives change.

The research record into the role of subtle energy in healing heart disease specifically is scant indeed. The most famous study on spiritual healing and heart disease was published in 1988 in the *Southern Medical Journal* by cardiologist Randolph Byrd of San Francisco General Hospital. Byrd took 393 patients in the coronary care unit who had had heart attacks or severe chest pain and randomly assigned half to be prayed for by born-again Christians. To eliminate any placebo effect (the power of suggestion), patients were not told of the experiment. And neither the physicians or nurses treating the patients knew who was being prayed for or not—so it was double blind. Each patient in the treatment group had three to seven people praying for him daily.

The results are still talked about ten years later: There were fewer cardiopulmonary arrests and less need for medication or mechanical breathing support in the group that received a daily intention for healing through prayer. Despite these differences, all of which were statistically significant, the mean time each group spent in the hospital remained similar, as noted in *Healing Research*.

Two other published studies are far more modest in scope and results. In *Medical Hypotheses* in 1982, researcher Robert Miller reported that forty-eight patients who had high blood pressure and who received distant healing treatments, experienced a decrease in systolic blood pressure. The probability the results were chance were less than one in a thousand. The control group of forty-eight patients showed no such result. No significant differences were found in the change of diastolic blood pressure, pulse, or weight between the two groups. Dr. Daniel Benor, who reviewed the study in *Healing Research*, concluded that the study demonstrated that healing could be "significantly helpful" in systolic blood pressure. But he noted that the study was flawed, because while the patients continued regular medical treatment, those treatments were not tabulated.

In the *Nursing Science Quarterly* in 1989, Janet Quinn, Ph.D., a nurse and Therapeutic Touch practitioner, reported that diastolic pressure was significantly reduced with Therapeutic Touch, with a probability that the results were chance being measured at less than seven in a thousand. Dr. Benor found the results "fascinating," considering that the patients were already receiving antihypertensive and cardiac medications. But Dr. Benor also found it impossible to judge whether the findings were clinically significant without being able to examine the raw data. "This finding warrants replication," he concluded.

A fourth study, published in the *British Medical Journal* in 1988 was even less conclusive. It followed 120 hypertension patients with systolic blood pressures of 140 millimeters of mercury or above or diastolic pressure of 90 millimeters of mercury, without or despite antihypertensive therapy. The patients were divided into three groups, with one receiving laying on of hands, another receiving distant healing, and a third group receiving no healing. The patients in the latter two groups sat in a room behind one-way mirrors so they were unaware of whether a healer was present during treatment. All three groups demonstrated a significant drop in blood pressure in the fifteen-week study. The researchers concluded the results were the result of the "Hawthorne Effect" where any attention produces measurable results.

These four studies imply that the domain of heart disease and subtle energy is a fruitful area for further research, but are certainly far from conclusive.

Rosalyn Bruyere is one of the few healers I came across who has worked with many heart patients over the years. Because heart disease is so complicated and affects so many systems in the body, from the kidneys to liver to digestion to brain function, "There's so much relief you can bring to people with this condition," she asserts. In her experience, she adds, "People who have advanced coronary disease have a kind of rigid tension about them, where they are never at ease. It's not just a little emotional healing. You're getting a quality-of-life healing."

It is not only the energy that she runs that is transformative, she says. As part of her therapy, she says, she once asked a film industry executive who was an ardent Republican to pray for Bill Clinton daily. "At first his response was, 'Yes, I'll pray for him to die,'" she recalls. "And I said, then you'll both die together."

To heal the heart, she explains, the metaphysical muscles must be exercised as well as the physical heart and arteries. "The hard one to get past is the unlovable. That's where the heart really develops," she says. "The capacity of the heart is to take any idea and see the other side." She advises holding something in your heart until it changes. She also suggests stretching your heart by giving, by letting others go in front of you, and by surrendering to God's will. On the other hand, the heart is restricted by controlling, judging, and ma-

nipulating. "'Bring your still mind to your heart,'" she says, of the famous expression. "Opinions out of your third chakra going into your
heart turns into judgment instantly." Judgment shrivels the heart.
(Healers distinguish between judgment and discernment.)

In 1982 Bruyere did a pilot study on heart disease with a team
led by a local retired internist, Dr. Arnold Hastings, now deceased.
The study, ambitious in design, was not fully completed and was
never published, because, according to Bruce Harshman, Ph.D., a
clinical psychologist in Los Angeles, of disagreements between
himself and Dr. Hastings. But the data and study design may be of
anecdotal interest to heart patients, cardiologists, and researchers.

The pilot study involved nine patients who each had had a heart
attack. Each was given a battery of tests, urinalysis, blood analysis,
EKGs, a stress test, and a Beck Depression Inventory, a widely used
psychological test. The defining mark for all the patients was a reversed ST segment on the EKG, a pattern in the EKG that indicates
a lack of blood flow to the heart. Patients with any other medical
disorder, such as diabetes or lung disease, were excluded. No angiograms were given because of the slight risk involved in the procedure, coupled with the lack of insurance coverage for the project.

Bruyere treated each patient once a week for ten weeks, doing
energy chelation and whatever else came up during the energy sessions. All nine patients showed an improvement in the ST segment, recalls Dr. Harshman. "It was reversed in each one
completely," he recalls. "We might have wished it spiked more. But
all the base-line scores changed. We were very convinced. The heart
data was there."

Bruyere has told her students that every one of the nine patients had had a spiritual experience that they had rejected. "And
that their heart disease occurred after this," says Needham. "Every
one of them. All of this stuff didn't come up in casual conversation,
but during the energy work."

Bruyere especially remembers the conversations she had with
one of the subjects, an engineer. "He was very interested in parapsychology. He had had experiences thinking he'd seen auras," she
recalls. "We chatted a lot about those kinds of issues. There was a
relief that came over his whole system—in being able to have the

discussion. He was just frustrated. Frustration was a big part of the issue."

Dr. Harshman says that the psychological follow-up tests were not completed for everyone, so the results are only anecdotal. But, he claims, "Two or three had significant changes in their attitude of life."

Dr. Reuben, a graduate of Harvard Medical School, has also had success in treating heart disease through spiritual healing. In Flow Alignment and Connection energy sessions with George Berger, a computer engineer for a television network in New York City, "where we have gone together has been so extraordinary," she says.

Berger, now fifty, had a heart attack and double bypass surgery when he was forty, considerably overweight and living a life of numbing excess. "My motto was, 'Why indulge, when you can over-indulge?'" he recalls. He began coming to Reuben for healings every other week in mid-1997. He had already gone through the Dean Ornish program. Even so, he developed four new blockages in his arteries and he suffered from angina. His chiropracter finally sent him to Reuben, who maintains a private spiritual healing practice in Connecticut.

Since he began seeing Reuben, he has ended a marriage that he decided was abusive, dropped his habitual rage, and begun to have transcendent experiences, something that had never happened to him before. "This is not something Nancy led me to," he explains. "This is something that was discovered [during the process]. It arose. It kind of came up."

In his first session, he recalls, they had a conversation about his heart disease. Then she asked him to get on the massage table. As Reuben began to do the healing he says he had a vision of a beautiful woman. "It was so vivid, I described it to her. Nancy showed me a picture in a book. It was that woman." The picture was of Swami Gurumayi Chidvilasananda, a Hindu guru of the *Siddha* yoga lineage. "I knew nothing about her. That really got my attention." Dr. Reuben, a practitioner of *Siddha* yoga meditation, believes Berger had an initiation. "I felt he had *darshan* [a holy audience]," she says.

In subsequent sessions he had visions. "I time travel. All these times I'm on the table, I'm transported. I see different things. All these things are being explored as alternative times or prior lives. It's hard for me to accept it totally. But I have to admit something is going on."

In other sessions, he says, Reuben asked him to journey into his own body. "We went into my heart. We went into my arteries. It was one of the most frightening experiences. We started where everything is pink and red. Then I got to a place that was sticky and dark like molasses. I couldn't see. I couldn't breathe. I got very frightened. We had to come out of there. Nancy suggested that perhaps we had gone into one of the blocks. We stayed away for awhile.

"We went into other places. We put light there. I can't describe what the light was. I would like to say it was a white light, but it wasn't. I'd like to say it was a clear light, but it wasn't. But I could feel it coming in through my head or feet. And all of a sudden physical things would happen inside my body, noisy things, temperature changes. My body would get red. Things were happening. And I can't tell you what. All the time, there's been a positive progression."

As the sessions unfolded, Berger began to see his life differently. He says he realized he was in an abusive marriage and had to get out. "I got married for the wrong reasons," he says. "I got married because I was lonely. . . . I was so lonely and so sad for so long. When I was a kid, I hated myself. You know, lots of kids don't like themselves. . . . After the first honeymoon, I was still lonely and depressed. The heart attack was the culmination of all of that. . . . I call it Jewish suicide. You're not happy where you are. And you can't figure a way out. So you kill yourself—in a socially acceptable way."

He says in the last eighteen months his lifelong rage has simply dissolved. "I finally understand that people do the best they can," he explains. "If you can accept that, you don't have to get angry at them if it's not what you need or want, or even if it hurts you. It serves virtually no purpose to remain angry for any length of time."

Now, he says, he sees other people differently. "People walk into my office. I never used to be able to get beyond physical appearances. But now I see their inner beauty. I had never experienced that before in my life. That is very intense."

His physical condition has stabilized. The blocks have stopped getting worse. His angina has also diminished. He stopped using nitroglycerin patches after working with Reuben for six months.

He believes the healings have made a profound difference in his life. "You have to tell me where these changes come from, if they don't come from this trip. I think if I had been like this twenty years ago, I would never have had a heart attack." Now, he believes, "People can heal themselves. And they can let the spirits help."

Not everyone has quite such a transformation. Susan Weiley has done some twenty-five sessions in the last fifteen months with the retired entrepreneur suffering from optic neuropathy, caused by a lack of circulation to the eyes. But they have not had a noticeable effect in his daily life.

The entrepreneur's eye trouble began when he retired. He has since rented an office and hired a secretary so he has some place to go, although Weiley says his sight is so diminished that he really does not do much once he gets there. "This is a man who is in so much denial that he's almost blind and he won't let anyone know," says Weiley. "When he comes to see me, he can't even see enough to know where to sit down. He has to keep appearances up. He won't let himself feel his vulnerability. He just won't go there. And he's a wonderful human being. This is just how you soldier on. He was a pilot in World War II. You don't weaken. You don't complain.

"I did a lot of reconstruction of his heart chakra. He had surgery. Anybody who has had surgery needs to have their aura and the chakra from that area worked on. The surgery cuts through energy lines, for one thing. And the illness itself shows up as a distortion in the field. There was a lot of clogging in the emotional level of the field. There were also a lot of places in the field in general where there was rigidity; the energy just wasn't flowing. It's reflected in his personality." In addition, she has worked on the energy field around his eyes, trying to open up the flow.

At the same time, she has given him a series of Kabbalistic healings, including *Nezach-Hod*, "because his sense of himself and his identity is so fragile." She's also done Healings of Immanence to open him to his higher Self and has infused him with the energy of the open heart with *Tiferet-Yesod*, another Kabbalistic healing. His heart chakra remains completely blocked. "And his vision keeps getting worse," she says. The vision will temporarily improve, she explains. "But he cannot hold it."

Even now he never discusses any emotional issues or expresses concern about his heart disease. "There is a level of disconnect that's amazing," says Weiley. "It's not what I see with my cancer patients. With my cancer patients, I can say in the first session, 'Why do you have cancer?' They'll be shocked by the question. But they'll have an answer. . . . With heart patients, the heart reflects the compartmentalization."

Other healers describe occasional anecdotal successes. Only further scientific studies can determine conclusively whether these are related to subtle energy shifts. Doris Dennard, the patient who nearly died on the operating table at Columbia-Presbyterian, may have been one such case, according to her long-time cardiologist, Major Geer, of Manhattan.

Dennard's heart trouble began in the late 1970s. Dr. Oz and Dr. Geer believe she suffered from congenital mitral valve disease, which her mother had also had. She first saw Marden in 1988 for atrial fibrillation, an irregular heart rhythm that can lead to stroke. "She said, 'I'm tired of fibrillating,'" recalls Geer. "She went to a healer. I had been treating her with medication so I could electrically shock her [back into rhythm]. But she chose to do it her own way."

Dr. Geer says on the next visit to his office her heart was back in sinus rhythm. "I figured it was coincidental," he says. "Some people convert [back to normal] on their own." But then Dennard's heart went back into an irregular rhythm a few years later, recalls Geer. She was hospitalized. "We kept trying to treat her. She says to me one time, 'I want to go home. Do what you can. Slow it down to the point you can. Let [the healer] Phil and me talk about it.'" Geer says he released her from the hospital, heavily medicated.

Dennard went back to see healer Phil Marden. Afterward, Geer says, she was back in normal sinus rhythm. "He converted her," he says. "I was totally amazed. I stopped to realize that what [the healer] Phil was doing was the same as what we were doing. But he was using a natural method. We take a defibrillator, an electric box with two paddles, and shock someone with a certain amount of voltage. Then they stay in sinus. Phil was directing the energy from himself into her. That in itself caused the same thing to happen. It was totally amazing, unheard of in my field. Of course," he cautions, "it's not been proven."

Marden says he used a technique he learned from Bruyere in which he found the frequency of Dennard's internal clock and, using his own *chi* and focused intention, stopped the clock that ran her heart for "a nanosecond" and reset it. Grief from a long forgotten incident that occurred in Dennard's childhood also came up during the session.

Dr. Geer recalls that Dennard stayed in sinus rhythm for "a long, long time." He notes, "It's unusual to stay in sinus rhythm for over six months if you have a heart condition like hers, where the chambers are very dilated and enlarged. I think [the energy sessions] had an influence on her overall condition." Dr. Geer says he realizes that the healing that seemingly helped Dennard is still scientifically unproven for her condition. But, he predicts, "As we learn more about it, we will apply it more."

Healers also talk about loosening and moving out plaque, as one technique to work with atherosclerosis. "There's a quality of the fingertips becoming lasers," explains Massachusetts healer Deborah East Keir. "I go in with my fingertips and it's literally with pulsed short bursts." Keir says she used this technique when working with Barbara Sullivan, a sixty-year-old psychologist, in 1995.

Ever since having had a heart attack in 1984, Sullivan had relied on a nitroglycerin patch and a calcium channel blocker to counteract her angina. But in November 1995 her heart pain was so severe that she found herself popping between three and five nitroglycerin pills a night. Her cardiologist told her she might need a triple- bypass operation. Sullivan joined a prayer chain. Before her angio- gram, she also had two sessions with Keir. Keir claims she focused on clearing Sullivan's arteries, where she says she felt blockage.

Sullivan says her pain disappeared. When she went for the angiogram, her arteries were clean. Without an angiogram before healings, however, there is no basis for comparison. Nevertheless, there are indications of some positive change in her condition. Her cholesterol, which had been at a count of 240, dropped to a count of 178. Her blood pressure, which had been at 140/80, subsequently measured 120/74. Instead of suggesting surgery, her cardiologist took her off the nitroglycerin patch. (She remains on a calcium channel blocker.)

Keir does not take credit. Healing work, she explains, is "very humbling in the sense that sometimes you feel something really happened and shifted. If a person isn't able to hold the frequency, they can come back the next week, and you're doing the same thing. It's not up to the healer."

Needham, a healer in New Hampshire, had a similar experience with an eighty-five-year-old man. He had had bypass surgery eight years earlier. He came to Needham for help in dealing with grief after the death of his wife. Two years ago, after eight months of healing sessions every other week, he reported to Needham that his doctor was thrilled because his cholesterol levels were lower and he had improved on his stress test. Needham is the first to point out that it is impossible to measure whether she affected her client's system or not. "But, she adds, "This is not the normal progression for an eighty-five-year-old man."

After heart surgery Pam O'Neil, a critical care and emergency room nurse for over twenty years and a student of Bruyere's for more than five years, quietly does healing at Good Samaritan Regional Medical Center in Phoenix, Arizona. She estimates she has worked on twenty-five heart patients post operatively.

During heart surgery, she says, "there's so much stuff going on. The sternum has to be cracked open. They cut right through the bone and then wire it up. So I try to repair it." She works on repairing the subtle gridlines of light so the cells will have a healthy matrix on which to grow. At the same time, she tries to "take the pain down." She only works in five- or ten-minute intervals right after surgery. "I haven't done any studies. But I can feel the immediacy of it. Usually the wound is very cold and very jagged. I just try to smooth that out." She says there is so much trauma to the body that the energy she runs has to be very soft.

On occasion, she says, the surgeons have to take the sternum out to close the patient up. "Then it's like a big hole there. It's—Oh my God. I can't do it by myself. Then you need a team [of healers]. There's like a vortex [from the heart] going backwards."

Christine Saball-Tobin, a psychiatric nurse at Austin Riggs, a private hospital in Stockbridge, Massachusetts, and a former teacher at the Barbara Brennan School of Healing, has also used her energy skills in a hospital setting. While she was a critical care nurse at Hillcrest Hospital in Pittsfield, Massachusetts, she used to assess what was going on with heart patients. In one case, she recalls, the doctors called a May Day code for an elderly woman. One of the physicians, knowing Saball-Tobin was an energy healer, turned to her and actually asked her whether they should continue efforts to revive the patient. "I could see her aura had separated from her body," says Saball-Tobin. "It [the aura]was actually over the physician. I said, 'I think she wants to die now.' At that point, he stopped the resuscitation. I did not tell him that I saw the aura over his shoulder."

In yet another instance, doctors were fairly sure that a sixty-year-old man had just had a heart attack. They were stabilizing him with a blood thinner. "I could see this man was very anxious," recalls Saball-Tobin. "I saw he needed calm and quiet." She says she expanded her own energy field to encompass the space around him and thus provide him with the sense of safety and calm he needed. When the doctors and nurses treating him came into that energy field, they automatically calmed down, she claims. The patient was vomiting, the sign of a particular type of heart attack. But Saball-Tobin felt the symptoms were more related to anxiety. Everyone on the unit proceeded as if he was having a heart attack, although it turned out he was not.

Once heart muscle has atrophied or died, there is little that doctors believe can be done to alter the situation. So the experience of Warren Nagel, a Manhattan businessman in his fifties, is somewhat unusual.

In 1992 Warren Nagel's heart muscle was destroyed by a virus. His ejection fraction (pumping efficiency) dropped to 50 percent or less of what is considered normal. He was perpetually short of breath. About 70 percent of people with the condition die within five years. His cardiologist, Dr. Frank Livelli, put him on a list for a heart transplant, the only long-term medical solution, at Columbia Presbyterian Medical Center. During the following year, Nagel's ejection fraction dramatically improved, returning almost to normal.

The improvement was temporary. By the end of 1993 Nagel's pumping efficiency was back down to 50 percent of normal; his other systems were also deteriorating. Nagel did not believe in healers. But he was dying. "I'd have gone to a witch doctor," he said when I met him at his spacious Manhattan apartment in February 1997. "I was ready to try anything." In early 1994 a family friend referred him to Dani Antman, a graduate of the Brennan school. "She started to tell me things about myself I hadn't told a soul, things about my relationship with my mother," he said. That got his attention.

Nagel saw Antman every week for a month. Then he stopped, partly because of financial reasons. (Around the time he was diagnosed with the heart virus, his real estate company also went bankrupt.) The other reason, he admitted, was she was getting "too personal." I said to her, she's not healing, she's playing shrink.

In the first session, Antman said she basically worked on clearing energy blocks in his heart chakra and legs. "I was opening up the energy to his lower body," she said. "It wasn't moving. His field was very gray. I wanted to get the physical body more vital." She also cleared an etheric chord connecting him with his mother. It had gotten tangled because of the difficulties in the relationship. In addition, she "received" a new heart template during the healing, which she put into his heart in the energy field.

In the next few sessions, she worked on clearing "a black hole" in the energy of his heart and on strengthening his *hara* to create a stronger intention to live. Over time, Nagel said, "Things physically changed. I didn't get worse. I pretty much stabilized." Tests showed that his heart function had not improved. But his arrhythmia disappeared. He was able to work and live a relatively normal life. "He plateaued at a good level of function. We did not relist him [for a transplant]," confirms Dr. Livelli.

Nagel's heart problems didn't disappear, however. In September 1995 his cardiologist performed a triple-bypass operation. As Nagel told me about the operation in early 1997, he seemed enthusiastic and healthy. Except for his thick gray hair, he had an almost boyish joy about him as he lifted his right pants leg to reveal a wide scar on the inside of his knee heading towards his ankle. Doctors took a vein from that area for his heart, he explained. After the operation, the leg wound would not close. Finally, in December 1995 the doctors scheduled him for a skin graft operation the following month.

Nagel returned to Dani Antman. "I went back to her because I knew it worked," he said, then corrected himself. "Or I wanted to see if it worked." Antman restructured the subtle lines of light around his leg.

Two weeks later his leg wound had just about closed. "Probably the fear of a skin graft got you to heal," his doctor joked. Nagel confessed he had gone to a healer. "Whatever you're doing is working," Nagel said Dr. Livelli replied. "I don't know if it was her, or you were taking care of it. I'm not going to disbelieve that what she did helped."

Nagel returned to Antman for several more sessions in the first few months of 1996. Antman's overall diagnosis of Nagel: "He was definitely not heart-satisfied." Antman, by then studying Kabbalistic healing, brought in *Tiferet*, the *sefirah* that helps one see one's self with love and connects a person with his or her longing for spiritual fulfillment. When I asked Antman to demonstrate this *sefirah*, she sat quietly, a few feet from me in her office. After a moment, I could feel almost a burning sensation in my heart, which shocked me. Antman hadn't touched me.

She chose *Tiferet* because Nagel had begun to talk about his heart's longings. "When a person allows themselves to long, it sort of counteracts their hopelessness. If they don't have a longing, part of them dies. When the longing comes back, they are more alive. The heart has something to live for."

Antman said Nagel's longing was for physical health "and to be out of pain, and to be emotionally happy in his relationships." Spiritually, she added, "He didn't know. We had interesting talks about that. He listened to Hasidic music. There was a longing in that. But there wasn't a conscious connection to a longing for God." In a later session, "We went back to why [the things he longed for] had atrophied in his life."

At one point, he confessed that he sometimes listened to a tape of a Jewish cantor singing Hebrew songs, although he was not at all religiously inclined. After listening to that tape, he would get an image of an old man. "'If you saw him, would you recognize him?'" Nagel said she asked. "She goes to this book, opens a page and points to a picture: 'Is this the man?' It was the man. Whoever the picture was, that's the person I was seeing. That just convinced me that Dani . . ." he cut himself off. "Whatever. Maybe I'm crazy."

Antman also began addressing deep issues "around confrontation and hate" with his family of origin. She brought in *Nezach-Hod* from the Tree of Life, energies to help him take pleasure and strength from his own essence. After seven sessions, Nagel decided not to continue. He did not feel comfortable with the personal issues she wanted to explore. "It was hard for him to face making changes in his life," says Antman.

Nagel felt pleased. He was stable. He recalled that at one point, Dr. Livelli said, "If I could figure out your case, we could write it up." Dr. Livelli says he might have said something like that, but only about the original, unexpected (and temporary) improvement in his heart function. As for spiritual healing, "If this is all the placebo effect, I'm 100 percent for it," he explained. But, he noted, he did not think it was part of his role as a doctor to recommend or investigate such practices.

Warren Nagel had five extra years with his own heart beyond what doctors had predicted for him. But in October 1998 his kidneys began to fail and he became short of breath. His reprieve was over. Dr. Livelli put him in the hospital to wait for a new heart. The wait will be four to six months. "I'm fine," Nagel said from his hospital room, clearly short of breath. "It's just a long wait."

Antman says she has no idea if another heart patient with the same problem could achieve a similar outcome. Indeed, even before Warren Nagel came to her, he had shown an ability to stabilize his own heart. "Each person comes in with a very unique situation," she says. "We're not just looking at the presenting complaint, but the soul's journey. And the healing each time would be unique. And the outcome would be unique."

Rosalyn Bruyere, however, believes subtle energy can support actual reversals in cardiomyopathy. The film industry executive whom she asked to pray for President Clinton also had a heart that had been badly damaged by a virus. After a series of healings, his doctors took him off a list for a heart transplant. In addition to prayer, Bruyere says she worked to stimulate his heart and lungs, "Everything that had to do with the breathing parts." Three years later, his heart remains stable.

What do these anecdotes really mean? Doctors do not yet know. Most of them are not even interested in finding out. For this reason, controlled double-blind research studies of heart disease and energy healing will take time. Dr. Oz himself is still learning the ins and outs of energy healing. In heart patients who are very sick, Oz found no physiological effects in patients from twenty-minute Therapeutic Touch sessions. He's not surprised, he says. These are patients, he says, who are on "whopping doses of chemicals. I don't think the mind is going to have the ability to control the body's responses in those circumstances," he says. "Effectively, we're in the middle of a nuclear war. Therapeutic Touch may be the equivalent of planting trees or growing flowers.

"The other possibility is that I have the wrong practitioners," he concedes. Briefly, the complementary care unit (now a department) accepted volunteers. Some of the top healers in Manhattan offered their services. But basically, hospital policy has restricted practitioners to hospital personnel.

Dr. Oz says that in preliminary studies he has found what any healer knows: different healers get different effects. In a study of healing on cancer cells in vitro, only one of three practitioners had a consistent 15 percent effect on the tumor cells. That practitioner, Frank Haung, has been studying a form of Chinese energy healing for eighteen years. The average nurse has far less training and experience in energy healing, notes Dr. Oz.

As Dr. Oz discovered, a wide range of abilities exists between practitioners who have had extensive formal training. In the not-yet-published results of an experiment designed to measure the ability of healers to create a corona discharge in a time-varying electrical field (also known as Kirlian photography) while sending *chi*, only three of four healers trained by Rosalyn Bruyere had a very noticeable corona on the day they were studied; two were able to create especially strong coronas. "I couldn't do it no matter what I did," says Dr. Oz. "If I pressed harder, if I hyperventilated, I couldn't do it."

Dr. Oz's other laboratory experiments have had disappointing results. Dr. Oz intends to continue his research. Currently, he encourages patients to listen to Sufi tapes. "It's five-tonal music, which is supposed to resonate with certain energy fields in the body," he says. "For me, what is most enticing about [energy] healing is that if it works, there's a whole different way to explain how the body might work."

Dr. Oz is one of the few doctors interested in exploring healing and heart disease. And, he admits, it is "an extremely delicate situation. The hospital and university are being criticized by their peers. They don't want Columbia [University] being taken over by radicals."

Ann Massion, M.D., a research psychiatrist at the University of Massachusetts, is the only other researcher known to be focusing on heart disease and healing. She is designing a study to examine the impact of Kabbalistic healing on heart disease.

Rosalyn Bruyere has volunteered to do healings as part of an experiment at Columbia Presbyterian. "I'd like to change the outcome for heart patients." But at the moment, no such formal study of healing and heart disease with Bruyere or any other healer is in the works.

Eleven

Cancer

Marilyn Schneider, a healer and the former nursing director of a long-term care facility in Cincinnati, Ohio, knows more about cancer than she sometimes wishes she did. And she's learning more about it every day.

A slim, well-coiffed woman in her mid-sixties and the mother of five grown children, Schneider's dance with cancer began in June 1989, when she woke up one morning in her suburban home to find that she was completely jaundiced. She ended up in the hospital the same day, with a diagnosis of advanced pancreatic cancer. Unlike a lay person with no medical expertise, she did not have to be told she was facing an extremely painful death. The cries from pancreatic cancer patients she had tended as a nurse still rang in her ears.

Schneider had just completed her freshman year at the Barbara Brennan School of Healing. For whatever reasons, no one had noticed anything amiss in her energy field during the year. That did not shake Schneider's faith in healing, however. From the beginning, she followed an alternative course along with the standard care. Schneider's doctors urged her to have emergency surgery immediately, since the tumor was completely obstructing her internal organs. Everything in her training as a nurse had taught her to obey physicians. But when she met the recommended surgeon, she was convinced she would die if she put herself in his hands. "He was so arrogant," she recalls.

Schneider began working long distance with Jason Shulman (who later founded A Society of Souls). She believes he gave her the strength she needed to find the right surgeon. The two had never met and Shulman lived in New Jersey, several states away. But during their first conversation, he described Schneider's tumor with such accuracy, it was as if he was reading the CAT scan. On the higher dimensions, explains Shulman, "location is indistinct. Where does love reside? In your heart? In your brain? In your arms when you reach out to embrace?" Likewise, he says, in the higher dimensions, "Where is the self located? Or the body? The body is located throughout space."

Shulman set to work charging Schneider's cells to give them extra life force. He also began to coordinate the pulses between Schneider's liver, pancreas, and spleen. "These organs were not in harmony," he explains. "A lack of relationship means a lack of possibility." Schneider says she felt comforted. "I felt surrounded by a presence," she says. "No one could have given me more of a gift."

Five days later, Schneider found a surgeon, Dr. Thomas Maynard, whom she felt she could trust. The night before the surgery, Schneider slept at home. She had one more phone conversation with Shulman, who planned to hold a focus of attention for Schneider during the actual surgery. "Is there a window by your bed?" he asked.

"Yes," Schneider said.

"Is there a tree by the window?"

"Yes," she said, startled. A ficus tree was by the window.

"He just wanted me to know he was right there with me," she says. "A lot of the fear went away."

The surgery was supposed to be a standard Whipple, a complicated operation in which the head of the pancreas is removed, along with the bile duct from the liver. The intestines are severed and reattached. The operation has a 5 percent mortality rate. But when Dr. Maynard opened Schneider up, he saw that the tumor had enveloped her portal vein, which services the liver. Almost any surgeon would have simply closed her up. If the liver was cancerous, she was as good as dead.

But Maynard cut a flap in the vein. Pulling it back, he saw that the tumor had not yet penetrated the vein's interior. He considered cutting out a piece of the vein and sectioning the two ends together, something that is never done. The patient could hemorrhage to death. The chance of failure, and a lawsuit, was high. Maynard says he suddenly knew it would be okay. "There are innate things, intuitive things, that happen with all of us in whatever we do," he says. "Something tells me where to move my hands. I have an ability to do things that isn't book-learned." And this was one of those moments. "She had a fatal disease—no ifs, ands, or buts about it. Unless something heroic was done, she was going to be buried quickly and die pretty miserably." The surgery lasted a grueling eight hours.

The five-year survival rate for pancreatic cancer in general is only 3 percent. Maynard estimated Schneider had just a 1 in 100 chance of surviving. Yet Schneider made a remarkably rapid recovery. To this day she does not need insulin shots, only a pancreatic enzyme. She has never had a recurrence. But physical healing was only one aspect of her journey. Before the operation, her healer, Jason Shulman, saw one of the causative reasons for Schneider's cancer. "This cancer is connected to your mother," he told her. "What happened to you between the ages of three and six?"

Schneider had no idea what he was talking about. Shulman let the matter drop. She needed her energy for the surgery. But almost a year after the operation, Schneider went to see Shulman in his office. "I did not even get on the healing table," she recalls. "We were just talking about what was on my mind."

All of a sudden, she says, "Jason seemed to be moving further and further away. Suddenly, I was right back to my grandmother's couch in the living room. I saw my uncle come in. . . ." Schneider says she suddenly had a flashback: She saw that when she was about four years old, her maternal uncle forced her to perform oral sex on him. But the worst part, she says, was her mother's response, which she had repressed all these years. "We are not to talk about this," her mother replied. And then her mother continued to send her on visits to her grandparents and uncle. She even sent Schneider alone on a vacation with the uncle. She broke down sobbing.

"Mothers are supposed to protect their children," Schneider says simply.

After these memories of sexual and emotional abuse surfaced, Schneider's forty-year marriage to Bill, a retired human resources executive, was reborn. She also found herself more assertive about her own needs. For the nearly ten years she was the director of nursing at a long-term care facility, she had never once taken a vacation from being on call twenty-four hours a day. She put others before herself, always. Before she got ill, "I was afraid of living," she says. But after recovering from cancer she was grateful to be alive.

Five and a half years later, she had one last visit with Maynard. He gave her one more CAT scan. It showed she had no cancer. "You know you are a walking miracle," he told her. He called in his entire staff to meet her and see for themselves someone who had survived pancreatic cancer. Indeed, Schneider's survival was so unusual that she once got a call from a physician in Iowa who wanted to talk to her; he had pancreatic cancer and could not find a single survivor in his own state.

Since then, Marilyn Schneider has done healing work with more than fifty cancer patients. In 1995 she also developed an entirely unrelated lung cancer that was excised. It recurred in the beginning of 1998. She knows intimately, as both a survivor and a healer, what cancer is really about. "It's about arrested growth," she says. "It's about not giving yourself enough space."

Cancer. The word is almost synonymous in our psyches with fear and death. The second leading cause of death in the United States, cancer often emerges without warning, frequently after growing silently for decades. Approximately 1.38 million new cases of cancer were diagnosed in 1997 alone (not including carcinoma in situ, early localized tumors, and nearly 900,000 cases of basal and squamous cell skin cancers). After five years, only 40 percent of those people will be alive according to the American Cancer Society. Approximately 560,000 people in the United States died of cancer in 1997, or 1,500 people a day. No one is immune. Cancer strikes children, the elderly, and men and women in the prime of their lives, often seemingly without rhyme or reason.

Since President Richard Nixon signed the National Cancer Act in 1971, the United States has been waging a "war" on cancer. The overall costs of cancer reached $107 billion in 1998. During the last twenty-five years, scientists have made important new discoveries about how cancer works. But the combined death rate for all cancers has dropped only 2.6 percent between 1991 and 1995. Treatments, when they do work, can sometimes be almost as debilitating as the disease itself.

Cancer is a disease in which a person's own cells grow out of control. Scientists have found that cancers appear to be caused by genetic mutations that occur in normal cells over a long period of time. "It normally takes decades for an incipient tumor to collect all the mutations required for its malignant growth," explained Robert Weinberg, Ph.D., a professor of biology at the Massachusetts Institute of Technology in a 1996 issue of *Scientific American* devoted to cancer. In some cases, oncogenes, which play a role in normal cell growth, mutate. In other cases, suppressor genes, which control cell growth, get damaged. Most cancers are not caused by inherited genes. According to leading cancer experts writing in the *Scientific American* special issue, just 10,000 deaths a year are the result of inherited "cancer" genes.

These discoveries, however, do not fully explain the fundamental cause of cancer. We have some 30 trillion cells, and cells in our bodies go awry all the time. Most people's bodies destroy rebel cells before they become tumors. Even women with the cancer-promoting genes BRAC1 and BRCA1 do not have fates that are totally predetermined. In fact, the gene confers only a 56 percent chance they will develop breast cancer and a 15 percent chance they will develop ovarian cancer by the time they reach seventy, according to a report in the *New England Journal of Medicine* that was cited in the *New York Times*.

"Everyone is so impressed when someone gets over cancer," says Dr. Elisabeth Targ, head of psychosocial oncology at California Pacific Medical Center in San Francisco. "The fact is, every single one of us gets over cancer every single day. The question we should really be asking is not 'Why do some people get sick?' but 'Why aren't all of us sick all the time?'"

What causes the genetic mutations that lead to cancer? It depends on whom you ask. The American Cancer Society lists tobacco use and dietary factors as two of the leading causes of cancer. Environmental factors are also noted, from carcinogens to radiation. Possible emotional or spiritual precursors are not even considered. Leading cancer experts writing in the aforementioned *Scientific American* shared the American Cancer Society's perspective. A chart of the leading causes of cancer listed thirteen major factors, with not a word about emotional factors.

Healers have a radically different view.

Sluggish, murky, heavy, dark, maroon, gray: These are some of the descriptions healers use in describing cancer cells. Medical researchers have found that cancer cells have a negative electrical potential compared to healthy cells. Healers describe cancer in similar terms.

"Cancer cells are low frequency, low amplitude cells, and, like embryonic cells, are undifferentiated tissue," says Rosalyn Bruyere, who has laid hands on thousands of people with cancer during her career. "That's why they grow the way embryonic cells grow. It was very popular in the seventies to believe that cancer was an unconscious death wish. It's more complicated. It's more like: 'Give me consciousness, or give me death.'"

More than any other disease, says Bruyere, cancer frequently is a soul's way of addressing power issues. "In cancer the body believes that the tumor that has been created should be protected and attended to in the same way as an injury, so it sends its blood supply to the tumor and feeds it," she writes in her book, *Wheels of Light.* "The body uses the wrong kind of power for the wrong thing in the wrong place." Bruyere and other healers say this misuse of power is holographic in a person's life. "As a general rule," says Bruyere, "cancer patients consider themselves undeserving. . . . They have difficulty accepting and using power properly. . . . When cancer patients reorder their psychological inventories, their bodies can and will fight the disease.

"Where [cancer] relates to power," she adds, "it involves whether we clearly identify something as an enemy, or whether we accept a certain amount of negativity. . . . Does someone else's negativity infect you? Or can you clean it up?"

To illustrate what a power issue might be, Debra Schnitta, R.N., who has studied with Rosalyn Bruyere and Amy Skezas, the founder of Flow Alignment, gives the example of a twenty-eight-year-old Indian-born woman who came to her for help. She had thyroid and ovarian cancer. During the session, Schnitta says, she *saw* "a very large and beautiful soul, looking for a way to express that. I told her, 'You're a very powerful woman.'"

Schnitta recalls that the woman did not want traditional medical treatment, in part because the doctors wanted to remove her thyroid. "I said she needed to see a physician," Schnitta says. "I told her, 'You're very sick.' She cried and cried and cried." When the woman didn't schedule another appointment Schnitta did something she normally doesn't do. She called. "I said to her if she wanted to die, she had to tell me. And she said, 'You're telling me to be powerful. You don't understand. In my culture, I can't go there.'"

Schnitta says here was a woman who needed to open her heart and speak her truth in order to heal. "In essence, she was making a choice to leave the planet. So many times we think it's about fixing the body. But really it's about the larger lesson. The 'hello' is what the soul needs to proceed in its incarnation in this lifetime."

Healers say that the underlying cause of the power imbalance is specific to each person. It is often something about which the person has little or no conscious awareness. The pattern is so integral to who they are that it just feels normal. Diane Munz, a Los Angeles woman who struggled with breast cancer on and off for ten years, told me that after working with Rosalyn Bruyere last year, she began to understand that she had not allowed herself to own her emotional power. "When Rosalyn says, 'You've never known how you impact people,' she's right on the money," said Munz, who was just thirty-three when she was first diagnosed. "It's always been part of my insecurity growing up: Am I the only one who feels this way, so intensely? People around me didn't seem to feel this way. It was confusing."

In the case of a baby with leukemia, Denver healer Melanie Brown believes some of the teachings were for the baby's mother.

"The mother had to take her own power," says Brown. "She was a very passive person, especially with men and authorities like her father. In fighting for her daughter's life, she took on doctors and got nurses fired. She sat vigil over this child. If she were the one with the disease, she would have died. She wouldn't have fought the way she did for her child."

The family took the baby to Duke University for a bone marrow transplant. "The statistics were not great," Brown says. "They saw nine or ten babies with better stats die around them." But more than two years later, the baby is thriving. "They consider it a cure. Her bone marrow has switched over," says Brown. "And the family has gone on to have another baby, which they were very frightened to do."

In many cases, healers find that cancer patients have suffered some kind of abuse, whether emotional, physical, or sexual, in early childhood, or some kind of traumatic loss. "If I ask a cancer patient have you in some way been silenced, without hesitation, every single one of them will say yes," says Marilyn Schneider. Often, adds Brown, "If it's abuse, it's not physical. It's more of the subtle emotional stuff, like not being validated, having to be perfect, judging yourself harshly."

Schneider explains that the cancer patient frequently ends up taking care of others as a substitute for expressing their own needs. They drive themselves endlessly, she says. On the surface, they appear active, dynamic, happy, productive. But underneath, basic needs are not being met, and basic emotions are not being allowed. The cancer cell is the part of the being that is in rebellion, she explains. It wants "complete freedom. It forgets it has a function in a system."

This was Dr. Dan Kinderlehrer's experience with a patient who came to see him with melanoma. She had had surgery seven years earlier. Then, unexpectedly, the cancer recurred. This time, her oncologist gave her six months to live and told her he had nothing more he could do. "The first day in the office, we talked about her life and her lifestyle," says Dr. Kinderlehrer, who is both a physician and a healer. "This was a woman who worked nonstop from the moment she got up until the moment she went to bed at night. She was doing productive things, but she never stopped. She was volunteering, starting her own business, and teaching. She was a wonderful woman. By her own admission, she said her lifestyle was crazy.

"I said to her, 'If this is so crazy why are you doing it?' 'Because I'm trying to kill myself,' she said," Dr. Kinderlehrer recalls. "She said it was because she felt badly about who she was. She had been terribly abused by her father and mother. Doing all these things was the only way to extract a piece of self-worth."

Dr. Kinderlehrer says the woman lived three years longer than her doctors had predicted. "The way she lived was by stopping," he says. "She gave up everything. She said, 'I'm just going to heal myself.'"

Healers stress that cancer is not about punishment, although deep down many people who develop cancer feel it is just that. "Frequently, people walk in with cancer and they feel they did something wrong," says Schnitta. "They didn't do anything wrong. It's just how some part of you has chosen to go through a lesson."

Nor does the mystery of cancer begin and end in the emotional realms. "If you got out all your rage, it doesn't mean you're going to survive," says Kabbalistic healer Shulman. "It is a mystery. It is God's will."

"The process of incarnation is a problem to begin with," he continues. "You sign on and—as they say on the T-shirt, 'Shit Happens.' Everyone here on Earth will be dead in 120 years. The slate is wiped clean. . . . This is the system, so either it's nuts. Or there is a deeper reason."

Most physicians and psychiatrists do not even stop to consider whether there might be emotional antecedents to cancer. But Dr. Bernard Siegel, a surgeon who has treated many cancer patients, finds, like healers, that many of his cancer patients have not been well loved as children. "In fact, I would estimate that 80 percent of my patients were unwanted or treated indifferently as children," he writes in *Love, Medicine & Miracles*. And, like healers, he considers this lack of love a causative factor in cancer. "Even laboratory rats, when prematurely separated from their mothers, become more susceptible to cancer," he notes.

Dr. Siegel cites comments such as, "We always wanted a boy instead of a girl"; or "Your father was drunk—we didn't want more children"; and even, "I wish I'd had an abortion instead of you," as leaving indelible marks on the psyche that are much deeper than most people imagine. "Such messages lead to a lifelong feeling of unworthiness. . . . Psychological shaping in the formative years plays a large part in determining who will develop a serious illness." And he adds, "I wouldn't be surprised if cancer in early childhood was linked to messages of parental conflict or disapproval perceived even in the womb."

Dr. Siegel also notes that cancer patients are exceptionally nice. "The truth is that compulsively proper and generous people predominate among cancer patients because they put the needs of others ahead of their own. Cancer might be called a disease of nice people. They are 'nice' by other people's standards, however. They are conditional lovers. They are giving only in order to receive love. If their giving is not rewarded, they are more vulnerable to illness than ever."

New York psychoanalyst Jane Goldberg, author of *Deceits of the Mind and their Effects on the Body*, is another professional whose experience concurs with that of healers. Dr. Goldberg, who specializes in treating cancer patients, says she finds that a serious disturbance in the primary nurturing relationships is typical. "Having been frustrated in the original search for closeness. . . . they have come to feel that neediness is bad," she explains in *Deceits*. "Nevertheless, the need remains, on the unconscious level.

"In an attempt to get the needs satisfied while at the same time hiding the need, they erect a persona of independence, security, and satisfaction," she adds. "The adult personality that is prone to the development of cancer then is one that is inordinately pleasant, not prone to feelings of anger or aggression and emphatically interested in pleasing the other."

Some medical studies support the view that emotional distress may predate the development of cancer. Researchers led by Dr. Caroline Bedell Thomas at Johns Hopkins Medical School took personality profiles of 1,337 medical students beginning some forty years ago and followed them for several decades after graduation. As Dr. Siegel notes, she found that the traits of those who developed cancer were almost identical to those who later committed suicide. Almost all the men who subsequently developed cancer had been inhibited from expressing emotion, especially aggressive emotions relating to their own needs. They had also suffered from loneliness and less satisfactory relationships than others in the study.

Lawrence LeShan, Ph.D., an experimental psychologist, had a similar conclusion after conducting personality studies of seventy-one "terminal" cancer patients. As Dr. Siegel notes, Dr. LeShan found that an underlying despair, more subtle and more difficult to discern than depression, existed in sixty-eight of these patients prior to the diagnosis, but in only three of eighty-eight other clients he surveyed who did not have cancer.

In another study done in the 1950s, as Dr. Ornish notes in *Love & Survival*, the Western Electric Company in Chicago gave 2,000 middle-aged male employees a questionnaire to assess emotional factors, including depression. Those who were depressed were twice as likely to have died from cancer twenty years later, when the sample was surveyed again.

Drs. Siegel and Ornish cite other studies showing that cancer patients who express their sadness, anxiety, and hostility live longer. Still other studies have found that people who eventually develop cancer report less emotionally close relationships and support before their illnesses.

Despite these studies, most doctors and researchers focus almost entirely on the biochemical aspects of cancer. Treatments are designed to attack cancer cells, not resolve the underlying feelings that may be directing the immune system. In contrast, healers say they try to help clients repattern their energy at every level.

"There are certain traits," explains Schneider. "It can be helpful to point out. It's not that you're doing something wrong, but that we give ourselves away. It's that doing, doing, doing. And not learning how to take care of yourself. It requires a total life change. I think I've done the work. But there's always more. It's so easy to fall back into those patterns. It's so ingrained."

Healings are not a substitute for traditional medical care. Everyone I interviewed had some form of surgery, chemotherapy, radiation, hormone treatments, or a combination. And no two cancers—and no two courses of healings—will ever be exactly alike, according to healers.

For example, Jane Ely, a shamanic counselor and a former senior teacher at the Brennan school, has helped two men handle prostate cancer. The first man, a recently retired Dupont Corporation researcher in his early sixties, was already on a spiritual path. Healing treatments and spiritual counseling were part of his treatment plan from the beginning. His doctors recommended partial removal of the prostate, which he agreed to after discussing the decision both with his wife and with Ely. Then, after surgery, he had sessions with Ely to support his physical and emotional healing. Ely repaired his field on all levels where the surgery had disrupted it. She did this by recharging the subtle meridians and grid lines around the prostate gland as well as the area of the body which had been cut.

She also worked on the emotional issues around the surgery, dealing with "a lot of fear about loss of functioning, loss of control and power," she says. He declined to be interviewed, but Ely claims that within six months to a year, "he was up and running." She reports that he had the least invasive surgery possible and regained sexual functioning within six weeks. "Energy medicine can really help repair the field, which then in turn helps the physiology," she asserts. Of course, there is no way to know definitively how much of that effect can be attributed to the healings without medical studies.

Ely's second client with prostate cancer was not on a spiritual path. When his odyssey began he was in his late fifties, the head of a major program at one of the top business schools in the United States, with a Ph.D. from the London School of Economics. He had lived a relatively charmed life, except for occasional emotional challenges. "I come from a traditional professional world," he says.

In keeping with his belief system, when his cancer was diagnosed in November 1993, he sought out a leading urologist and followed the traditional medical protocol without question. On the Gleason scale, which measures biopsy samples, his cancer rated an eight on a scale of two to ten, meaning it was fast growing and aggressive. "It turns out younger folks are more likely to have an aggressive form," he says. "There's no bang to the psyche I've had that was like that."

Within weeks, he had his prostate removed during a surgery that lasted four and a half hours. The trouble came afterwards. The pathologist found cancer right up to what had been cut, suggesting that the professor still had cancer cells in his body. His oncologist urged a thirty-week course of radiation. The professor was not happy. "It was the same course of treatment as if I had chosen not to get surgery," he says.

He reviewed the medical literature to make a decision and found there was no evidence that radiation therapy would prolong his life. "How can you recommend this?" he asked his doctor. "Because it's the accepted practice," he says the oncologist replied. The professor then consulted twenty leading experts in oncology from such prestigious institutions as Sloan Kettering in New York, Johns Hopkins in Maryland, and Stanford University. All but two said they would take radiation. It did not matter.

"I had already decided," he says. Statistically, he had a 75 percent chance his cancer would recur. He focused instead on the 25 percent shot he had of beating the disease. "I was concerned that radiation does terrible things to the body," he explains. "It destroys the immune system, which is the one hope you have. And the possible side effects include loss of bowel function. It doesn't burn just diseased tissue. This was the major break."

The professor began investigating alternative therapies, while monitoring his health with regular ultrasensitive PSA (Prostate Specific Antigen) tests from Stanford University. Eventually, he began working with alternative practitioners who used Electro-Acupuncture by Voll (EAV) analysis to measure subtle energy frequencies as a diagnostic tool. One of them referred him to Jane Ely in April 1996 for healing sessions. "There was a network," says the professor.

In the first session, he recalls, Ely did a shamanic extraction of the cancer energy. It was utterly bizarre, he says. "What would I think if I was looking in the window. I'd think, 'This guy was off his rocker.'" During the session, he says, Ely asked the cancer why it was there. "Then she removed it," he says. "She got tough, tough, tough. It was like she was talking to a thug." After that session, he claims, EAV no longer measured any cancer energy in his field. "That was a miracle," asserts Ely. "His physiology just changed overnight after that particular session. Sometimes it happens like that. Sometimes it doesn't."

The professor began to see Ely every month, for double sessions each time. Each session was different. Once Ely did a soul retrieval to bring back "lost parts." If he hadn't experienced it himself, he says, he might not have believed in it. But, he says, "She identified some things from my past. In one of the scenes she visited, she saw a playground where I was being beaten up by other kids. I did live one-half block from a playground and every so often I got beaten up. It was very real."

Ely says in these and other sessions she often focused more on the professor's emotional issues than on his physiology. "When he came in his energetic field was rigid, meaning that there was no emotional aspect apparent," she recalls. "He was truly what I would call a thirsty soul. He was dying without his emotions. Our spiritual work was about helping him find it so he could live. When he realized there was safety and security in having emotions, his entire field brightened," says Ely. "The emotional bodies started pulsating and got bigger and bigger. He literally turned rainbow colors in his field."

In May 1996 after just three sessions with Ely, the Stanford ultra PSA test showed a prostate specific antigen level of .02 nanograms per millileter, on a scale where .07 reflected a 99 percent chance of recurrence. For a year his tests had ranged from zero to .01 except for one brief spike a year earlier. Worried, the professor immediately had another sample taken. The test showed an astounding PSA level of .19. A test done by a second lab confirmed the results.

Ely assured him the tests were simply picking up toxins that had been stored in his body that were now being released. The next day he had another PSA sample drawn and sent to Stanford for analysis. The test showed he had zero prostate specific antigen in his body. "I was amazed," he says. "First I called the head of the PSA laboratory at Stanford. 'Have you changed your test in any way?' I asked. 'Have you ever seen a PSA go up so fast, and go down to zero?' He said, no, he had never seen a test go up like that and back down. He had no explanation. You either have cancer or you don't. And no cancer has a doubling rate like that."

For the last two years the professor's PSA tests have been effectively zero. "The experiences I've had are not inconsistent with an energy paradigm," the professor says. "Something important is going on." His new view is not something that he shares with the elite physicians he knows. "I just don't go back [to the doctors]," he says. "There's nothing they can do for me. And they don't understand."

Occasionally, healers appear to support a person's ability to make a dramatic physical shift. But even in these so-called "miracle" cases, healing follows both spiritual and physical laws. Just as getting sick is a process, it always takes time for the body to heal. Peter Wimmer's case is a good example. A man in his late fifties, he was diagnosed with incurable prostate cancer in August of 1997. His PSA test score was over 50 on a German scale on which anything over 5 is considered dangerous. His doctors put him on hormone reduction therapy, but they told him he had just three months to live. Medical pictures showed that the cancer had spread outside the area of his prostate.

Wimmer did not believe in healers. But his daughter Astrid called Gerda Swearengen, a recent Brennan school graduate who is a German-born American citizen, the same day her father received the diagnosis. From Virginia, Swearengen did distant healing sessions for Wimmer in Germany every other week. She worked on the prostate gland, clearing energies out, and also restructured both the energy field and the organ. She says she also worked telepathically and energetically with his psychological issues. "He had a lot of issues having to do with self-esteem. He was very controlling," she says. "He had an overpowering mother." She says in some sessions she held the energy of the Divine Mother and Kali—the Hindu feminine aspect of the destroyer—to bring the energy of Mother into balance in Wimmer's energy bodies.

In the first three months, Wimmer did not get much better. But he did not get worse. The PSA test scores dropped to 45. Six months after the diagnosis, the PSA tests measured 30. More than a year later his PSA measured 2.5. Finally they dropped to zero. "My dad is living like he was before," says Astrid, who is the only one in the family who speaks English. She says her father's doctor still cannot believe it. Swearengen does not know if her client will remain cancer free. She notes he was not interested in making emotional changes. And, she adds, she cannot predict what would happen in any other person's situation.

Healer Melanie Brown, a former director of physical therapy at Ontario Community Hospital, in Ontario, California, has worked with more than a dozen cancer patients and has seen how widely responses can vary. She does not believe that living or dying is the most essential goal, although she understands the longing. "It's really about how moment to moment we choose to walk the journey with God or without God. It doesn't mean we'll be physically healed. Everyone gets diseases and has tragedy. It's part of the human journey."

Brown says she knew, while still a student at the Brennan school, that working with people who had cancer would be one of her life's tasks as a healer. As a homework assignment she once had to answer the question: "What is your world task?" When she meditated, the answer came: to work with cancer. "Why do you think we trained you for three years in a cancer facility?" she heard a voice in her head ask. Before moving to Denver, Colorado, she had worked for three years at City of Hope in Los Angeles, a ninety-six-acre cancer research facility.

Ironically, Brown's first cancer client gave her an optimistic view about the power of spiritual healing. In February 1990, while Brown was still a student, a woman with metastatic cancer in the bone, liver, and brain came to her for help in dying. Further chemotherapy and radiation were no longer options. "She had already failed chemo. She ended up with an enlarged heart," explains Brown. "She was in a terminal cancer [support] group when I got her. I honestly thought my job was to help her die."

Brown primarily cleared chakras and spent sessions charging the woman's energy field. During the healings the woman began to remember episodes in which she had been severely abused by her mother, who was later hospitalized during the client's childhood as a schizophrenic. The client later confirmed these memories with her maternal uncles. "As this material came up," Brown says, "She began clearing from the illness."

The abuse had left this woman unable to care for and honor herself fully. "We did a lot of work around nurturing herself. That's when I began to realize that's what cancer is about—having needs and taking care of them. Her mother-in-law got brain cancer in the middle of this and her husband flew [his mother] to Boulder so that his wife, who was technically dying of cancer, would take care of her. She agreed to do that. . . . We worked a lot on it, but it was a huge issue."

Four months after the healings began, in May 1990, CAT scans showed that the woman's cancer had disappeared. "The thing that was so amazing was watching the doctors go nuts over it," says Brown. "One physician said, 'Well, you know you are still filled with cancer.'"

Not long after, Brown learned the limits of healing in the current paradigm. A woman came to her for help with a seven-centimeter tumor, the size of a large nectarine, in her breast. Simultaneously the woman got an initial round of chemotherapy. No one can say for sure why, but the tumor dissolved. It's something that happens, but only rarely. "I was aware when it went away," claims Brown. "I could see it when it was there. And then I was told to do a certain technique. I was told to lift the tumor out. And what the guides did was kind of broke it into pieces and mixed it with something. They had me put it back in. It was like gold flakes were mixed in." Brown says the tumor had been shrinking anyway. But then by the next session it was gone. Doctors could not find anything on the MRI either.

Nevertheless, the doctor recommended a mastectomy, just in case cancer cells too small to show up on an MRI still lurked. Afterward, the pathology report did find microscopic amounts of cancer. Brown believes even that small amount of cancer would have dissolved in the course of further treatments. "What I realized is, you feel you've done a good job, like taking away a seven-centimeter tumor. And then they recommend a mastectomy." But, she adds, "I'm not sure I would have made a different decision. . . . She said 'my children mean more than this breast.'"

Cheryl Jacobs, a mother of two young children living in Ann Arbor, Michigan, also had a cancer that retreated in an unusual way during the course of healing sessions. Again, it did not change the medical outcome. Jacobs, an organization development consultant, had just turned forty when she got sick in July of 1995. She complained of terrible abdominal pain, but an emergency room physician sent her home. Three days later her gynecologist performed laparoscopic surgery and concluded she had a massive infection. She received intravenous antibiotics for eight days, but no cause for the infection was found. Doctors continued to watch an abdominal region that appeared to have scar tissue. They weren't especially concerned. But Jacobs was. In September she went to see local *chi gong* healer, Gabriel Chin.

After scanning her for mere seconds, Chin announced, "This is dangerous. Get it out." Jacobs insisted to her gynecologist that he remove the mass. He told her not to worry. When doctors finally operated in November, they discovered that her appendix was riddled with cancer; it had burst months earlier but her body had sealed off the infected area. Further tests showed that the appendix was cancerous and the cancer might have spread to her ovaries. An abdominal wash was positive for cancer cells.

Cancer of the appendix is so rare that no standard protocol existed. "Normally, you die," says Jacobs. "They wait for the cancer to grow. Then they cut it out. Then they wait for it to grow again. And they cut it out."

Jacobs immediately began daily *chi gong* sessions with Chin. She also added distant healing sessions with Marilyn Schneider to work on the emotional and spiritual issues. In February of 1996, at the recommendation of a Mayo Clinic team, she underwent a radical hysterectomy, along with removal of her abdominal lining, 40 percent of her colon and the tumor that the first team had somehow missed. Subsequent tests found that none of the tissue or organs removed were cancerous. Even more inexplicably, this time no cancer cells showed up in the abdominal wash.

Jacobs believes she knows when her cancer "really cleared up," as she puts it. About two weeks before her visit to the Mayo Clinic, at Schneider's direction, she had a conversation with her cancer during a meditation. She had been having conversations regularly. This time, she says, "I called up the cell and said, 'So tell me something I don't know.' It sure did," she recalls. The voice told her something about herself that she didn't know and had trouble even believing. "My body became electrified. I started sobbing." But at the same time, she says, "I had to struggle to trust what I heard. Over the next few days I surrendered to it."

A week later, she did the same meditation again. This time she had a very different experience. "In a second the interior of my body changed. It opened up into a dome shape. The ceiling of the dome had all these very uniform rectangular shapes. Each one had a dot in it. And the dot was black. It was like ceiling tiles. Everything was identical," she recalls. "A voice said, 'We are united.'"

Jacobs says at the time she felt the vision was meaningful. "Cancer cells run wild," she explains. "They're not uniform." She thought then that perhaps the loose cancer cells had gotten pulled into the tumor. But she was troubled by the dark spot in the cells. She went ahead with the surgery because she did not want to take any chances. "I'm not entirely at peace with everything that happened," she adds.

But in working with Marilyn Schneider, she says, she learned "how much of my life I had spent being a facade of what I thought people wanted me to be. . . . If you do that long enough, you don't know who you are." She says she did not even listen to her gut for all the years of her first marriage, staying in a relationship that didn't serve her. "Healing is not hocus-pocus," she says.

For a while, she believed if you create an illness you can cure it once you learned the lesson. But now she sees that is much too simplistic. "That thinking has evolved for me. It's part of my life pattern and journey that I am in this place. . . . We don't know what our contract is." And, she adds, "The journey, and why things happen to us, isn't about one thing. It's so layered."

Jacobs says she is often still driven by the idea that there is something she must do to get her life in order. At the same time, she feels that the most important thing she is learning is just to be, and to be connected to her Self. "Being is about surrender. That is hard to do," she admits. But, she adds, "If I totally surrender, then I move into the energetic field, the possibilities of the universe."

She finds it especially strange when people say to her, "'Now you can go back to being normal.' There are people who recreate the life they had before," she says. "I find that an appalling thought. Not because it was awful, but [because] it had led me to cancer. Why would I go back?"

Marilyn Schneider has treated people who have come to her with brain, breast, bone, liver, prostate, skin, and lung cancer. In the seven years she has been treating cancer patients, she has seen only one pass over—a young man who came to her when he already had a twenty-pound tumor in his abdomen. He wanted help in dying, she says. This does not mean all her clients are cured. Some of them have been struggling with cancer on and off for more than a decade.

Her work with Susan, a married social worker in the Midwest, has been especially long running. Susan, who works in a hospital and who is married to a physician affiliated with a hospital, asked to be identified only by her first name, fearing repercussions for her husband and herself from their medical colleagues if they discovered that she had pursued an alternative treatment such as spiritual healing.

In 1991 Susan, then thirty-eight, had a lumpectomy. Soon after, she began distant healing sessions with Schneider and decided to have a prophylactic double mastectomy, the most drastic treatment available in Western medicine. (Because her mother had had breast cancer, she was in a high-risk group.) Her early healing sessions focused on the mastectomies and reconstructive surgeries.

"We did a lot of work around the aspects of being a woman," says Susan. Physically, she says, she had hardly any scarring from the surgeries. (Schneider worked on the lines of light in the energy field around the area of the surgery so the tissue would have a healthy matrix on which to grow.) "When I went to get a mastectomy bra, the woman [in the store] said, 'You've been out of surgery three or four months,'" she recalls. "I had been out two or three weeks." After the reconstructive surgeries, which also went smoothly, the sessions tapered off.

When the cancer recurred in her bones in 1995, Susan underwent radiation. She had no treatment burns, and she credits weekly healings. The radiation cleared up some areas but the cancer showed up in new areas. As doctors switched her to chemotherapy, Susan also became the recipient of group healing sessions, something both Jason Shulman and Rosalyn Bruyere recommend when dealing with cancer and other "big" illnesses. (Bruyere says the client gets more frequencies, because each healer is unique. And, she notes, when a man and a woman work as a team the configuration can be especially powerful. "You get Osiris, Isis, and Horus," she says, referring to the Egyptian names for the Divine Father, Divine Mother, and Divine Child.)

After the first group healing, Susan's tumor markers dropped 110 points. "It's funny," recalls Susan. "My physicians kept saying, 'I've never seen anything like this.'"

"I did not throw up once during my chemo," says Susan. She was on Kytril, an antinausea drug, but many people who take the drug get sick anyway. "My doctor thought that was pretty amazing." After her fourth chemotherapy treatment in April 1997, her blood chemistry was normal. Her metastatic cancer, to all appearances, had gone into remission. Just to be safe, her doctors administered a fifth treatment in May 1997.

Susan's remission ended six months later. On a new round of chemotherapy her tumor markers have dropped from 1200 in July to 240 in October 1998. "There are times when I say, 'Why can't I just get rid of this?'" she admits. Still, she believes the healing sessions have been an enormous support: physically, emotionally, and spiritually. "Let me say this, I wouldn't want to go through chemo without having healings."

On a spiritual level, she says, her cancer has helped bring her closer to God. "Some of this is a recognition that this is God's work," she explains. "It's not all in my control. We really only have today. We don't know what tomorrow is going to bring."

Marilyn Schneider, too, knows about recurrence. In April 1998 doctors at Johns Hopkins Medical School removed Schneider's left lung after a cancer she had had in 1995 recurred. "I never get sick," she says. "I only get cancer." She began a round of chemotherapy and group healing sessions. In July, after four cycles of chemotherapy, all traces of the cancer were gone. A month later, however, doctors found three cancerous spots in her right lung. They were too small to biopsy. For now, the doctors are just watching.

For Schneider the experience has been yet another, painful spiritual initiation. Her granddaughter gave her a card with a saying from Mother Teresa that sums up her feelings on some days: "I know God wouldn't give me anything I can't handle. I just wish He wouldn't trust me so much."

The teachings have been on many levels, she says. For many years, Schneider has been doing her *sadhana* (spiritual practice) with the guidance of a Hindu spiritual leader. She considered herself a "recovering" Catholic. But recently, one of the healers she is working with got very specific guidance. Kabbalistic healer Kim Summers heard a prayer that she says she knew was meant for Schneider: "May the miracle of Jesus Christ and His love and knowledge descend upon you and guide you. May you speak to Him as your brother. May His love and benevolence flow to you and overflow to others. For He is Christ and Christ to all those who believe."

Directly before the session when the prayer came in, Schneider had been thinking about her intense devotion to Christ as a child. "I went to mass every day. Even in high school, I rode my bike to early mass with the nuns every day." Schneider says she believes it is time for her to open her heart again to Christ and to make peace with her Catholicism. In general, she says, "There is so much support. It's overwhelming. Letters come every day, from people I haven't seen in ten or fifteen years, telling me what our relationship meant, thanking me for things that happened years and years ago. It's been an amazing time."

No one, including Schneider, knows what will happen next. Her husband Bill, diagnosed five years ago with Lou Gehrig's disease, a progressive nerve disease, has recently deteriorated. Schneider is planning on resuming her practice. But it is also possible that she and her husband have a soul pact to depart around the same time. "I don't know what's in store," says Schneider. "My affairs are in order. I have to be realistic. But I am not afraid. I think the hardest thing to deal with is the grief of leaving all the people I love.

What's really hard is seeing the grief of my children. I'm certainly not going to give up."

The stories of these healers and cancer patients may be intriguing. But they are just anecdotal. The few studies that have been conducted provide only a tiny bit of additional information. Dr. Fahrion's study for the National Institutes of Health, as noted earlier, found modest success when people with basal cell carcinoma received as little as ninety minutes of healing treatments over the course of three weeks.

In *Healing Research* Dr. Benor found only two other controlled studies with statistically significant results. The first was conducted in the 1960s by a researcher at the University of Chile. He found that a mental intention by healers to reduce tumor growth in mice significantly reduced tumor growth, compared to the control group. An intention to increase tumor growth also reduced tumor growth compared to the control group.

Dr. Benor was not surprised. "This is in line with many healers' claims that a *native intelligence* in the healing process guides healing to act only in directions that are beneficial to the healee, in line with the intentions of the healer," Dr. Benor noted.

Twenty years later, a researcher at the University of Utrecht examined whether distant healing could inhibit the growth of leukemia cells growing in a culture. In one experiment a healer increased the rate of cell growth in the treated cultures by 38.93 percent over the control group. In a second experiment, untrained people increased leukemia cell growth 27.51 percent compared to the controls. In the last experiment, the healer decreased the leukemia cell growth in vitro by 18.5 percent compared to the control group.

The researcher concluded that energy-based healing probably was not real. Dr. Benor, on the other hand, found these studies provocative. He believed the reasons why the healer increased cell growth in one trial and decreased it in another lay in subjective information that only the healer could have provided. "If healing can kill cancer cells in the laboratory, there is no reason to believe it could not also do so within the body," he concluded. (Technically, the cells are not killed during healings; the energetic support is withdrawn.)

More recently, in 1997, Dr. Mehmet Oz at Columbia Presbyterian Medical Center in New York and several coauthors measured whether healers could influence tumor cell growth in vitro on four different cancer cells. The findings did not reach statistical significance. However, the healer-treated cells all showed lower cell growth compared to the control groups. "It is highly improbable that random error alone could generate the association we observed between tumor cell inhibition and our healer's treatment," Dr. Oz and his team noted.

In another study, led by researcher William Braud, Ph.D., a well-known British healer caused 200 to 1200 percent changes compared to controls on cervical cancer cells in vitro by laying hands on the flasks in which they were being cultivated. In one of these experiments the healer reached a 38.02 percent deviation from chance, achieving a statistical significance of .00002. But overall, Dr. Benor, who reviewed it in *Healing Research*, did not have access to the data to analyze the results independently. Therefore he categorized the study's results as inconclusive.

Of course, trying to measure healing effects by looking at a test tube reduces the nature of healing. Spiritual healing, after all, is not simply a pill or radiation substitute. The effects can go far beyond physiological changes.

Diane Munz, who ultimately succumbed to cancer, told me during the last year of her life that she was just grateful for healing sessions. They took the pain away, connected her to herself and brought a new kind of love into her life. Once, Rosalyn Bruyere, whom she saw for healings in the last year of her life, came to her in the middle of the night in a dream. "The incredible thing is I thought I was just dreaming. But I woke up realizing, 'Gosh, I don't have any pain.' I had been having chronic pain in my hips. I had dreamed I was in her healing room."

When she told Bruyere about it, she recalled, "Rosalyn said, 'I know. I was there. I'm terribly sorry. It's a great invasion of your privacy. But I was dreaming and sometimes when I'm dreaming I send the energy out.' . . . Can you imagine someone coming to you in your dream?" asked Munz. "I just didn't have that belief system. It's hard to convey what a big deal it was. It was such a holy experience."

Healing really is not about curing. Even if the emotional and spiritual levels are healed, the body does not always have time to catch up. "If you do this work you might still die anyway," notes Bruyere. "Sometimes a situation has gone too long with too many components to be easily healed." Besides, she adds, "Spirituality is not going to save us. That idea is left over from early views of religion. The point of religion is living well, not saving yourself."

If dying is honored it can be a time of profound transformation. Dying is both a time of completion and a birth into a new phase of existence, notes Marcella Thompson, of the Healing Light Center Church. "You see the important thing is to be loved," says Thompson. "Over and over again I have seen that."

Melanie Brown recalls a man with lung cancer, a department head at Colorado University, who had an awakening in the last months of his life. "He was very well connected," says Brown, adding that one of his major issues was that "he was totally identified with his ego."

In many of the sessions, Brown says she worked with *Tiferet*, the *sefirah* in the Tree of Life, which helps people connect to their longing for their soul's fulfillment. She also did healings involving *Tiferet-Yesod*, because of a lack of sense of Self that she felt he carried.

"He spent a lot of time in healing sessions realizing all the times he had judged people, pushed them away, insisted he was right," she says. Around the time he was told by doctors that he had just three months to live, he had a revelation.

"He had a pool he wanted to have heated," recalls Brown. "But it was going into winter. No one had the parts. He called a plumber who fixed it in five hours. As [the plumber] worked, his pants were down, with his cheeks showing. He was judging [the plumber] the whole time. At the end, the plumber refused payment. 'This is my gift for you,' he said. 'I know you have cancer and don't have long.'"

At that moment, Brown says, her client "realized he'd been judging people his whole life, felt he was superior. His son had never lived up to his expectations. He reached out to his son and embraced him. When he got bad news, he got into bed with his wife, and they would hold each other, crying in joy and sorrow."

Two weeks before he died, he had a retirement party from the university. "Everyone knew it was to celebrate his passing," she says. "It was incredible to see how many lives he had touched."

Spiritual healing, like cancer itself, is ultimately not about the physical body, but the soul's journey.

Twelve

AIDS: An Odyssey

Joseph Carman, a former dancer for the Joffrey Ballet and the Metropolitan Opera, recalls the moment that he first realized that AIDS was a spiritual path. He was at one of Barbara Brennan's weekend introductory intensives in 1991 and raised his hand to ask a question. "I'm HIV positive," he said. "Can you give me a reading? What's going on in my body?"

Everyone in the room turned around to stare. Carman, now in his midforties and retired, still has a dancer's physique. A down-to-earth man, he claims he saw Brennan's energy field change, and believes he saw her as Heyoan, her spirit guide. "I saw her as this old sage sitting there." First Brennan talked to Carman about his adrenal system, which controls the body's fight-or-flight response. She said his adrenals were overtaxed. Carman didn't know much about clairvoyance, although he was open to spiritual guidance. He had spent three months meditating in Ganeshpuri, India, in 1982, under the guidance of Swami Muktananda. He felt Brennan was on target.

"I was abusing my body with performance schedules," he recalls. "And I had been addicted to cocaine at one point." Brennan explained that when a person's system runs on fear and stress, it burns the body out. Eventually, "you don't have fight power," Carman explains.

Then came the clincher. Brennan began to channel Heyoan, her spirit guide. In a slower, more deliberate cadence, Brennan/Heyoan announced: "We here in the spirit world have the greatest honor and respect for anyone who has chosen to take on the path of AIDS." The comment hit Carman in the gut. "I cried. I had never thought of it as part of a spiritual journey—that AIDS could be a gift, part of a path. The room changed. Everyone got extremely silent. It was so incredible for everyone there. It was very powerful. I carried that with me for quite a while."

Almost nothing pushes our buttons like the word "AIDS." AIDS is caused by HIV, the human immunodeficiency virus. It is a sexually transmitted disease in a world in which sex is closely associated with sin. Until very recently, AIDS was considered to be generally fatal and incurable. Because it emerged in the United States as a "gay" disease, it is also associated with homosexuality in a culture that is homophobic. Nearly two decades after it was first identified, AIDS is still largely a disease of culturally marginalized people. In the United States, the disease now afflicts the poor and the drug addicted, as well as the gay population. Elsewhere, AIDS is devastating large parts of the Third World. In some sections of Africa, as much as 25 percent of the population is HIV-positive.

From the scientific perspective, HIV is an especially wily virus, the equivalent of a biochemical Trojan Horse. It is so delicate it cannot live outside the body. But once inside, it is insidious, patient, and extraordinarily adaptable. HIV co-opts the body's defense system by attaching to specific lymphocytes in the immune system known as T-4 cells. These are the very cells which are supposed to activate and coordinate other parts of the immune system in an attack against invaders. There the virus hides, growing silently.

Over time the T-4 cells die, making an infected person increasingly vulnerable to germs that others fight off with ease. Eventually, many people with HIV infections waste away as their bodies are devastated by opportunistic infections. The process by which HIV infection progresses to full-blown AIDS can take a decade or more. About 5 percent of infected people are considered "Non Progressers." They may never get AIDS.

The first cases of AIDS were reported by the Federal Center for Disease Control and Prevention in 1981. Today, the disease is considered an epidemic. Approximately 650,000-900,000 Americans are infected with HIV, and a new person is infected with the virus every thirteen minutes. Some 380,000 Americans have already died of AIDS-related illnesses since the virus was first recognized. Worldwide, more than 30.6 million people are infected with the HIV virus, including more than a million children. An additional 16,000 people become infected every day.

Back in the early 1980s, people who developed AIDS usually succumbed within a year or two. But in 1996 protease inhibitors came on the market. These powerful new drugs keep the disease in check. Some scientists believe AIDS may be changing from a fatal disease to a manageable chronic illness, somewhat like diabetes. But no one knows how long these drugs will work. In some people the virus has already become drug resistant. Between 10 percent and 30 percent of the people who take the drugs do not respond to them or have extreme difficulties with side effects. In addition, they can cost upwards of $16,000 a year, making them out of reach for most of the people with AIDS in the world, including some in the United States.

From a spiritual perspective, too, AIDS is a complex challenge. Each person's journey with AIDS, as with any disease, is unique. Yet certain themes are fairly consistent, according to a number of leading healers. They believe that HIV-positive men and women have taken on a significant world service: bringing our dark feelings about sex into the light.

"Gay people are like messengers," explains Eetla Soracco, a gentle, patrician woman who began working with men in Los Angeles who were infected by HIV before anyone knew what the virus was, or how it was transmitted. "It's like the Jewish situation in Germany. Rosalyn [Bruyere] says they chose as a group before they come in to be sacrificial lambs. Jesus was a sacrificial lamb. And the Jews came in [to the Holocaust] to raise the consciousness—to keep the memory alive that man should not do this to man. Gay people have also chosen to give us a message about love and caring and equality. It doesn't matter what you do in your bed. You're still a valuable person."

Maria Bartolotta, a Los Angeles healer and former student of Bruyere's who apprenticed with Soracco, has ministered to more than thirty men infected with HIV in the last thirteen years. She, too, concurs. "This is a group karma," she says. "I'm not talking about something God has visited on us. Karma to me is not paying dues. It's about [beliefs] that we're holding in the physical and emotional body that we have to heal."

"Because it's a sexually transmitted disease, and because we have such a charge on our sexuality and a view that sexuality is bad, it's just like herpes in young kids," she says. "HIV targets the very core of what we need to heal as a culture and a race. All of us have sexual self-hatred and guilt. That's why the thing that has been going on with [President Bill] Clinton is so important. . . . Where there's self-hatred and darkness, God doesn't come in. How many people do you know who masturbate, and ask God to bring light in as they do it? How many people even realize that orgasm is supposed to bring in light?"

Healers believe the sexual shame and guilt may be even stronger in the gay community than in the culture at large because gay sex is so often disapproved of. This is something gay men grapple with every day of their lives. "Many gay men have always felt anxious or confused about sexual issues, and many of these feelings may have nothing to do with HIV," states a pamphlet from the Gay Men's Health Crisis. "After all, much of society is homophobic and disapproves of gay sex—HIV or no HIV."

Like the Gay Men's Health Crisis, Soracco, Bartolotta, and other healers stress that the HIV and Herpes viruses are not the cause of sexual shame, guilt, and judgment. But the way we react to these viruses are indicators of the negative feelings and beliefs we need to transform. The issues raised by the devastation of AIDS in Africa and other Third World countries, Bartolotta adds, are slightly different. "Africa has been victimized forever," she says. "We haven't honored what each culture holds. . . . Instead of honoring each piece of the deity, we've made a hierarchy of good and bad and better and worse. When you have thousands of years of bias, it's in the psyche. It's in the cells."

Healers say AIDS also offers an opportunity for us to look collectively at how we, as individuals and a society, have been separating sex from love. This separation is pervasive in the culture at large. It is depicted in many movies and on television, and it is acted out on college campuses, in bars, and in everyday life. Men, especially, are literally encouraged "to score" as proof of their virility and value. Some aspects of gay liberation culture have served to magnify this issue, too. "Love goes through the heart," explains one healer. "If [sexual energy] gets stuck in the first chakra [as a purely physical thing], it turns on itself. Some gay sex is not about love, but [about] how much you score. It's about performance." Or, as healer Alix Young notes, with AIDS the question is: "Where has the sexuality been assaulted. Can we look at that?"

Neither the heart nor the body is truly satisfied by sex that is separate from love, according to healers. Indeed some people seek even more sex in vain attempts to find the love for which they yearn. "I walk away from sex feeling like I did something wrong," confessed one twenty-six-year-old gay man in "B-2K: Beyond 2000," a Gay Men's Health Crisis pamphlet designed to be a conversation between gay men about sex. "So to get over those feelings, I go out and trick again. It's like this crazy cycle."

Explains Bartolotta, "I'm saying to these guys, 'God Bless you, you've been raped. You've been sodomized. You've had a lot of partners.' The damage is this was taking place outside of love. Anal sex isn't a bad thing in itself. It's when it's taking place outside of love. Many people don't bring love and light into the sexual act. . . . It's something you have to learn. Self-hatred and guilt will keep it out. There's no love in a rape. There's no love in a trance. Sometimes we have to have many experiences on the way to learning to bring love and light in."

Rosalyn Bruyere puts it succinctly in her book, *Wheels of Light*. "Whereas a bacterial infection indicates the need to change how we *feel* (usually with regard to anger), a viral infection indicates the need to change how we *think*, not our opinions, but a "wholesale change" in consciousness. . . . One change in our collective consciousness that must emerge from these viruses is the awareness that sexual union is the sacred joining of two life forces. We must begin to be more selective about the kind and quality of energy with which we choose to merge."

The most important thing for someone with HIV is to strengthen self-love and self-knowledge. "I'm not talking about narcissism," says Levent Bolukbasi, the founder of the IM School of Healing Arts in Manhattan, who has been doing healing work with more than a dozen HIV-positive men. "I am talking about true love. . . . What needs to happen is for people not to judge themselves. Once people see themselves without the judge, things begin to change. . . . If you are made to feel wrong [because of sexuality] from the beginning, it affects you very deeply."

Bolukbasi, who goes by his first name, Levent, notes that the immune system's need for heart energy is quite literal. The T-cells, the target cells of HIV, are formed when stem cells migrate from the bone marrow to the thymus gland, where they undergo division and maturation. "T lymphocytes learn how to differentiate self from nonself in the thymus gland," explains the Merck *Manual of Medical Information.*

The thymus gland is directly above the heart. "It's the gland directly associated with the heart chakra," Levent explains. "The thymus knows the Self. It's a great educator of the T-cells. There's great wisdom there."

Eetla Soracco, who devoted herself to AIDS patients from the earliest days of the AIDS crisis, learned about self-love the hard way. What she witnessed as a young woman in Europe during World War II made her want to die. At twenty-eight, the mother of three young children and married to an American man, her body finally complied: She developed an inoperable cancer in her pituitary gland. "I know the moment I started creating it," she claims. "I had the death wish. Every morning I woke up in the same room with the same wall paper and wished God would take me in my sleep." Healing sessions with Rosalyn Bruyere helped bring her back to life. But she also had to do inner work on her own. "I didn't love myself unconditionally," she says.

Soracco, who is now radiant and serene, says she hated herself so much that she could not bear to look at her own reflection in the mirror. "I had no good feelings towards this person," she recalls. "I was so ugly. So fat. I felt I could not do anything." Day by day, she confronted herself in the mirror. She says it was one of the hardest things she ever did. "One day, I kind of twinkled a little bit," she says. Eventually she learned to love her Self. "This is what we come here to learn," she says. "If it was easy, we wouldn't pay attention."

The love that Soracco and other healers talk about is not the ordinary type of romantic or parental love most of us know. Such love may be powerful, but it is deeply entwined with need, narcissism, desire, self-worth. We typically love others because of what we receive, because they make us feel important, or worthy, or beautiful, or sexy. We often love ourselves just as conditionally, because we're smart, or beautiful, or popular, or successful. If the beauty or popularity or success ends, we cease to love ourselves. Unconditional self-love, however, does not shift according to circumstances. It just is. It radiates, the way the sun radiates light.

It is this steady force of love that Soracco says she brings to her HIV-positive clients. "I feel the most important healing force is love," she says. Many of the men she has treated have since passed on, but she believes their lives were enlightened. "Many of the men had difficulties," she says. "They didn't know who they were. . . . They needed someone to help them find their path. I helped them to look at their lives while they were in the dying mode and right some wrongs, and [to] love themselves unconditionally. So when they come back to another life, they would have more preparation."

In some cases, she believes, the extra energy helped sustain the men she worked with. One man managed to get the degree he wanted before he passed on. Others made lifelong commitments to lovers. And in other cases, she says, it was her job to help her clients pass on. "I couldn't prolong their lives, but [I could] prepare them spiritually. My patients died in a state of euphoria, with all the light around them," she says. "They were all different, but it was always the same kind of end, with a spiritual awakening. . . . When you are in a dying state, you are more open to the truth. Otherwise, you have a lot of defenses."

After more than a decade of working almost exclusively with the AIDS community in Los Angeles, Soracco retired to New Mexico, where she continues to do healings, recently participating in the study of distance healing and AIDS.

Los Angeles healer Maria Bartolotta, a petite, dark-haired woman, has also done long-term healing work with HIV positive men since the early days of the epidemic. In general, Bartolotta, who carries a range of "red" and "fuchsia" energies, works with people who have power issues. She works with many well-known Hollywood personalities; actors, athletes, and musicians. "The conscious people know they are carrying light on the CD or the screen," she explains. "So they come here for that."

She also works, at the other end of the spectrum, with many people who have been abused or raped as children and thus suffer from post-traumatic stress disorder. Immune system dysfunctions always involve power issues relating to basic life force and vitality. Some of her HIV-positive clients also fall into the category of people who are dealing with sexual abuse, as well.

Some of the sexual abuse that she helps to heal happened on the physical level. And, she adds, "I have just as many people who were molested on the subtle level—on the astral level—literally stuff happened at night in the dream time and from other people's thoughts and desires." She says she creates space for all the anger, fear, rage, and pain that her clients feel. "I'm very patient, kind, and compassionate. I'm holding them, letting them cry. I always run energy. . . . I've been down in the trenches with their blood and their tears and their bodily fluids.

"People will say how much they hate someone. I say 'Tell me about it.' I get them to actually move the rage. . . . I've had people who were so rabid, they were foaming at the mouth. People sometimes vomit, they have so much darkness coming out. In a sacred space, it can transform. Just the idea that someone is loving them as they reveal themselves. . . . They're allowed to feel what they feel. That's what brings them around."

Bartolotta says she is reparenting, repatterning, rewiring. "The truth is that most people did not have the kind of parenting where they cried and raged and the parent loved them. We were shut out. And when we expressed our sexuality, we were shut down. Sexuality was not given any light by the parent. I'm doing something that should have been done by the parent."

In Bartolotta's experience of HIV infection, it is "the guilt and the self-hatred around sex that will kill [someone]. And it's not just sex. It's power. It's abuse. It's also the anger at the perpetrator that they never dealt with. Any undercurrent of pain is a drain on the life force and, therefore, of the immune system. You have to get [the dark stuff] up and out in the presence of someone who can fill that space with light."

She also provides a basic energy cushion for her HIV positive clients that in some cases appears to be physically sustaining. "I have three or four men I see who have been HIV positive for fifteen to twenty years," she says. "I do think I have helped them. I'm giving my clients cushioning and padding, energetic support they never had as children."

But, Bartolotta adds, there are no rules. "I've also worked for years with men who are now dead. It's everyone's individual vessel, what they were told when they were first diagnosed, how many deaths they have witnessed" and many other factors.

"I had a guy who had buried 150 friends. I knew he wouldn't last. He had no reason to stay alive. How can you survive that?" Another man she worked with had a lot of physical vitality, what she calls "body *chi*." "But he was born a Mormon and there was a religious self-hatred piece. There was a self-judgment." On the other hand, she says, "I have had guys with zero T-cells who didn't get sick for two or three years."

One of those men, a corporate strategic planner, recalls having only 250 T-cells in 1990 when he began to see Bartolotta. At the same time, he began taking AZT. His T-cell count climbed to 650 within a year. "The fact is it wasn't the technology," he asserts. "When I would not do the work with Maria I did not have as good a well-being. It's not like if you stopped all the air went out of the balloon. I could see I would catch cold. My T-cells would be more erratic." This strategic planner says Bartolotta also helped him end a relationship "that was a big drain on me. She helped me to understand that what [the boyfriend] was going through was like an alcoholism. It was like an addiction. And I was enabling him." To clear the situation, he says, he had to let go of a lot of residual Catholic guilt.

Another man, Robert Cohen, a retired lawyer in his late forties, tested positive for HIV virus from a 1980 blood sample. He began to see Bartolotta in 1988 when his T-cells had fallen to 400. At the same time, he stopped taking recreational drugs and drinking alcohol and began meditating. Six weeks later, he had a follow-up blood test. His T-cells were almost 900. In 1990—the ten-year anniversary of his exposure to HIV—his T-cells fell to little more than 100. He began taking AZT, the original antiviral drug. Since then, he has only been sick once in 1995, with MAC (Mycobacterium avium complex), a serious infection that can be fatal with HIV.

"I'm very personally responsible," says Cohen. "I don't blame myself for having AIDS. No one knew anything. If I had known about it and done things, well, I would feel differently. . . . Over the course of the last ten years, I have maintained my wellness. Statistically, I shouldn't be here. . . . I'm a long-term survivor. But I have certainly progressed to [AIDS]. I think I'm a miracle man."

Cohen retired three years ago. The virus in his system has become resistant to the protease inhibitor cocktails. He now has a high viral load and a T-cell count of only 30. He still has sessions with Bartolotta every other week. "I don't feel a physical change exactly. But I feel better. We talk about everything. I rage. She's always amazed at this rage aspect I have. I see what idiocy we all go through every day. . . . People are fraudulent and misrepresentational—almost exclusively. . . . Maria is an environment in which I can express this rage."

"In my experience, the men who live the longest are the ones who have the most available rage," says Bartolotta. "They don't take the hit and collapse in on themselves. It allows them to fight. . . . The men with so much rage—they're flushing themselves. The red energy of rage seems to keep their systems ahead of the virus. They have so much energy. It's not like you have to have an open heart to stay alive. The goal is to have compassion for themselves and their perpetrators, but not before they have truly processed what they really feel."

For others Bartolotta has ministered to, it has been a matter of making someone comfortable as he moves toward death. "There's a feeling that happens when there's not enough *chi* to hold what you're putting in," she says, beginning to cry. "I cry when it happens. It's just they don't have enough receptors to hold light. . . . Rosalyn

[Bruyere] only asked us to take one vow, to fight for life until death wins. . . . I will fight to keep the body housing the soul until there's not enough *chi* or essence in the vessel. And then I will help the soul leave."

Long-term HIV-positive survivors who have worked with healers talk about both physical support and spiritual transformation. Terry Houlihan, thirty-nine, is another HIV-positive man Bartolotta has seen survive between fourteen and twenty years with the virus. He says HIV infection has transformed his life.

"As much as we think we're all so different, it all comes down to loving ourselves and each other," he says. "I treat everybody as an extraordinary human being, whether you're a homeless person, or a busboy, or the president of the United States. When I wake up I feel joy. I walk my dog in the morning and I feel such joy that I'm alive."

He has also seen others drop their prejudices and open their hearts. He sometimes visits his first boyfriend's parents, although he lost the boyfriend to AIDS years ago. "They are fundamentalist Christians. Yet they love me. There's not a time when I leave their house that I'm not choked up. I've reaped the benefit of the only thing their kid wanted—acceptance."

Recently, at the funeral for another friend, the friend's mother, who came from a background that normally condemns homosexuality, spoke. "'Just go home and love your kids,' she said. It didn't make any difference that [her son] was a fag," he recalls. "She just couldn't hug him any more. . . . All these people have had to go back to their small towns to die in their parents' homes and it's changed the consciousness."

Houlihan was already on a metaphysical journey, he says, when he discovered he was HIV positive in 1985. (He believes he was infected in 1981 by his first love.) But his interests did not include spiritual energy healing. "I was a true disbeliever," he says. In fact, he concedes, when he first met Bartolotta, who wears her long, dark hair loose, "I thought she came with a [witch's] broom."

In 1992 when his thirty-year-old partner, David Oliver, began to see Bartolotta for healings, he admits, "because I was not a believer, I did not participate in any of his contact with her. I didn't want to take away from the benefit he felt he got from it. I never even took him to her house."

Bartolotta could not help Oliver change the course of the illness, yet Houlihan believes, "Maria was able to bring him to a place of comfort that nothing else could." After Oliver passed on, Houlihan began to have sessions with Bartolotta. "When Maria puts her hands on you, you are immediately warm," he says. "It's just the charge she has. If I'm calm, I can feel the tingle in whatever part she's working on. It's pretty astounding."

Until the protease inhibitor came along, he says, he shunned Western drugs like AZT and used acupuncture, Chinese herbs, and rebirthing and had sessions with Bartolotta twice a month. "What Maria has become is part of my protocol," he says. "Had I not had Maria in my life, the journey would have been a darker trip. I think she made a significant difference in calming me down and bringing me back into myself."

Until three years ago, Houlihan says, "I lived my life as a dying man." Now, he has returned to acting and just completed a Ford commercial. He also teaches boxing and does some bartending for a catering company. "People look at me. I work out. I'm pretty well built. They would never guess I've lived for [at least] fourteen years with this disease coursing through my veins."

All in all, says Houlihan, "This whole thing has brought enormous blessings. So where is the bad part? Death is the price we pay for living, for being loved and being able to love. It doesn't come free."

Each person I interviewed had a different path. A married professor and father of two young children thought he might be facing the end when he began to have healing sessions with healer Alix Young in February 1995. He believes the spiritual dimension affected the entire course of his medical treatments.

The professor was diagnosed as HIV positive in the fall of 1993, after he had been having symptoms for a number of years. "This was my alarm clock, my wake-up call to take a closer view of what the design of my life and beliefs should be," he says. He focused more deeply on his family than he ever had before. He says he and his wife (who tested HIV negative) began to say the rosary together every evening.

He began a standard medical regimen that included AZT; nevertheless he declined rapidly. The Federal Center for Disease Control and Prevention considers anyone with fewer than 200 T-cells to be in the advanced stages of AIDS. By June 1994 the professor had fewer than 50 T-cells. Kaposi's sarcoma was spreading uncontrollably. Doctors radiated his face. Then lesions appeared in his mouth. Chemotherapy also failed. The combination of treatments and the strain of the virus put his hemoglobin "into the basement," as he says. By February 1995 he was getting blood transfusions every other week just to maintain his hemoglobin levels. "They said this was the end," recalls the professor.

"When I met him, he was in a rapidly progressive stage," confirms one of his physicians, family practitioner Dr. Gerald Bally, who has treated more than 300 patients with AIDS. "The rapidly increasing Kaposi's sarcoma lesions were affecting his functional capacity and employment. He was at a crossroads where you don't like to see patients go."

Around that time, the professor read Barbara Brennan's books. Enthralled, he called Toronto healer and Brennan school graduate Alix Young. "I wasn't looking for the logic. I was beyond that," he says. "I was free. I was able to accept the mystery. There was a door for me to knock on."

The professor's whole way of talking softens as he describes the healings. "She had a treatment room in the back part of her house," he recalls. "It was a room with windows all around it and the sun was always beaming in. It was always warm and comforting. . . . She acknowledged great learning from me. That was of great help, to know I was providing something for her, too," he says.

"My biggest problem, she had told me I was too much of a thinking person, that I had to let go of that to allow the guides to come in and work. I had trouble with that. She'd say, there's the cognitive side to you. Often, I drifted into slumber during the energy work. . . . My wife would ask: 'What does she do?' I'd say, 'I don't have my eyes open, so I don't know what she's doing. My wife would go, 'Oh,' and raise her eyebrows."

Young says that, to begin with, she worked on strengthening his auric field, to give his body the energy it needed to continue. "She saw the rips and tears. I remember her describing my energy field, and the holes that needed to be repaired," recalls the professor. Young also did *Gevurah-Hesed* healings because, with AIDS, "certain cells are attacking other cells. That signifies boundary problems." In other sessions, she embodied *Netzach-Hod,* so he could stand up for himself as he negotiated his way through the medical system.

During these healings, the professor's medical treatment took a novel turn that his doctors believe may have saved his life. First, Dr. Bally detected an infection, Parbo B virus 19, in the professor's system that nobody else had noticed. On a hunch he decided to give IVIG (gamma globulin). He believed it might clear up the infection and get the professor off the blood transfusions. In addition, he had a radical idea that it might knock out the Kaposi's sarcoma, something that was not in the medical literature.

"Gamma Globulin is the collected antibodies from blood donations that are purified so that all they are are antibodies," explains Dr. Bally. "Kaposi's sarcoma is caused by one of the human herpes viruses. Because the gamma globulin has a wide variety of antibodies, I thought it might keep the Kaposi's sarcoma at bay."

Dr. Bally, who turned out to be right on both counts, is now in the process of writing up his findings for a medical journal.

There is no way to prove it, but the professor is convinced that the energy healings actually influenced the course of his medical treatments. "I can't separate each one of these tracks," he says. "They are so closely entwined. . . . I walked out of the office after the [gamma globulin] thinking, "I can't believe how this has all happened through the aid of a guide. This was an illustration to me of intervention on my behalf of yet another dimension."

Many scientists and psychiatrists would, no doubt, say the professor was in fantasy. But he remains absolutely convinced. His journey brought him even more than stable health; looking back, the professor says he has developed what he calls an "intense centeredness."

Retired dancer Joseph Carman's journey has also been one of both physical healing and spiritual awakening. For him, learning to fight, the very thing the HIV virus dismantles, has been an ongoing lesson. After Brennan's clairvoyant reading, he attended two past-life regression workshops with spiritual teacher Chris Griscom in New Mexico. He says he recalled images from a past life as a sol- dier in World War I, "where I couldn't handle it anymore. I rolled out of a foxhole and asked to be shot. . . . And in this life and in that life there were a lot of young men dying. That was a very important connection for me."

Whether or not past lives will ever be validated by science, Carman says his experiences helped. He felt with AIDS he was hav- ing a psychological deja vu. "With AIDS, I had the feeling there was no way to live, that I had to check out," he explains. "The situation was too hopeless." He had flashbacks to that earlier experience for a year, he says. But some of the despair he was feeling cleared.

Later on, in the fall of 1993, he took an intensive week with Rosalyn Bruyere. After he returned home, Carman was diagnosed with Kaposi's sarcoma. "The teachings [Bruyere gave] were to pre- pare me for this news," he says. "She was talking a lot about initia- tion. . . . And it really was an initiation. I was being put through a test. How was I going to deal with this disease?"

In October 1996 Carman landed in the hospital. After his lungs cleared with the help of a protease inhibitor and an antiviral medi- cation, the Kaposi's sarcoma escalated on his legs. In February 1997 he flew out to see Bruyere. They spent three hours a day together for a week. She did hands-on work directly on the Kaposi's sarcoma. "She did the sound therapy, denser frequencies. It's like a motor. You can feel it," he says. "It's a pulsation."

Bruyere believes those heavy frequencies disorient the virus. She was also "amping" him up with extra energy. And she focused energy directly into the lesions on his legs, using what she calls a "pulsed laser" frequency to zap the lesions. "She was explaining to me the mechanism of how Kaposi's sarcoma works," recalls Carman. "It's not like regular cancer metastases. It's more like leprosy. Each lesion appears individually.

"I had a lot of lesions on my right leg, running on the outside. And she thought for a minute. 'You use the inside muscles [in danc- ing] to turn out,' she said. She had me do karate kicks on the table. I had a lack of stimulation and circulation [on the outside of the legs]. It's easier for the tumor to collect there. It also explains why Kaposi's sarcoma gravitates away from the center of the body."

Carman says he even had a lesion on the end of his nose. She worked on that, too. "She swears her hands don't get hot," he says. "But they were like a furnace. I swear the next day, it was gone. I had had radiation treatments, and it was still there. And she did it with her hands. I was staying with a friend. I got up the next morning and he said, 'That lesion on your nose is gone.'"

One day, when they were in the garden, she gave him cactus plants. "She was wanting me to plant new seeds," he says. "Everything has symbolism around her." Bruyere told him he had to nurture four things in his life: creativity, companionship, sustenance, and peace. "She was healing the Kaposi's sarcoma," he says. "That was important. But I was being transformed into a much stronger, wiser person." As a symbol of the fighting strength he needed, she also gave him a cougar claw, shamanic medicine, which he wears around his neck.

When Carman returned home, "I had a healing crisis. I went through this incredible depression. I'm not the kind of person who can't get out of bed." One night, at about 2 A.M., obsessed with death, he got up and walked around. He had two canaries. One of them, sitting on its perch, suddenly just fell over in his cage in front of his eyes. It had been perfectly healthy. Now it was dead.

After that, his depression lifted. He began writing his first pieces as a dance critic. Almost two years later Carman's viral load is undetectable and his T-cells have been stable at over 300, a result of the protease inhibitor he still takes. He is no longer on chemotherapy. The Kaposi's sarcoma has remained inactive, a typical result with protease inhibitors.

"She pointed my life in a different direction," he says. "I don't know how I would have done just with the drugs alone. Being in her energy field for three hours a day made me so much more of a warrior. She transformed me. . . . I'm still feeling the effects of it.

"And I've come out a better person for the journey," says Carman. He says it is not just because of healing sessions, noting: "No one who has survived AIDS would say it hasn't changed them."

Sometimes with AIDS, as with any disease, a healer's job becomes one of helping someone cross over in death, as Dr. Nancy Reuben discovered. In 1997 she worked part-time on the staff of a long-term care facility for indigent AIDS patients in Connecticut doing a healing circle once a week. Sometimes, she says, the nurses would also call her in to help when someone was having trouble dying. "They needed to die, and they just couldn't," explains Dr. Reuben.

Like birth, dying can be easier when it is assisted. Sometimes last wishes must be fulfilled and relationships resolved before someone is willing to take the journey out of the body. One woman, she remembers, lingered in a coma. When it was clear the woman was hanging on in a way that did not serve her, a nurse-practitioner who was a Franciscan nun asked Dr. Reuben to intercede. "I telepathically asked her and I scanned her. I realized one of her chakras, the sixth chakra, was askew," she recalls. "Everything else was aligned so she could leave. So I moved it into place. She also said telepathically that she had a problem with this person in her life. I got that it was a woman. This person really needed to know that the patient really loved her, and that even if they hadn't worked it out in this life, they would work it out eventually."

Dr. Reuben says she told the Franciscan sister about the "discussion" she had with the patient. That night, the Franciscan sister realized, the woman the patient wanted to make peace with might be her sister in the Southwest. She called the patient's sister and relayed the message. The sister said, "That's what I've been waiting for. Now I can accept her death." The patient died a day later. "This is an example of how you can help the patient and the family," says Dr. Reuben.

She got to know another patient, whom she also helped to pass over, through the healing circles first. He was unusual, she says, because his mother came every day and ministered to him, while many other patients were without visitors. "This patient was twisted up like a pretzel," says Dr. Reuben. "I don't know what had happened to his body. And he was demented. But I did the healing circles. On this one occasion it was on how to deal with each new illness." All of a sudden, she recalls, he shouted, "'Attitude.' It just came out of this body. So I felt that he was there on some level even though he had AIDS dementia."

Eventually, Dr. Reuben says, the nurses and even the patient's mother felt it was time for him to die. "So I went into his room, and I asked him out loud. I said, 'W—, would you like me to do a private healing session?' He said, 'Yes.'. . . You can't do therapy work with someone in this situation, which is why energy work is so helpful at the end of life," she explains. "So I did a session telepathically. I asked him what was going on, why he wasn't leaving his body. He said his body was all twisted up and he couldn't figure it out. I said, 'You really only have to align your energy centers.' So I harmonized my chakras and allowed his chakras to line up. Then, two things came through telepathically. The first one was that he said he had a real problem with a man in his life. Again, there was unfinished business. It was upsetting to him that it wasn't worked out. That's all I got. I told him it could be worked at some other time.

"He also said this was a test for his mother," recalls Dr. Reuben. "He was getting a lot out of his mother coming and ministering to her. He said he was testing her love. I didn't know what that was about. To me and all the observers it looked like she was Mother Teresa." Dr. Reuben says he also told her he was upset that his mother was saying to him every day, "'It's all right to leave.' He said that's not what he wanted to hear. He wanted to hear that she loved him."

She discussed the conversation with the patient's mother. "She said . . . the man he had a real problem with, 'That's his father. Even when he was little, his father wouldn't hug him,'" recalls Dr. Reuben. "So I told her the other thing. I said, 'I don't perceive you as anything but selfless with your son. But he said he was testing you.' And she said, he had always tested her. And she hadn't been so loving always, that he had been a very difficult child."

Dr. Reuben says he told the patient's mother that her son wanted to hear her say how much she loved him. "So she did that. And he died a couple of days later," says Dr. Reuben. "I imagine that it helped him in some way."

Dr. Reuben says these and other experiences have shown her that healing can occur at the soul level at any time. "When people are dying and can't talk for whatever reason, it's not the end of being able to work with them," she says. "Their spirit is alive and well. On a level we're not ordinarily used to perceiving, they yearn for connection. In the end, people die when they are ready. But I came to believe that I could at least help."

These stories, of course, are just anecdotal. The first double-blind study of distant healing and AIDS, published in December 1998 in the *Western Medical Journal*, suggests, however, that healings can affect the physical and emotional states of men and women with end-stage AIDS.

Researchers Fred Sicher, an adjunct associate scientist at California Pacific Medical Center, and Dr. Elisabeth Targ, clinical director of psychosocial oncology research at California Pacific, took forty people with endstage AIDS and divided them into control and treatment groups. All of them had fewer than 200 T-cells; a few had no T-cells. The people in both groups were closely matched for severity of illness and age.

The researchers then stripped away all the known means of influencing another human being's health: touch, attention, extra medicine, or sugar pills as well as any conscious experience of being treated. "What we were trying to do was eliminate an effect of expectation or placebo," explains Sicher.

"As a psychiatrist I know that the mind-body effect is extremely powerful," adds Dr. Targ. "We're doing everything we can to mobilize people's hopes and expectations in healing. There's a lot of evidence that if someone thinks they're going to be healed, they will be healed. And if you touch someone in a loving way, the person's immune system may respond. I wanted to know: where's the magic?"

To make sure the people in the study could not guess whether they were in the control or treatment group, Dr. Targ and Sicher had all the healers do their treatments at a distance. The patients never met any of the healers. After the patients agreed to participate in the study, they just went about their business. A few even traveled abroad. The healers were also scattered across the country. Those in the treatment group had absolutely no way of knowing that they were receiving approximately one hour of distant healing six days a week for ten weeks. All the patients were examined only three times: before the study began, after the healing sessions had been completed, and three months after the healings ended.

The forty healers who participated had varied backgrounds. Some had training in *chi gong*, one was a Lakota Sioux–trained shaman. A few were evangelicals. More than half had studied with Rosalyn Bruyere, Barbara Brennan, or Mietek Wirkus. Most of those who had studied with Brennan had also studied Kabbalistic healing or Flow Alignment and Connection. Mietek Wirkus, who ranks as one of the most studied healers in the United States, personally participated in the study.

"We tried to incorporate people from every walk of the healer field," explains Sicher. "We don't want to say we're endorsing any particular school of healing at all or any individual healer. We're afraid of being used by individual healers to promote their own practices. The whole field of healing is tainted with amateurism, fraud, and quackery. Many, many people who call themselves 'healers' are total frauds. And the intentions of others are ego based and financial. We tried to avoid all those people."

Some of the healers had very intimate experiences. Eetla Soracco did all her healings facing the altar in the healing room of her Santa Fe, New Mexico home, which she keeps lit with dozens of candles and the pictures of the Virgin and other holy saints and loved ones. She says she got to know each man she treated at the soul level, although they never met on the physical plane. "They had different characters and different personalities," she says. "These were special men." Each time she connected to one of the men, she says, they were never alone. "There were several spirit doctors, guides, angels. There is lots of help. The main thing is to ask for help."

Deb Schnitta, a Flow Alignment practitioner based in Pittsburgh, began the study while she was on vacation and did her first distant healings on a beach. "It was a very humbling experience," she says. "First of all, when you got the material, you realized how sick they were. They had almost no T-cells. They used a population that was really really sick."

Table 1. Baseline and AIDS Management-Related Variables

n	Treated 20	Control 20	Two-sided P[1]
Age (years)	42.9 ± 7.2	43.2 ± 6.4	0.80
Sex (% female subjs.)	10	5	1.00
Ethnic minority (% subjs.)	0	20	0.12
Education[2]	4.1 ± 0.6	3.9 ± 1.0	0.38
Baseline AIDS-related factors			
Years HIV positive	9.0 ± 3.5	7.3 ± 3.1	0.11
CD4 cell number/ml	90.3 ± 66.0	83.8 ± 70.9	0.55
No. existing ADDs	1.4 ± 1.3	1.3 ± 1.4	0.65
No. prior ADDs	1.9 ± 1.3	2.1 ± 1.4	0.58
ADD severity[3]	5.4 ± 3.0	5.0 3.3	0.49
Interventions during study			
Triple-drug therapy[4]			
Throughout study	70	80	0.72
At least 2 months	20	15	1.00
Protease inhibitors	90	95	1.00
Pneumonia carinii prophy-laxis	100	100	1.00
No. alternative therapies[5]	4.2 ± 2.6	2.7 ± 2.0	0.10
Support[6]	85	95	0.61
Psychotherapy	45	50	1.00
Baseline subjective measures			
WPSI score	1.64 ± 0.72	1.69 ± 0.80	0.86
POMS score	62.3 ± 46.7	42.8 ± 39.9	0.16
MOS score[7]	−0.01 ± 0.8	−0.01 ± 0.8	1.00
Baseline personal habits			
Smokers	0	25	0.06
Recreational drug use[8]	20	20	1.00
Alcohol use[9]	0.4 ± 0.6	0.8 ± 1.1	0.27
Exercise[10]	1.4 ± 1.3	1.9 ± 1.4	0.34
Meditation practice	60	75	0.50
Religious/spiritual practice	90	80	0.66
Belief in DH[11]	2.8 ± 0.6	2.9 ± 0.4	0.33

Data are means ± SD or %.
[1]Paired t test for continuous variables, Wilcoxon signed-Rank test for variables with outliers, McNemar's test for binary variables; all tests are of matched paired differences. "Matched" refers to variables used for pair matching.
[2]Some high school = 1, high school graduate = 2, some college = 3, college graduate = 4, graduate degree = 5.
[3]Boston Health Study opportunistic disease score.
[4]Simultaneous use of a protease inhibitor and at least two antiretroviral drugs.
[5]Acupuncture, psychic healing or prayer, Chinese herbs, yoga, biofeedback, guided imagery, Chi Gong, nutritional supplements or vitamins, special diet, group therapy or other.
[6]Number of subjects reporting study participation support from family or community members.
[7]Normalized mean score for 10 factors.
[8]Four subjects in each group used crack cocaine or oral amphetamines; one treatment subject also used IV amphetamines.
[9]No alcohol = 0, once or twice a week = 1, several times a week = 2, heavily on weekends = 3, daily = 4.
[10]No exercise = 0, once a week = 1, two or three times a week = 2, four or five times a week = 3, daily = 4.
[11]"I doubt it" = 0, "Maybe" = 1, "Probably" = 2, "Yes, definitely" = 3.
(Western Journal of Medicine, Vol. 169, number 6)

What stands out most in her mind is her experience of AIDS. "I'd feel the presence that was the AIDS illness," she says. At first, she wasn't sure if she was just experiencing something specific to the patient she was working. But after the second or third client, she began working on a woman, and she too, had the same energy. "There was an AIDS energy signature. It's the characteristic of AIDS at an energy level. It would be like on a crisp fall day, you go the whole year, and then it's fall again and your mind clicks into the experience of all falls. It's a specific texture. It's a very slow, sluggish feeling. I felt the cells were covered in something, so it was like they were moving uphill, and it was very difficult for them to move.

"Sometimes I would work on organs that were affected," Schnitta continues. "Then it was easier. The cells were more receptive. The tissues were more receptive. When I moved into the feeling I associated with AIDS, it was like a tire moving along, then going flat. It was like—Thunk! Every time I got in contact with the AIDS virus, it was much thicker, much slower, much more difficult to penetrate."

She says she could actually sense two different immune systems: the old healthy one and the one functioning in the AIDS paradigm. "The only way to support the part that was sluggish was to strengthen the other part of the immune system. . . . If you push against the slowness that's there, it just gets slower. It was obstinate and it had a purpose."

The other thing she experienced was that AIDS fed on fear. Not just fear at an individual level, but at the level of the world collective. "It's not just any fear, like the fear of crossing the street," she explains, "but more the fears of sameness and differentness, exclusivity and inclusivity."

This had implications for her healing strategy, she says. "If you went in and induced anything that was fearful in the body, it would be detrimental." She says in some cases, the healthy immune system "even if it was stronger, wasn't interested in engaging. It was used to something that had engaged it, and it was not a very safe environment. Sometimes I would sit and sit and wait. There was one young gentleman, it was the sixth session before I finally felt something shift. I finally had contact with the healthier part of his immune system."

Washington, D.C. healer, Susan Ulfelder, did very physical work also. She says she energetically removed a large viral mass from one patient's spleen. With another man she worked intensively on the lymph glands. "I was literally repairing lines, repairing chakras, pulling things out and putting things in. I've seen the study written up as being based on prayer. It was not based on prayer. I didn't just sit there and pray for someone. I was literally pulling globs of virus out of their fields."

Jim Ambrogi, a Kabbalistic healer with no training in auric healing, had one of the most abstract experiences. He says he had no direct connection with the personality or body of the person he was working with. He focused mostly on patterns of energy, he says.

For some healers, the feedback on the so-called inner planes was so loud and clear it was like a face-to-face conversation, only more dramatic. Flow Alignment practitioner Catherine Karas recalls tuning into a man for the first time during the pilot study, in September 1995. "I heard a voice as loud as could be saying: 'Get out of here,'" she says. "That was the most profound thing that happened to me." It was in that moment that I woke to the efficacy of distance healing. . . . I was speechless. It was so loud. It was so clear." On the other hand, she did not have much conscious experience of the virus itself. "AIDS was irrelevant to me. I was working with a person, not a disease. The disease was irrelevant."

Many healers did the healing work completely on the inner or psychic planes. But Kate MacPherson, a teacher at the Brennan school, used three pillows arranged on her healing table as a stand-in for the patient. "The bottom represented the feet, legs, hips. The middle represented the torso. The last pillow represented the shoulders, throat, neck, and crown. . . . These pillows became that person. I would work up the pillows, doing a chelation, chakra work, a *hara* healing or a core star healing." She, too, felt very connected. "With one fellow, I felt as though he was my son. I got such a heart connection to these guys."

At the end of the study, significant differences appeared between the twenty patients in the control group and the twenty who received distant healing. "Some people did get dramatically better during the study," says Sicher.

The patients in the control group collectively developed twelve new illnesses compared to the treatment group, who experienced only two new illnesses. The probability that this was a chance occurrence was statistically four in a hundred. The illnesses that the treatment group developed were also ranked as being far less severe: .8 on a scale of 1 to 3, compared to 2.65 for the control group. Group three illnesses include things like Kaposi's sarcoma skin lesions, thrush in the throat and lungs, and regular pneumonia. Group two illnesses include encephalitis, Cytomegalovirus, and PCP (Pneumocystis carinii pneumonia). Group one illnesses include illnesses such as Kaposi's sarcoma in the lung or gut and Mycobacterium avium complex, an often deadly infection.

The people in the control group collectively clocked twenty-six doctor visits compared to eighteen visits for the patients treated with distant healing. The people in the control group collectively clocked twelve hospitalizations, compared to three for the treatment group. The hospital visits were, on average, significantly longer for patients in the control group: 6.8 days, compared to one-day stays for those who received distant healing.

Despite these statistically significant differences, there were no significant differences in the T-cell counts. T-cell counts for both groups went up slightly.

The groups also showed differences in their mood states. All of the patients in the study were given a Profile of Mood States, a widely used measure of emotional distress, at the study's inception and at the close of the experiment. The overall mood of the treatment group improved by fourteen points, while the control group's mood collectively deteriorated twenty-six points on the mood test.

The results of an earlier pilot study, conducted before protease inhibitors were available, were even more dramatic. All ten patients in the treatment group lived, while four of ten patients in the control group died. But, notes Sicher, in that study there was a difference in age groups that might help to explain those results.

Surprisingly, most of the benefits of the distant healing in the final study actually appeared after the treatment period had ended.

Table 2. —Medical Course Over 6-Month Study

Medical Outcome	Treated (n = 20)	Control (n = 20)	Two-tailed P[1]
Outpatient visits	185 (9.2 ± 5.9)	260 (13.0 ± 7.0)	0.01
Hospitalizations	3 (0.15 ± 0.5)	12 (0.6 ± 1.0)	0.04
Days of hospitalization	10 (0.5 ± 1.7)	68 (3.4 ± 6.2)	0.04
Illness severity[2]	16 (0.80 ± 1.15)	43 (2.65 ± 2.41)	0.03
ADDs acquired	2 (0.1 ± 0.3)	12 (0.6 ± 0.9)	0.04
ADD recoveries	6 (0.3 ± 0.6)	2 (0.1± 0.3)	0.23
CD4$^+$ change (/µl)[3]	31.1± 54.9	55.5 ± 102.0	0.55
Deaths	0	1	1.00
Change in POMS score (distress)	−25.7 ± 46.0	14.2 ± 49.0	0.02
Change in MOS	0.2 ± 0.8	−0.2 ± 0.8	0.15
Change in WPSI	−0.2 ± 0.6	0.1 ± 0.9	0.31

Data are n (means ± SD) or means ± SD.
[1]Wilcoxon signed-rank test for the first seven outcomes; paired t tests for the last three outcomes; McNemar's test for number of deaths. Due to clumpiness of the data for variables near $P = 0.05$, the randomization test was also performed with the following results; hospitalizations, $P = 0.06$; days of hospitalization, $P = 0.04$; ADD severity score, $P = 0.03$; ADDs acquired, $P = 0.06$.
[2]Boston Health Survey opportunistic disease severity score, includes ADD and AIDS-related illness (Table 3).
[3]n = 19 in the control group (one subject died).
(Western Journal of Medicine, Vol. 169, number 6)

"If we had just looked at the intervention period alone, we would not have had a significant study. It's what happened in the following months," explains Sicher. "Life-threatening illnesses have taken a long time to develop. The effects of the healing effort are not going to occur immediately."

Sicher believes the reason is easy to understand. "It's not like going in and having surgery. It's something that, at least I suspect, affects someone at the soul level. Then there's a subsequent physiological effect. Suppose you lose someone who is very close to you," he continues. "It's like a body blow. It can really put you down in the dumps. And then three months later, you might develop an illness." In his view, healing works the same way. The soul effect comes first and then the physiological results appear later. But in healing, the effect is positive, while in trauma, it is negative.

Sicher and Dr. Targ are the first researchers to look at time-delayed healing effects. Sicher believes the findings are significant for all studies. "If other studies had looked at delayed effects, they might have had more significant findings," he asserts. As it is, no one, including Sicher and Dr. Targ, have any idea how long the

TABLE 3. —Distribution of AIDS-Related Illnesses Acquired During the Study

n	Treated 20	Control 20
BHS severity group III (ADD)		
Kaposi's sarcoma (visceral)	0	1
Mycobacterium avium complex	1	1
BHS severity group II (ADD)		
Cytomegalovirus	0	2
HIV encephalitis	0	1
Coccidiomycosis	0	1
Wasting syndrome	0	1
Pneumocystis carinii pneumonia	1	1
BHS severity group I (ADD)		
Esophageal candidiasis	0	2
Kaposi's sarcoma (cutaneous)	0	1
Recurrent pneumonia	0	1
BHS severity group I (AIDS-related)		
Pseudomonas sepsis	0	1
Meningitis sepsis	0	1
Oral leukoplakia	0	1
Kaposi's sarcoma metastasis (cutaneous)	0	1
Renal insufficiency	0	2
Oral thrush	1	5
Herpes (genital/rectal)	1	3
Oral ulcers	1	0
Anemia	3	1
Bacterial infection	5	8
AIDS-related illnesses not scored by BHS		
Cervical dysplasia	1	2
Diarrhea	2	6
Peripheral neuropathy	5	6

Data are number of cases; presence or absence was based on blind medical chart review.
(*Western Journal of Medicine*, Vol. 169, number 6)

effects of healings might continue. Their study only looked at the first three months after the treatments ended.

Dr. Targ and Sicher also cannot explain exactly how the healers were able to affect the health and emotional states of the patients they treated at a distance, although, as Sicher acknowledges, attributing it to the quantum realm is a popular concept. Explanations don't worry either Dr. Targ or Sicher. "At this point, all we're doing is demonstrating an effect," says Sicher. "That's fine. Science does not require the understanding of a mechanism in order to demonstrate an effect. For years, no one knew how morphine, quinine, or even aspirin worked."

Helene Smith, Ph.D., head of cancer research at California Pacific, was impressed by the results. She had funded the study even as she was dying of breast cancer. When the results started to come in, Dr. Smith wanted some of the "drug" for herself, recalls Dr. Targ. Although the study measured healing, she assumed it meant that prayer also worked, and she asked her medical colleagues, "How many minutes are you praying for me?" says Dr. Targ. "And we did. I believe it helped her. I've never seen anybody perform as well as she did, as sick as she was."

Dr. Smith worked on the study from her bed until a week before she passed over. After the healers completed their part of the study, Sicher also asked the healers to do volunteer healing sessions for Dr. Smith, who was by then in the last stages of dying. Catherine Karas says she knew when Dr. Smith had crossed over. "Her energy became less contained, more abstract, more expansive," she claims.

Sicher and Dr. Targ believe the implications of the study are profound. "We have a study that says we're all interconnected in meaningful ways that can really benefit our health," asserts Sicher. Adds Dr. Targ, "I think things can only get better. People would spend more time contemplating their connection to one another, be more aware of that, be more loving. If everybody knew that every thought affected somebody else, they might be more careful with what they're thinking."

Dr. Targ notes, however, that "One study never proves anything. . . . What this study is is a call to action."

Strangely, the mainstream medical community has been underwhelmed by the study. When Sicher, who devised the study, was looking for a medical doctor to team up with, he first went to one of the most prominent AIDS doctors in San Francisco. "He laughed in my face," recalls Sicher. "He said, 'If you were from a pharmaceutical company and had a new drug, I might help you. But give me a break. I'm in a serious business here.' You know it was just utter, total contempt."

Leading scientific and medical journals *Science*, the *New England Journal of Medicine*, and the *British Medical Journal* all turned the study down for publication. Says Sicher, "When you talk about someone in Albuquerque or Matawan, New Jersey, trying to affect a very sick person in San Francisco, people are going to think you're talking about something that's impossible."

It seems odd that more AIDS doctors would not be interested in the results of such a study, or in designing additional studies. The study and the reports of healers and clients suggest that spiritual healing gives people a cushion even when T-cell counts do not change. But many more studies need to be done before such conclusions can be considered scientifically reliable.

It might be interesting, too, if future studies looked not only at psychological shifts, but spiritual shifts as well. As compelling as the design of this one study, it did not measure all the effects of spiritual healing that healers and HIV-positive men and women talk about.

Clark Dingman, the former president and CEO of Samaritan Hospice, now in Marlton, New Jersey, puts it succinctly. He had been given three months to live when he began working with a spiritual healer in April 1996. "The allopathic medicine wasn't enough. I wasn't sure I wanted to go on," he admits. "I'm no longer the person that I was. Jane [Ely, the healer with whom he worked] would describe it as a reincarnation in the same body. It's true I don't think about things in the same way. . . . I see this disease as a gift. I worked with God to become a new person."

Part Five

Thirteen

Beyond Healing

"You are a wonderful being. You are composed of many parts. . . . As you grow into the light these parts begin to take on a higher and higher level of smoothness, efficiency and peace. . . . Now we will dance together. . . .

"It is your soul and greater consciousness that brought you here. . . . You are becoming a doorway of peace, a doorway of Flow, of Alignment, and of Connection. There is nothing you need to do but follow the flows. . . ."

The voice, dreamy and soothing yet also deliberate, was that of Amy Skezas, the founder of Roselight, an educational organization that trains leaders and teachers of energy work in San Rafael, California, and a graduate of the University of Pennsylvania School of Law and former corporate law associate. Ethereal music, "Receiving the Pattern of our Divine Self," amplified the message as it played from a tape deck.

Skezas, a dark-haired, solidly built woman with unusually vivid blue-green eyes, was lying on the floor, looking as if she might be asleep. All around, spread out on the floor of a meeting room in a Novato, California, hotel were forty or so students, including a physician, a half-dozen nurses, a tax consultant, a business consultant, a Columbia University Ph.D. candidate in Tibetan studies, and a dozen or so graduates of the Barbara Brennan School of Healing.

Most of them were lying nested in blankets, in various states of meditation. A French-African physicist (who dropped out of graduate school just before completing his Ph.D. to pursue quantum physics as a "light worker" instead) sat lotus style, with his legs crossed.

It was the beginning of an eight-day workshop in June 1997 on Skezas's signature course, Flow Alignment and Connection. Skezas emphasizes group work, a partnership between human beings and spirit guides. It is a concept that might cause many of the law partners with whom she briefly worked to question her sanity. Yet it is consistent with the experiences of healers. The higher the energy, as Barbara Brennan herself teaches, the higher the spirit guides with whom one can connect. In order to take Flow, students must first awaken their Light Body, which includes higher harmonics of the chakras and *hara* as Barbara Brennan teaches them. The Light Body exists in dimensions closer to the causal realms and further away from physical reality. It usually takes six months or more to awaken the Light Body. The process is accomplished through specific transmissions of light through sound, muscle contractions, resonance, and harmonic induction.

"It's group work," Szekas told her students. "You are not in charge. Think of an orchestra or members of the band. . . . You're relieved of the illusion that you are in charge. It does not relieve you of responsibility." At the same time, Skezas is emphatic that Flow Alignment and Connection is not healing. "It looks like healing. It smells like healing. But it ain't healing," she told her class. "It's exploration of consciousness."

Hindu saints and Tibetan masters often talk about the world as a "play of consciousness," as Swami Muktananda put it. Skezas, too, conceives of the whole world as a play of consciousness. Before being certified as a Flow Alignment and Connection practitioner everyone in the workshop will have to complete a session with something nonhuman, such as a flower, a tree or a dog. Each person will also have to complete a session on a situation as energy and explore potentials for transformation.

Skezas teaches students to lay hands on people, but she also teaches that energy work can be done as easily, if not more easily, by intention and connection to high realms of light. One can influence a person or a situation through light without *doing* anything—when *doing* is defined by the Newtonian paradigm. Hands simply are not necessary. "The practice works because you get out of the little self. You literally get out of the reality of separation," she says. "If you aren't out of the little self, you aren't doing Flow Alignment and Connection."

Even the way Skezas teaches reflects these beliefs. Lying on the floor, looking as if she is asleep, she claims she is anything but idle. She says she is transmitting frequencies of light to each student to awaken consciousness during what she calls a "journey." "I get into an expanded state of consciousness first, and I connect with my team [of spirit guides]. Then I become one with you. It's like a swallowing. I am blended with you. In that place of blending, my grace enlightens you. Now, that's not little Amy. It's a very high form of energy. In that layer of reality, that localization and separation doesn't exist. I find that which is in me and also in you. It's different with each person."

Skezas teaches students to use an invocation to call in spiritual light and move into the frequency band of Flow Alignment and Connection. But her major gift to students is the transmission of light that awakens their consciousness. Skezas knows just how radical what she is teaching is. No hands; no doing necessary. Influencing just through being, intention, and light. One morning she told the class: "We are training revolutionaries."

Like scientists, healers and "light workers" are always looking towards the unified field where everything becomes one. Skezas sees every *thing*, not just human beings, as filters for that oneness. She likens the manifest world to a series of Play-Doh molds that shape the clay. "If you put the Play-Doh through a triangular hole, you get a triangular shape," she explains. "The filters are structures. There's the All There Is, the Tao or God, and then we have all these filters.

"Obviously a lot of other people know about this," she says. In fact it's stated plainly in the Hindu, Tibetan, Sufi, and Judeo-Christian religious texts. But unlike many other teachers, Skezas encourages her students to experience every *thing* as part of the oneness. In her cosmology, everything is malleable to some degree or another. "Flow Alignment and Connection has to do with taking anything—a toaster that doesn't work, a broken leg—and checking out the structure, seeing where it's aligned, where it's not aligned, where it's connected, where it's not," she says. "Flow is the thing that moves through the pipe."

"Flow is about stepping into the light, letting go of restrictions," she continues. "I'm very interested in power. That's the real power. Not power over. But power to participate, so people are not out of the loop. So people can create their lives in meaningful ways."

"In Flow, I'm taking you to a level that underlies all structure. . . . Even atoms are structure. I would say Flow is more fundamental than even atomic energy. I would say in our universe, everything that is manifested and destroyed happens through a process of Flow Alignment and Connection. I see it in those terms. I am trying to teach people who come to me about the fundamentals of creation."

Although Skezas is not teaching healing, many of the people who attend her workshops are healers. They use the transmission of light from Skezas to amp up the energy base in their own healing practices. Among healers, Barbara Brennan graduates, in particular, have trained with her.

For many the experience of Flow is counter to everything they have ever learned about healing, although it is a logical extension. "All I did was lay on the floor and I got it," says Cheryl Ann Bartenberger, a Barbara Brennan graduate. "I didn't think I got very much because I didn't do very much. My belief system was challenged. It was so easy. It just happened. Flow Alignment changed my life. It had a major impact and it still does. Out of all the techniques and skills I've learned, I did Flow with the most grace and ease. And it's the most practical."

"You can't underestimate the power of doing that work," adds San Francisco healer Catherine Karas, one of Brennan's first graduates. "Amy is a very powerful transmitter."

Others become disenchanted over time. "I don't use it anymore," says Alix Young, a graduate of the Brennan School, who studied Flow for five years but now favors Kabbalistic techniques to reach the higher realms. "I didn't notice great shifts or long-lasting effects. It's a bit too broad, too unfocused for me."

Still others are fond of Flow exactly because it goes beyond the boundaries of traditional healing. "My definition of healing is helping to evoke the connection with God," explains Thomas Ayers, Ed.D., a graduate of the Brennan school and a Flow practitioner. "Flow can include any business, a political party, anything that's human, anything that has structure. The intent is to invoke the light within, not to bring light into it. The light is already there. Even the darkest heart has light within it. It may take a couple of eons to emerge, but it will. The hands-on model is too small. It's the difference between a ballroom and a broom closet."

Skezas does not lecture on the relationship between energy, illness, and emotions. She spends all of five minutes in her Flow workshop discussing the chakras. She is not training healers, although healers may benefit from her training. She is interested in patterns of energy, and in creating patterns of harmony and bliss. "I'm not trying to fix anything," she explains. "What I'm trying to do is illuminate a person's situation and help them go to the next level. I'm not looking for a specific result. But there's an incredible laser-like focus. Anything I turn my radiant awareness to is illuminated."

She often seems genuinely less interested in the Earth plane than in higher dimensions of mind. Yet she is also down to earth. She is a keen business woman. She charges $1,400 for her eight-day class on Flow. Her private sessions are $200, which is on the high end. She does not believe in scholarships or discounts because then, she claims, there is no even energy exchange. She has tried it, she says. "It never works." And she tells her students if they call themselves "light workers" instead of healers, they will be more likely to stay clear of legal wrangling with the American Medical Association.

So, too, Skezas is not especially interested in being a guru. When I asked her to explain her work, she would frequently answer: "Well, what is your experience?" Part of it is a reticence to talk about the implications of what she is teaching. And in part, she would rather connect through what healers call "the inner planes" than have a regular conversation with most people. She even allows students to take some classes long distance. It sounds odd. But for

Skezas teaching is synonymous with transmissions of light. Most of her courses have very little in the way of what we think of as factual information.

Students who do courses long distance pay their fee like everyone who attends the class physically. Then they tune in from home and Skezas tunes in to them from the workshop. "This looks and smells like bullshit on first glance," Skezas admits. "But not if you understand what I do is not dependent on time and space. The question is: 'Do I want to get those thunderbolts in my energy field?'"

Skezas does give a blast of energy. Once, while observing (and, as it turns out, absorbing) her Flow class, I was late for one of the sessions. Skezas gestured for me to lie down next to her while the students gave each other hands-on energy sessions. Skezas was transmitting energy in her usual way. First I drifted into what felt like a drunken sleep. Then I went into a revery in which I saw subterranean links between areas of my life that felt impoverished. They looked separate in ordinary reality. But they stemmed from the same something. When I woke, I was in tears.

Another time, I asked Skezas about Physical Atomic and Cellular Evolution (PACE), a subject she tackles in her own ethereal way. She ended up sending a transmission long distance. Around that time, I went through several days where I was revved so high I didn't sleep much. During that same time, my fairly new computer had a melt down. (The fan inside broke.) Tracking how PACE worked was more difficult—for me at least. But around the time of Skezas's transmission, I began to see into people's cells and physical bodies in a different way than previously.

Skezas teaches all of her courses as a series of inner journeys and transmissions. For instance in Physical Atomic and Cellular Evolution, she does not teach anything that would be recognizable to a quantum physicist. Rather, she focuses on a kind of metaphysical experience:

"So for this journey, putting your body in a comfortable position, letting yourself relax as if you are on a beach in the sun, feeling and sensing the many grains of sand beneath you . . .

*as if somehow, with an exquisite sensitivity and awareness you
could perceive the individual grains of sand beneath you . . . as
if everywhere there is a solid surface you could begin to perceive
it as if it were made of grains of sand, thousands of them, tiny
irregularly shaped pieces of matter, smooth or rough, an entirely different world than you normally perceive. . . . And now
imagine that with us you are entering a smaller world, a world
of atoms. . . ."*

Amy Skezas always wanted to know how the world "really
works," as she puts it. The daughter of an oral surgeon and a school
teacher, she grew up in western Pennsylvania. "I had a lot of difficult
experiences as a child, a lot of trauma and pain," she recalls. "But I
also had a lot of joy." She describes herself even then as "dissociated
from my body." As a young teen away at boarding school, she practiced hatha yoga, studying from a book, *Yoga for Beauty and Health.*
Once, she claims she went into a deep meditation and woke to find
herself floating up at the ceiling of her room. Terrified, she fell back
into her body.

After graduating from Cornell University with a major in international relations, Skezas converted from Judaism to Greek Ortho-
doxy to marry her college sweetheart. Together they moved to
Philadelphia so he could begin medical school. A year later, Skezas
began law school. With visions of empowering the disenfranchised,
she worked in a clinic helping people get their food stamps. Every
night, she says, she also made dinner for her husband.

It was while she was in law school that a neighbor introduced
her to Rolling Thunder, a Cherokee Indian shaman, mystic, and
healer. "When I saw that guy, I knew he was different from me. And
I wanted that," she says, admitting, "I didn't know what *it* was." At
workshops, she watched Rolling Thunder in action. "They were doing things like what Jesus did," recalls Skezas. "They exhibited some
knowledge of how things worked." Later she also studied with Sun
Bear, another Native American shaman and healer.

Skezas's husband became increasingly nervous about her pre-
occupations, especially after she did a massage on a neighbor, and
wholly untrained, performed what Sun Bear later described as an

exorcism. "The walls felt like they were sweating," Skezas recalls. "All of a sudden I felt this presence breathing down on me like a Tasmanian Devil." The presence was attached to the woman asleep on the massage table. Hearing Rolling Thunder's voice in her head, she ran to her kitchen, threw sage from her spice rack into a pot and boiled it. (Sage is a purifier.) When the room returned to normal, the woman sat up and stretched. "I feel like a burden has been lifted from me," she announced.

When her husband accepted a residency at a northern Pennsylvania hospital, Skezas became an associate at Sayles, Evans, Brayton, Palmer and Tifft, the leading law firm in Elmira, New York, which had Corning Glass as one of its big clients. The money was great; the hours decent. Skezas helped set up 401k plans for corporate clients and assisted in enough litigation to witness what she calls "my blood lust." She quit before the end of her first year. In a month, she was pregnant. She gave birth to a son in 1987.

Skezas devoured Barbara Brennan's book *Hands of Light* and planned to enroll in the Brennan school. Instead, she ended up studying with a team of California teachers, Sanaya Roman, a trance channel, and Duane Packer, Ph.D., a geologist, who were developing a way to awaken the Light Body.

Roman and Packer do not emphasize hands-on healing. They teach students how to use subtle energy for manifestation, and for creating greater ease and grace in living. They claim to channel guides, Orin and Da'ben, and to this day refer to their guides as if they are partners, a habit Skezas adopted. Roman and Packer taught Skezas how to "look" at things as light and to work with things and situations at the level of unmanifest light. They now run a lucrative spiritual tape and book business that has a worldwide customer base. They taught Skezas how to awaken her Light Body in 1989.

That same year, Skezas claims a spirit guide, whom she calls "Athabascar," taught her Flow Alignment and Connection. Skezas calls Athabascar "a being of light." Many people think of spirit guides as an aspect of one's higher self. From this perspective, guidance is just another word for inspiration. Skezas insists Athabascar is a separate being. She claims when she opens to "his" energy, "everything rises to a higher level of order and harmony." Whether one asks her a spiritual question or where she wants to have dinner, she might "check" with Athabascar before answering.

As Skezas turned inward to Athabascar, the problems in her marriage became more obvious. "I grew up with [my husband]. I love him. I respect him," she says. "He was uncomfortable with all this light work stuff. And I didn't know how to trust. It was harder and harder for us to live together."

Skezas packed her bags and moved to San Francisco, leaving her baby behind. "I went through a lot of anxiety myself about what she was doing," recalls Judith Truestone, a friend and a shamanic teacher from those days. "To leave a law practice, I could understand that. But I felt maybe she needs to find a different law firm. . . . When she left the baby I had a lot of concern, not only for the baby but for her own guilt later on. . . . I was concerned. People do a lot of things and regret them."

Says Skezas, "My guidance was to leave my son there. I was told that was the best thing for my baby. I still miss my kid a lot. But I made the right choice. I have to tell the truth. . . . My son has three parents, a baby brother and a baby sister and a mom he comes home to every day and who loves his father. My child is imprinting that."

Skezas began teaching Flow to a handful of people in 1991. Since then some 300 people have studied Flow. Recently she has certified a handful of students, including several in France, Holland, and Canada, to teach Flow to their own students.

A few people who do not have much experience or training in energy work are befuddled when they take Flow. Others adore it. Some Brennan graduates claim that it transforms their practices. Pauline Dishler, R.N., the retired director of the School of Anaesthesia at Allegheny Valley Hospital in Pittsburgh, recalls working with a woman whose liver was damaged from Hepatitis C. The client's blood tests for liver function came down to 90 after just three Flow sessions. Before learning Flow, Dishler had only seen a drop of twenty points over three or four sessions. It might have just been the accumulation of healing treatments, but Dishler asserts, "I felt the shift had occurred when I did Flow."

Dishler says the higher frequencies that she accesses with Flow allows healings to unfold with more ease. "Rather than me going in and restructuring a chakra, in Flow Alignment, I can put my hand on the client and the chakra will restructure itself. . . . There's a different shift when it's my soul to the client's soul."

Dr. Nancy Reuben, who also combines Flow with traditional auric healing, concurs. "I used to help people externalize more," she says. "I work with a lot of people with a lot of anger and in the setting of Flow, I have seen that energy transform without a lot of screaming and drama. . . . I think it has something to do with the nature of the frequencies."

Ultimately, what most sets Flow apart from traditional healing is its open-ended style. Skezas encourages Flow practitioners to apply Flow to everything. Judy Eggleston, a former tax associate with Arthur Anderson and Company and an adjunct professor of accounting at George Washington University for a decade, has used meditation strategies in her private tax and business consulting practice. Using her training in the Light Body frequencies and sometimes using Flow, she says she simply visualizes a business as a grid of energy.

"If I look at IBM back when they were having problems in the eighties, it was this huge central core, not at all proportional to the wavy lines emanating from the pattern. IBM was middle-management heavy. Now, if you look at it, it's much healthier. There's a much smaller generating core and a lot more flow."

Eggleston has done the same kind of meditations for CEOs of small companies. In one case, she claims, she was able to *see* as energy that an executive needed to be removed. "He was an impediment for growth. I was able to describe [his position in the organization] accurately enough that the CEO knew what I was talking about. It was someone they had been thinking of asking to leave for some time."

More recently, she has been setting up her own organic foods business, Platt Valley Organics, named for the Platt River Valley in Nebraska, where she owns several farming businesses. She says before she began creating the business, she set up an energy grid. "I look at it once a month to see if anything has shifted or changed. And I energetically make changes."

She also uses her energy skills to set up meetings. "I literally bring a person into my space [in meditation] to see what happens. . . . If this person comes into my field as energy then there is a reason for me to meet with them. Sometimes, they just hang neutral on the edge, and it can go either way. Sometimes, I have a person get shot out of the field."

The idea that one's consciousness could affect anything and everything, including a business organization or a meeting, was a claim that seemed rather extraordinary to me at first. Of course, I then felt compelled to test it.

I started with something simple: a session on a pink zinnia I bought at a local supermarket. The flower had no scent. But as I meditated on the flower and *saw* it become more full of light, it seemed to release a delicate fragrance. I thought it might just be my imagination.

Later I became more bold, still believing I was just playing with something that couldn't possibly be "real." I was a passenger in a car with two friends. We were driving back from the country to New York City on a Sunday afternoon. The road soon became thick with cars, and one of my friends began to grumble. I decided to try a Flow on the highway traffic. Sitting in the front seat, I went into a Flow meditation in which I visualized clear sailing down an open road. The trip ended up being very smooth.

I came out of the meditation just as we reached the turnoff for the George Washington Bridge. Traffic for the bridge on the turnoff was backed up for miles. Just ahead on a deserted stretch of highway a large traffic sign announced: "Alternative Route to the Bridge." We ended up at the toll plaza in just two minutes. When we reached the toll plaza we turned on the radio. An announcer reported a half-hour wait for the George Washington Bridge. We zipped past the toll plaza in less than five minutes. But it is not possible to know whether or not the Flow had anything to do with the ease and grace we experienced, or if it was just a coincidence.

Another time, I tried a Flow on an inanimate object, a computer printer that was making a dark streak across every page. During the Flow, I meditated and went into an altered state. I saw the computer printer (which belonged to a friend and was in her home office across town) as lines of energy. I literally felt as if I merged with the printer in a state of bliss. From a state of surrender, I then used my "imagination" to reconnect the lines that seemed to have frayed. Afterwards, the printer worked normally. I was astonished. It did not seem possible to me that my "imagination" might have affected the printer.

I mention these experiences because they are a window, as it turns out, into a different view of reality, one that goes beyond all traditional concepts of healing. Such experiences are not, of course, dependent on any one technique.

For example, I first heard about grids from Gerda Swearengen, who was at the time a student at the Brennan school (where grids are not taught). She was able to see energy grids naturally without any training. She, like Eggleston and Light Body teachers Packer and Roman, believe such grids exist in the causal dimension beyond the aura. Rosalyn Bruyere also teaches about grids. In keeping with her Native American teachers, she calls them webs. On the causal dimension, she teaches that we all have individual webs and we are also linked by universal webs. These grids exist around everything—people, organizations and things—and can be accessed by anyone who can see them.

Even the experiences I had using Flow are not truly unique to Flow. For example, I had similar results using a Healing of Immanence a year before I ever sat in on Skezas's Flow class. That situation involved a healing I did on an infestation of moths.

Friends on Long Island had moths in their house, which were eating holes into some of their clothes. In a meditation from my apartment in Manhattan, I witnessed the divinity of the moths. Two weeks later, their cleaning lady pointed out the moth nest, which she had found underneath the living room rug. She apparently had known about the nest for some time, but never mentioned it. Together they took the nest out of the house. That was the end of the moth problem. I will never know if the healing had any influence on the situation. Nevertheless, the coincidence was intriguing.

Another mind-bending experience occurred in a quite mundane setting: Ollie's Chinese Restaurant in Times Square in New

York. I was having lunch with William Gough, the founder of the Foundation for Mind-Being Research and a former Department of Energy executive, who organizes meetings for leading scientists and energy workers focused on the new paradigm. While we were waiting to order, Gough picked up a spoon.

"You see this?" he said. As I watched, Gough, a man in his sixties, with a tremendous enthusiasm for the mysteries of the universe, twisted the handle of the spoon 360 degrees as if it was a plastic straw, and then he did it again. When he was done the handle of the spoon had two knots in it.

I picked up my spoon. I assumed if he could do it, I could do it, too. I had heard about spoon bending. I always assumed it was a parlor trick. The spoons in the restaurant were probably just very flimsy. I pushed with all my strength but the handled didn't budge. "How did you do it?" I asked. "Is it a trick?" I demanded to see his spoon. I could not budge that spoon either.

"I asked the same thing the first time I saw this. I couldn't believe it was real," Gough confessed. "But I watched my own twelve-year-old son bend a spoon. You have to decide for yourself."

"Well, how did you do it?"

"You just intend it. You gently intend it. That softens the molecules of the spoon. Tests show that the molecules literally change their shape in spoon bending."

I sat quietly in Gough's energy field for a minute, knowing from all my discussions with healers that my field could resonate with the know-how in his field. Then I tried to bend the spoon again. I held the spoon and focused on it with love. Ever so gently I thought to it: bend. I did not insist. I just allowed. I suddenly loved that spoon. Suddenly, as I pushed on the spoon, it was like plastic in my hand. Before I knew it, I had twisted the handle 360 degrees. I was shocked. And very pleased.

Gough told me that a group of scientists from one of the top engineering schools in the United States had learned to bend spoons at a recent retreat for scientists he had organized. When they went back to the lab, they tried another spoon-bending session. All the lights in the building blew out. It turned out that the copper wiring in the fuses had bent along with the spoons.

279

Shamans also bend material reality in this way all the time. Every time Rosalyn Bruyere runs a workshop, she bends the space with her intention and her focus. Bruyere claims that together with her partner, Ken Weintraub, she has chanted over a dead car battery—and watched it come back to life. "If we are living light we can only affect things. We can't *not* affect them," she explains.

For most healers the focus is strictly on healing illness and dis-ease. Occasionally, however, Bruyere nudges her students to broaden their perspectives. "When I need to find an object in the city of Los Angeles," Bruyere told students at a recent intensive, "I can go through an intellectual process, using the Internet or the yellow pages or asking experts. Or, I can clear my mind, see what it needs, and put it in my energy field. The very next place I walk into, it will be there. It can help me find just the right table for a specific corner. I don't need to see the table, but just see the corner beautiful and filled."

In the same way, Bruyere added, "I can find missing books, manuscripts, and people." The trick, says Bruyere, "is you must quiet the intellect for tracking. Otherwise, the intellect obscures tracking." For the most part, however, Bruyere is far more interested in healing bodies and souls. She only worked on the car battery she says, because there were elderly people in the car and she didn't want them to be kept waiting in a stalled car. "Otherwise, I would have waited for the roadside repair service like everyone else."

Most healers, however, do not focus at all on the broader implications of intention, love, and consciousness. A few are even put off by it. Jason Shulman, for instance, could not understand why I would want to spend the time creating harmony on the highway. The broader uses of consciousness and intention are, in a sense, the frontier.

Consciousness, above and beyond its effect on health, is more the domain of a few innovative scientists. "Congratulations," said Dr. Robert Jahn, dean emeritus of the School of Engineering and Applied Science at Princeton University, when I confessed that I had tuned into a printer psychically and that it worked more smoothly afterwards. "It happens all the time. You're just acknowledging it. You're just being honest."

"Most people have so suppressed this capacity that they are straight-jacketed into this causal deterministic world they've created," Dr. Jahn said. "But it is available to anyone who can play the game."

As a scientist, Dr. Jahn knows what he is talking about. For more than twenty years, he and researcher Brenda Dunne, a psychologist, have been exploring what they call "The Margins of Reality" in laboratory experiments.

Fourteen

Love and Desire: The Frontier of Physics

If you had asked Professor Robert Jahn, a professor of aerospace sciences at Princeton University, back in 1977 what effect our thoughts and intentions have on the physical world, he would have had a ready answer: none.

At that time Jahn was the dean of the School of Engineering and Applied Sciences at Princeton. He specialized in applied physics: plasma dynamics, ionization kinetics, rocketry, advanced propulsion systems. He worked on technological advances like magneto-plasma-dynamic thrusters. NASA and the U.S. Air Force funded some of his research. Like any good scientist, he put his trust in empirical data: hard, beautiful, crystal clear numbers.

Dr. Jahn still relies exclusively on "hard" data. But these days he is less focused on advanced space propulsion than on the frontiers of physics and consciousness. For twenty years, he has been directing one of the most extraordinary physics/engineering/consciousness projects in the world, one that he and medical researchers believe is a powerful analog to spiritual healing. If anything, its implications go even further than hands-on healing in transforming our ideas about the nature of reality.

As Dr. Jahn tells it, it all began when an undergraduate student majoring in electrical engineering and computer science wanted to design an electronic device to study low-level psychokinetic effects—mind over matter. The student wanted Jahn to act as a faculty adviser. Jahn was highly skeptical. Mind over matter was a great idea—inside a science fiction thriller. But after much deliberation, he gave his approval. He felt the student would learn by doing the project, even thought he was sure it would fail.

When the student graduated two years later, Jahn had to admit the project had been successful. It had been so successful that it raised disturbing national security questions. If people could *intentionally* affect electronic information, what did that say about the integrity of missile silos, aircraft cockpits, and other highly sensitive computer-based systems? The right person or people could, theoretically, influence the computers that run something like a "Star Wars" program. They would not need any guns or missiles. Only their minds.

Dr. Jahn, a rather conservative, quiet, elder statesman of science, knew he had stumbled onto phenomena that affected more than a few computer systems. He was looking at data that might shatter basic ideas about physical reality. It was almost too much to bear. "If we were not in mixed company, I would use an expletive at this point," he said when I visited him in his Princeton University office. "I was sort of clasping my hands to my head saying, 'Why me?'

"On the one hand, I saw the immense implications of this thing," said Dr. Jahn, who picks his words carefully. "We are talking about the role of human desire, human intention, and human will on the way the world works. There's an interconnectedness and there's a subtle influence potentiality here that legitimizes prayer, that legitimizes hoping, that legitimizes creativity. You don't have to accept [prayer or interconnection] cold turkey on the basis of authoritarian dogma. It can be demonstrated in the lab."

On the other hand, Dr. Jahn knew such research was so radical it might not advance his career. In the end, he said, he felt he had no choice. "Sooner or later you have to look at yourself when you're shaving in the morning. I heard a sermon once in my church, one of the best ones I ever heard. It was given by an assistant minister who happened to be female, who was later dismissed. But the last lines of the sermon were: 'I did not dare. What a burden to carry through eternity.' That's pretty much it. You can live for this world. Or for something bigger. That's really the basic choice."

In 1979 Dr. Jahn founded The Princeton Engineering Anomalies Research (PEAR) laboratory to study the effects of the human mind and human desire on the creation of reality. In many ways, the PEAR lab is the result of a marriage of minds between Jahn and Brenda Dunne, a developmental psychologist and the manager of the PEAR lab. Funding came from the Fetzer Institute, private philanthropist Laurance Rockefeller, and several other foundations. To this day, the lab is tucked away in the basement of a Princeton engineering building near the machine shop.

The lab itself is a warren of small rooms, with various computers and random-event generators lining the walls, and one low couch (in front of the biggest random-event generator in the lab) where a Noah's Ark motif runs wild with a melange of stuffed animals (gifts from visitors to the lab). Many people at Princeton have no idea research into telekinesis is being conducted on the campus, at all, let alone by senior scientists.

Several years ago, when Dr. Jahn spoke about his work at a conference on alternative medicine hosted by Dr. Larry Dossey, about 800 doctors, nurses, and other health-care workers gave him a standing ovation. But many of his engineering and physics colleagues are less enthusiastic.

When the prestigious engineering journal *IEEE Spectrum* published a paper "The Persistent Paradox of Psychic Phenomena" by Dr. Jahn and Dunne in 1983, the journal received 2,000 requests for reprints. Yet when Jahn and Dunne suggested writing an update a few years later, the editorial board said their readers had no interest in such a topic. Editors at another journal declined to publish one of their papers because, they explained, they had to protect readers from unfounded claims.

Recently, Nobel laureate physicist Steven Weinberg, Ph.D., attacked the PEAR research. "We understand enough to know there is no room in nature for telekinesis or astrology," wrote Weinberg in *Dreams of a Final Theory*. "Should we not test this to make sure there is nothing to them. . . . But I would not recommend the task."

"It's always been this way with novel ideas," said Dr. Jahn. "Verily, I say unto you it is easier for a camel to go through the eye of a needle than for a physicist to understand the nature of reality," added Dunne in a separate conversation later.

"As I tell my ten-year-old visitors [who come to the lab on school trips], if you want to become scientists you have to be able to say two very hard things," Dunne continued. "You have to be able to say: 'I don't know.' Because if you already know everything there is, you can't learn anything new. And you have to be able to say, 'I was wrong.' Because if you aren't willing to make mistakes you're not going to find out something novel and amazing. And these are two things that are not taught to scientists. You have to be open. Open is the opposite of closed."

For twenty years now PEAR has explored the same basic question: Does consciousness have an impact on inanimate objects and mechanical phenomena?

The PEAR studies are ingeniously simple. They use random-event generators, machines that involve some sort of random physical or binary process (similar to flipping a coin). The operators, or subjects, are ordinary people who claimed no psi abilities. They never touch the machines but are asked to focus on an intention, such as increasing the outcome in a positive direction (more "heads," so to speak), a negative direction (more "tails"), or not at all. They also state their intentions and record them before beginning their sessions. Sometimes when they focus their intention, they are thousands of miles from the actual machines. At other times, they focus their intention before the machine is turned on, or after it has been turned off.

By May 1996 50 million experimental trials had been performed, containing more than 3 billion bits of binary (heads/tails; yes/no; on/off; or 0/1) information. Over the years, Jahn and Dunne have reported their findings in peer-reviewed publications such as the *Journal of Scientific Exploration, Alternative Therapies,* and *Foundations of Physics* as well as in technical reports. Their findings illuminate the nature of human consciousness and its ability to impact the physical world.

Here are some of their key results:

- **People affect machines but the effects are subtle, accumulating significance over repeated efforts**: A majority of the operators did not achieve individually significant results. But when the scores were combined, correlations were found between the prestated intention of the operator to produce a specific result and the result generated by the machine during a run. In fact, PEAR calculates the possibility that the results of all trials were mere chance at one in one billion, or .000000001.

- **Every intention counts, even the intention to have no impact:** When operators were asked to establish a baseline reading, the baselines they created were too perfectly random to be random. For instance, out of seventy-six baseline runs, statistical laws predict that seven or eight of these runs will exceed the .05 mark in one direction or another. (Yes/no; heads/tails; 0/1.) But operators establishing baseline readings did not create a single run with a statistical deviation from random.

- **Signature performances**: Some of the individual operators had distinctive and replicable patterns in the ways they influenced the machines to deviate from random. Jahn and Dunne call this characteristic outcome a "signature." These signatures tended to remain constant from machine to machine and from test to test. An analogy might be the continuity of style of a musician over a series of performances and even using a range of instruments.

- **Male and female performance is distinct:** Men tend to produce results in keeping with their prestated intention more often than women. But women tended to create a bigger overall effect. Dunne speculates that in an untrained population, men may naturally have a stronger intention; women a greater natural capacity for resonance.

- **The power of pair bonding**: When two operators jointly participated in a given experiment they created a "co-operator" signature unique to the pair. This signature was not a combination of the two people's individual signatures but something entirely unique, as if the pair was a distinct entity. Co-operators of the same gender were less effective than male/female pairs. "Bonded" male/female pairs produced the highest scores of any operator pairs.

- **Intention transcends space:** An operator produced the same signature effect on machines whether he was seated next to the machine in the laboratory or focusing on the machine from thousands of miles away.
- **Intention transcends time**: Operators could exert their intention to influence the random number generating machines several hours before or after the machines made their actual run and achieved similar effects to what they got when they focused their intent during the machine's run.
- **The power of surrender and unconditional love**: The most successful operators spoke of a sense of "resonance" or "bond" with the machine, "of surrendering their sense of identity to merge with the machine into a unified system; of exchanging roles with the machine; of 'falling in love' with it or having 'fun' with it."

Random Event Generator: Cumulative Deviations from Theoretical Mean, Operator 10, All Local Data

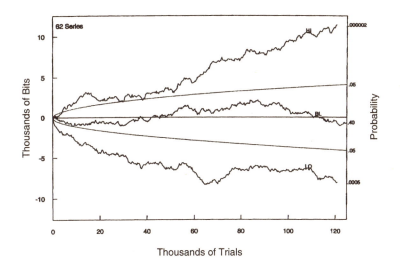

Operator 10 influencing the results of a Random Event Generator. Baseline (BL) represents chance. The high line represents results of operator's intention to increase above chance. The low line represents results of operator's intention to decrease below chance. (Courtesy Princeton Engineering Anomalies Research Lab [PEAR Lab]

Dr. Jahn and Dunne believe they have empirical data on the most powerful physical force in the world: Love. Just as mystics and saints have always claimed.

"The successful strategy for [intentional influence of matter] involves some blurring of identities between operator and machine. . . . And, of course, this is also the recipe for any form of *love*: The surrender of self-centered interests of the partners in favor of the pair," Dr. Jahn wrote in *Alternative Therapies*.

"Love! Even by the most rigorous scientific experimentation and analytical logic, it appears that we have come upon nothing less than the driving force of life and of the physical universe: Love, with a capital L."

"Where have we seen this before?" asked Dr. Jahn during our meeting. "Some people love their cars. Some people love their pianos. Some people love their baseball gloves. Some people love their cats and dogs. When you get into a bond with something, transcendent experiences happen. . . . It's a collective experience that becomes almost ineffable, but you know it when you've got it. . . . The reality changes."

The same thing happens at every level of reality, Jahn and Dunne note. Even when two atoms get together, they share electrons. The system becomes bonded. The atoms merge. Hydrogen and oxygen are transformed into something entirely new: water.

Based on their observations and empirical data, Jahn and Dunne have created a model of consciousness, a phenomenon that has long baffled scientists and thinkers in all disciplines. Their model borrows from quantum physics. They postulate that:

- Like elementary particles (matter) and light (energy), consciousness (a processor and generator of information) exhibits a wave/particle duality. Like quantum particles, consciousness can "circumvent and penetrate barriers and resonate with other consciousnesses and . . . aspects of its environment."
- Consciousness "atoms" can combine into consciousness "molecules" that have characteristics distinct from their constituents, just like physical atoms and molecules.

- Some form of "consciousness" can be conceded to the machine, in the sense that, like humans, it too is a system capable of exchanging information with its environment
- The bonding process, even of atoms in physical situations, is ultimately inexplicable.

Dr. Jahn and Dunne and other scientists have also looked at the effects of group consciousness. Roger Nelson, Ph.D., another scientist working in the PEAR lab, found that during a sacred cere-mony conducted by a shaman, a portable-event generator in the room became less random. A control run at a different time with the same generator showed completely random results. He repeated the experiment during a group meditation at a sacred site in Egypt. The

Random Event Generator Trace during Healing Ceremony

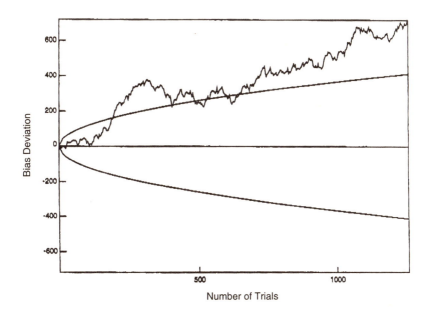

Cumulative deviation of Random Event Generator trace during a 20-minute healing ceremony performed by a Shoshone Shaman at Devils Tower. The horizontal line shows the expectation for the random walk described by the accumulating deviations, and the parabolic en-velope shows the locus of the 0.05 probability for so large a deviation as the database increases. (Courtesy PEAR Lab)

random-event generator became significantly less random than during a control period with no focused intent at the site.

Intriguingly, the PEAR team also ran random-event generators at academic conferences and business meetings. But these events showed no unusual deviations.

The Pear team concluded that when there is "a high degree of subjective resonance within the group," a consciousness field effect occurs. Dr. Dean Radin, the former head of consciousness studies at the University of Nevada, Las Vegas, also reached similar conclusions about a consciousness field effect. He studied major group events as they were unfolding.

In one study he ran two random number generators during the 1995 Academy Awards when millions of Americans were tuned into the show. One generator ran at his home, as he watched the show on TV. The other ran in his lab twelve miles away. Both he and an assistant logged the high interest events (like Best Picture) versus low interest segments (such as commercials). The high interest segments correlated to the least random series of numbers, with the odds against chance reaching 1,000:1. A control run of the random number generator produced only chance, or random, results.

When Dr. Radin ran a similar experiment during the O. J. Simpson trial verdict, the machines generated numbers that were the least random at the exact moment the court clerk read the verdict when five billion people had their attention focused on the event.

Altogether, more than twenty such studies have been conducted by Dr. Radin, the PEAR team at Princeton University, and Professor Dick Bierman at the University of Amsterdam. The studies, like those above, showed subtle but unmistakable shifts away from randomness when groups of people focused on one thing. After the assassination of Israeli Prime Minister Yitzhak Rabin, the PEAR team even retrospectively examined the data from a continually running random-event generator in the lab. The period of five minutes surrounding the event showed a powerful shift from randomness and an extraordinary effect size.

Random Event Generator Data at Time
of Assassination of Israeli Prime Minister Rabin

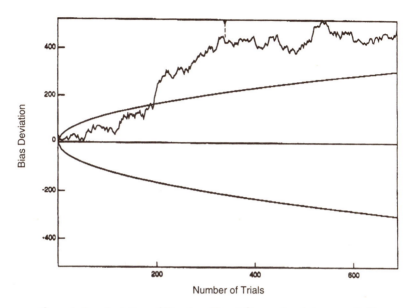

Cumulative deviation of Random Event Generator data recorded in Princeton at the time of the assassination of Prime Minister Rabin. The graph shows a ten-minute period of time exactly centered on the time of the shooting. The horizontal line shows the expectation, and the parabolic envelope shows the locus of the 0.05 probability for so large a deviation as the database increases. (Courtesy PEAR Lab)

Dr. Radin believes these quantum-like field effects show that many people focusing on the same thing bring coherence to situations. "These studies have profound implications for the understanding of social order and disorder," asserts Radin in *The Conscious Universe.* "They suggest that a previously unsuspected cause of global violence and aggression may literally be the chaotic, malevolent thoughts of large numbers of people around the world."

Dr. Radin, too, has developed a hypotheses about the nature of consciousness, including:

- Consciousness extends beyond the individual and has quantum-field-like properties, in that it affects the probabilities of events.

291

- Consciousness injects order into systems in proportion to the "strength" of consciousness present.
- The strength of consciousness in an individual fluctuates from moment to moment. Some states of consciousness have higher focus than others. Ordinary awareness has a fairly low focus of attention compared to peak states, mystical states, and other nonordinary states.
- A group of individuals can be said to have "group consciousness." Group consciousness strengthens when the group's attention is focused on a common object or event, creating coherence among the group.
- Physical systems of all kinds respond to a consciousness field by becoming more ordered. The stronger or more coherent a consciousness field, the more order will be evident.

All in all, the findings of PEAR and of related research are laboratory analogs to the experiences of healers and mystics through the ages. Dr. Jahn and Dunne have not won any Nobel prizes, however.

"Colleagues who were near and dear to me for most of my career now look at me rather strangely," admitted Dr. Jahn. "When you try to broach these topics, they shuffle their feet or look at the ceiling or excuse themselves to go to the water cooler." If they bother to look at the numbers, added Dr. Jahn, "they will desperately try to find things wrong with it. They will resort to quite illegitimate strategies."

For centuries now scientists have viewed human beings as machines. They have seen consciousness as nothing more than an epiphenomenon of nerves firing. They poke and prod brain cells, even though, as Dunne notes, "Looking for consciousness in the wiring is like looking for Johnny Carson in the tubes of the TV set." Scientists view the world, too, as a machine. "Do you want someone to come up to you and tell you you've been doing it wrong your whole life and, sorry, you've missed the whole show?" asked Dr. Jahn. "I think that's where the resistance comes from. They don't want to be told they've been wrong."

But if our love and our desires and our wishes help to create reality, we are looking at a very different world. If we can bond with other people and even with machines and can create experiences and results from these bonds, we are helping to create reality. "It changes science. It changes technology. And it changes people," said Dr. Jahn. "And," he added, "the implications for medicine are immense." But especially, he noted, it changes what it means to be human.

Sterilizing the soul out of scientific research had its purpose, he noted. "Let's be fair about it," he told me. "It's taken us a long way. It's a magnificent accomplishment. But to progress much further [science] has got to reassimilate the subjective part of experience. . . . A totally objective paradigm . . . seems so transparently inadequate to me."

Some people have their awakening at the feet of a guru. Dr. Jahn had his awakening in the lab. Jahn believes we are all interconnected, all parts of the One. He has seen it in the cold, hard, crystal clear numbers that he has always trusted. When it was time for me to leave his office, he got up and hugged me. "There is room aboard the Ark," he said.

Fifteen

The Future

When I was at the very beginning stages of my research into spiritual healing I asked Mother Meera, a Hindu woman who radiates a very clear light, what she meant when she alluded to the transformation of humanity.

"Do you feel it in yourself?" she asked.

"Yes," I replied hesitantly. At that time I doubted whether one human being could be more spiritually awake than another. But after sitting in her presence, I had had the most vivid dreams of my life. They were so vivid that I knew that they were not dreams, but teachings. One dream was actually a nightmare in which someone was murdered. I woke up in a cold sweat, aware that that "someone" was my own ego.

That same night I also dreamed that I had written a celebrity profile for a magazine, as I did in those days. But much to my chagrin, the magazine had run it with someone else's byline. It was a very direct message about my focus: I should look more to the content of what I wrote than to recognition. The two dreams were related; they were stern teachings.

"That is the transformation," Mother Meera said to me through her translator, Adilakshmi.

At the time I was disappointed. A few dreams? Some teachings that were designed for me personally? That was the big transformation? It hardly seemed cataclysmic. Of course, that was before I understood how energy works.

Now I see how my thoughts, feelings, beliefs and intentions affect myself, other people and my environment. Your thoughts, feelings, beliefs, and intentions also affect everything and everyone around you, including you and the cells in your body. We are helping to create the world in each moment. We have a choice: to be in fear, or anger, or numbness. Or in love. We usually cannot change overnight, but we can always move ever so slightly in the right direction. Releasing patterns that constrict us can sometimes be excruciating. But each time we do so, life expands. And the more we heal ourselves, the more we hold light for others.

I can give some very small examples of what this means in daily life. Once, as I was experimenting with the energy centers in my Light Body (the band of energy beyond the aura), I went into an electronics store to return something. The saleswoman started to give me a hard time, even though I had my receipt. I began to gather myself for a battle, and all the pleasures that go with it. Then it occurred to me to spin my heart center. The woman behind the counter became much nicer. It was almost as if I had flipped a switch. In a way, I had, and it had affected both of us.

Another time, I was at a writer's conference at a small New England college. By day, it was a luxurious setting. But sleeping in a dorm again was not much fun. The mattress was coated in plastic, and every time I turned, I slid all over the place. When two people ended up under my window, four stories down, I was ready to murder them. I listened to one person's voice go on as "good night" turned into an Olympic conversation. The more I hated that person, the more he seemed to drone on.

Eventually, I meditated. Soon I found myself sensing the person below. I realized he was talking to fill himself up. I felt sad that I had been so angry. I focused all of my being on becoming love. For a moment I let go of all of my needs. All of my desires. I cannot describe how blissful I became. I even loved this man who was talking. Indeed, we had a soul-to-soul communion. A minute or so later, he said good night. He had needed connection and he had gotten it.

Cheryl Ann Bartenberger, a recent Brennan school graduate, tells a similar story. She was in a grocery store waiting on a long checkout line. The tension and agitation was building in everyone on the line, the bagboy, the cashier, and a couple of unruly children. She realized that she had a choice: She could jump on the bandwagon via harmonic induction and take on and reinforce anger, frustration, and disgust. Or she could choose peace. "So I went into the state of grace and radiated it 360 degrees around me." She says the children calmed down almost instantly. And everyone else around her slowly relaxed. "I no longer limit my healing abilities to the healing room," she says. "It is amazing what can be created with love."

These are just small stories. Dr. Gary Schwartz, who teaches energy medicine to the postgraduate doctors at the University of Arizona, also has an example of what it means to choose love instead of despair or self-pity. "I know a woman who was dying and couldn't get out of bed. So she spent the last year of her life just radiating love. She didn't ask for anything in return. Can you imagine?" he asks. "There are so many people who don't feel they have any purpose to life. What would happen if they, too, radiated love?"

The inverse of the principle of love is also true. Most of us know people who are always having computer glitches, or car trouble, or some other ongoing difficulty. One energy worker I know once got furious with his computer; at that moment all the computers in the government defence agency where he was working blew out. Some scientists believe such incidents are not a coincidence.

"I have a friend who, when he gets angry, the light bulbs on the street blow out," says Dr. Elmer Green, the biophysicist who has studied the physiology of healers and Hindu yogis. "When [healer] Mietek [Wirkus] gets upset about something, the microwave won't work, the TV won't work. These are all macro effects [of vibratory activity]."

When we get angry at someone our rage also reaches them. The more *chi* or consciousness we have, the more power we have to influence the world. This is one reason it is so important for anyone embarking on a spiritual path to dissolve negative emotions and intentions.

We live in a sea of energies, some light, some dark. Dr. Schwartz at the University of Arizona Medical School believes that the fact that obesity in the United States has reached epidemic proportions may be related to the starvation occurring in North Korea and Africa and other parts of the world. He says he had this revelation when he pondered his own sometimes-excessive hunger in the midst of so much plenty.

"'What was I trying to suppress?' I asked myself," Dr. Schwartz says. "When you think about energy and information, everyone is connected to everyone else. . . . Millions of people are dying from starvation. And we are doing virtually nothing about it as a species. Yet all of this pain, all that energy, is still racing around the Earth from an energy point of view. When you realize that energy can affect our biological systems, you have to ask: What are we doing to ourselves?"

The tiny group of scientists researching spiritual energy and consciousness believe that as more people heal and move to a higher "vibration," or a more coherent heart focus, society will change. "What I really think is that the planet is going through a paradigm shift," says Rollin McCraty, director of research at the Institute of HeartMath. "The shift isn't what people think it is. It's from logical awareness to heart awareness. That's the next level of human consciousness.

"We will move into a much more loving, intuitive, higher speed domain," says McCraty, who believes we could even reduce wars, famine, and inner city violence. "Then the planet will make a big shift. I think that really could happen. I think we'll see the proof of it in our lifetime. The heart has the intelligence to do that."

Dr. Elmer Green agrees. "The destiny of the planet is to become spiritual and for all the vibratory characteristics to raise up to the point where it is all spiritual. It may take thousands of years. But we have to go through the step we're taking right now, where we become aware of the astral [auric] plane." He believes, no matter how long it takes, the process is inevitable for one simple reason: "The powers of God are in every human being."

Whatever the ultimate results, it seems clear that we are on the verge of a new era, an era in which subtle energy will become part of the known world and a part of science.

A small number of doctors and hospitals are making tentative efforts to explore or incorporate energy medicine. For instance, at the Program in Integrative Medicine, launched by Dr. Andrew Weil at the University of Arizona Medical School in 1997, energy healing is one of eight complementary disciplines included in the two-year postgraduate fellowship. Since its inception, Rosalyn Bruyere has been a visiting faculty member, teaching the fellows, some of whom have been practicing medicine for as long as a decade, as well as larger groups, about energy medicine and spiritual anatomy. She has also laid hands on the fellows, to give them a personal taste for how subtle energy works. Dr. Weil hopes these doctors will become leaders in the new integrative medicine of the 21st century.

The Alliance Hospital Group in Cincinnati, Ohio, also retained Rosalyn Bruyere as a consultant for a new alternative treatment center, beginning in 1997. There, too, she is helping to help train the medical staff in energy healing and energy anatomy.

The most innovative program of all, however, may be at the University of Pittsburgh Medical Center, where Lewis Mehl-Madrona, M.D., the medical director of the Center for Complementary Medicine, oversees a 21-member team of alternative practitioners. The center provides energy healing, acupuncture, spiritual counseling and other alternative treatments to some 300 patients a month. They come from across the United States, including the West Coast.

"A lot of studies have been done on spirituality and health," explains Dr. Mehl-Madrona, who is trained in emergency medicine, psychiatry and Cherokee medicine. "Almost all of them show that spirituality is incredibly important. We try to help people come to a spiritual practice. . . If you don't have a practice, we'll help you find one. We believe it is an important aspect of getting well."

Dr. Mehl-Madrona recently completed a study comparing five-year outcomes in a group of patients treated only with conventional care and a group that also received counseling and healing from Native American healers. In the study, published in *Alternative Therapies*, he found that most people were better five years later. But those who had received the Native American healings, whether they suffered from cancer, infertility, depression, back pain or several other ailments, were significantly better. Most surprising, patients with diabetes and agina, who deteriorated under traditional care, showed significant improvement when they received Native American healing, which combines ceremony, energy medicine, life-style modification and spiritual counseling.

"What the study says is that this program adds significantly to conventional medicine." But, he adds, "The thing to keep in mind is that this center should not exist. The fact [that these treatments] are separated out is a testament to the narrowness and blindness of physicians. In our century, physicians have decided only drugs and surgery work. That's nuts. . . . I call it techno-arrogancy."

California Pacific Medical Center in San Francisco and Stony Brook Medical Center on Long Island, New York also have complementary care programs which offer chi gong, movement, meditation, guided imagery, and massage—and energy healing and homeopathy. "We're trying to bring a new vision of wellness," says Dr. Elisabeth Targ of California Pacific. "The whole spiritual dimension is something that is new. Spiritual is a loaded word. It's about meaning and connectedness. It's about: What is my place on this earth? That's very important. The locus of change is being placed with the patient. You have to do some work. It doesn't all come in a pill."

Research projects on energy healing are also being conducted at California Pacific Medical Center in San Francisco and at a few other hospitals. Courses on complementary medicine are now offered at 53 of the 124 medical schools in the United States, according to a recent survey published in *Alternative Therapies*. The offerings at a dozen of these schools, including the University of California at Los Angeles, Dartmouth Medical School, and Indiana University School of Medicine, touch on energy medicine, spirituality, and health and on modalities such as Healing Touch or Therapeutic Touch.

The same shift is occurring abroad. The United Kingdom has more than 8,500 registered healers, and physicians there receive postgraduate education credits for attending courses on energy healing, according to *Healing Research* author Dr. Daniel Benor. Healers are able to purchase liability insurance similar to the policies covering physicians.

In Poland and Russia, some medical schools include instruction in energy healing. In Poland, according to Mietek Wirkus, healers are licensed by the government after demonstrating that their treatments have worked on a specific number of patients.

Meanwhile, in Vienna, Austria, the Danube Hospital is launching an alternative medical group connected with the oncology department. Anita Ritt-Wollmersdorfer, M.D., a psychiatrist who has been studying healing with Rosalyn Bruyere, will oversee a team of ten healers in a year-long pilot program.

China, which has a long tradition of subtle energy healing via acupuncture and *chi gong* masters, currently leads the world in research into subtle energy.

Ultimately, I believe, the entire medical system will undergo a transformation. In the medical system of the future, doctors will look at energy as more primary than biochemistry. All doctors will be educated in spiritual anatomy and its relationship to physical anatomy. Many doctors will continue to practice what we consider physical medicine. But physical medicine will change.

As our technology develops, we will take readings of more and more subtle energy measurements. We will not need to remove perfectly healthy organs to prevent disease or to diagnosis it. We will not have to wait for cancer to grow into a tumor before it can be detected and treated. We will not have to wait until someone has a heart attack to know they have congestion in their arteries.

We will be able to measure subtle energy disturbances, much the way we can now measure and understand brain waves and heart rhythms, technological developments of the twentieth century. Medicine will shift from treating disease to treating nascent energy imbalances. Indeed, we will look back at the medicine being practiced today in the same way we look at the blood-letting of previous centuries, as primitive.

Eventually, spiritual healing will become a standard discipline, much the way psychiatry became part of medicine during the twentieth century. In the popular culture, spiritual concepts will be as accepted as psychological ones are today. We will even accept the existence of intelligence that exists without physical form, much the way we have come to accept the existences of microscopic life forms. Some medical professionals will be drawn to work with the soul, while others will focus on the physical and auric domains.

This shift does not have to wait for the twenty-second century. The truth is that spiritual healing could become a licensed profession tomorrow. We already have the technology to measure who has the ability to facilitate healing and who does not. In fact, it is easier to measure the physiology of healing than of psychotherapy. (Actually, the most talented psychotherapists are probably holding a healing state that could be measured physiologically.)

As researchers at the Menninger Clinic and elsewhere have demonstrated, in a healing state a healer develops a marked increase in alpha waves. The heartbeat also becomes coherent. There is also an entrainment of brain and heart frequencies between healer and client. Most healers show changes in the electrical charge on their skin, as well.

It would be very easy to certify healers based on a combination of measures. We will ultimately have organized peer review of healing talent. We will also develop tests to measure a healer's ability to create positive physical, emotional, and spiritual changes in clients. Tests to measure a healer's ability to change the structure of water or influence the growth of cells in vitro could also be established.

In addition, we will expect healers to demonstrate the physiology of a healing state: increased alpha waves, a coherent heartbeat, and changes in the electrical charge at the skin during healing. All that is needed for such testing are common medical devices such as EKGs and EEGs. A combination of these elements would be important, because in some very high healing states, Dr. Green found, there were no signficicant electrical changes measured at the skin.

In addition, orthopedist and researcher Dr. Robert Becker, who was twice nominated for a Nobel prize, has suggested using a superconducting quantum interference device (SQUID), a sensitive magnetic-field detector. More primary research with recognized healers would be needed before this could be implemented. But Dr. Becker believes that with a SQUID the "magnetoencephalogram"—the magnetic signature of each healer—could be measured. (Just as we all have electrical charges around and in us, we also have a magnetic field. Each one of us has our own astral "finger-print.") For some years, Dr. Becker has urged such measurements of healers. But the equipment has never been lent for such research.

Many healers are just as happy to be unregulated, given what is going on in health care today, where financial considerations are often more primary than the highest good of the patient. But recognizing healing as a profession would give the public more protection. Right now, just about anyone who has taken a weekend course in healing can call themselves a healer.

The truth is that healing requires talent and formal training, just as musical, or athletic, or legal skills do. As Flow Alignment and Connection practitioner Catherine Karas puts it: "Yes, you can have anyone do healing, like you can have anyone play the piano. But they're not going to play like [concert pianist] Van Cliburn. . . . If you're talented, you're going to do better. And if you're talented and trained, you're going to do even better."

Currently, this new era is in its infancy. To realize the potential, we must research all aspects of psi and of spiritual phenomena. We must, as Dr. Robert Jahn and Brenda Dunne at Princeton University propose, begin to understand empirically how it is that we interact with the physical world and help to create that world. As Dr. Jahn and Dunne urge we must create "a science of the subjective."

No one can predict where this research will lead. I am sure that, as we study this area and as people begin psychic and spiritual training earlier, the abilities of healers as a group will blossom. The same will be true of the psychic and spiritual abilities of everyone in the general population.

Ultimately, however, the effect of this research will reach far beyond the doctors' and healers' offices, according to Dr. Jahn and Dunne and others. Consider that when Isaac Newton described gravity in the seventeenth century, no one could have imagined his equations would help take us to the moon. And when James Clerk Maxwell derived the equations for electricity and magnetism, no one could have predicted radio, television, electric lights, satellites, faxes, or even elevators. Analogous expansions will occur when we understand subtle energy.

Already, in China, scientists at the Institute of High Energy Physics have reported that *chi gong* masters have changed the polarization plane of laser light and influenced the decay rate of radioactive material in laboratory tests. *Chi gong* masters also changed the molecular properties of tap water, saline solution, and glucose solution, as measured by laser Ramon spectroscopy. These experiments have not been replicated in the United States. But William Gough, founder of the Foundation for Mind-Being Research, who spent more than thirty years overseeing new research for the Atomic Energy Commission and the Electric Power Research Institute, has examined the studies and believes they have important implications for our future. He believes such experiments should be replicated in the United States.

Nevertheless, even basic medical research involving subtle energy and consciousness is still routinely turned down for funding. For instance, when the United States Army put out a call for research proposals on breast cancer, Dr. Elisabeth Targ, who co-chaired the study on AIDS and distant healing, submitted a study on distant healing and breast cancer. Her study got the top score for design, but it was not funded. "They had two complaints," recalls Dr. Targ. "First, they didn't think it would work. Second, they didn't feel it would translate. What would they do with the information? they asked."

Microbiologist Garret Yount, Ph.D., an associate researcher at the Complementary Medicine Research Institute at California Pacific Medical Center, also had trouble getting funding for a study of the effects of *chi gong* on the molecular and genetic structure of cancer cells in vitro.

"There's tons of money for the inside-the-paradigm stuff, all the boring stuff," says Dr. Yount, who began his research after his father received *chi gong* sessions and recovered from "terminal" leukemia. There is also money, he notes, for alternative treatments that fit the current paradigm, like herbal treatments, which can be "fitted into a marketing stream." But research on subtle energy, he says, "scares some scientists. That's my interpretation. What's more apparent is the hostile reaction. They think I'm a wacko. And they don't like it."

Increasingly, as I researched healing, I wondered where the intense resistance to energy healing really comes from. There are abundant studies and anecdotal reports that suggest healing may be more than placebo, that it can alleviate suffering and help create cellular and emotional changes. Why wouldn't doctors rush to explore this area? They rush to try every new pill that comes on the market, and every technological device. Furthermore, doctors all take the Hippocratic Oath. I believe they want to alleviate the suffering of their patients.

Since its rise in this century, allopathic medicine has made extraordinary advances. Yet we simply do not have all the answers. We cannot effectively treat half of the 27 million people who seek to control something basic—their blood pressure. And we lose 60 percent of all cancer patients within five years of diagnosis. Altogether, approximately 100 million Americans suffer from chronic illnesses that doctors cannot cure.

Medicine, in general, is not always as "scientific" as many people believe. Doctors can give patients statistical probabilities about the course of their illness, but they can never predict exactly what will happen to any one individual. Doctors can explain disease processes with stunning elegance, but strangely they do not even investigate why some people recover from "terminal" illnesses.

Meanwhile, adverse drug reactions cause 106,000 or more deaths a year, according to a study published in April 1998 in the *Journal of the American Medical Association*. This means drugs given in normal and appropriate doses are, conservatively, the sixth leading cause of death.

If healing caused as many deaths as prescription drugs, I would understand why doctors would be up in arms against energy healing. But such healing, when practiced by someone holding an intention for the client's highest good, does not have adverse side effects. Why wouldn't doctors want to add it to their "arsenal" of treatments?

The scientists who are committed to researching psi and spiritual phenomena believe the explanation is simple. Basic values have to change. The highest healing comes from holding the highest and purest intention towards all beings and all events at all times. To put it more simply: the highest healing comes from love. As Dr. Green notes, "Everything is mind, but it is love that moves it." Yet it is not your ordinary love, but an unconditional impersonal love.

This means that a physician cannot just adopt spiritual healing as another weapon in the arsenal after a weekend workshop. An inner transformation has to occur. And a societal transformation, as well. Right now doctors as a group do not even think love is "scientific." It is not even addressed in medical schools. Nor has love been considered an appropriate topic for medical or psychiatric research, where it is usually translated as "caring" in scientific papers.

"They would have to give up everything, change their values," explains Dr. Green. "People talk about Jesus, but they don't talk about what Jesus said to do. They say, if you believe in Jesus, you're saved. But Jesus said you have to become like the Father in Heaven and you will be saved. And that's what the Buddha said and Krishna said. It's the most difficult thing there is. And for the whole race to get that way will take thousands and thousands of years. . . . Right now is a real transition."

In healing, love is the engine. Techniques are mere pathways. I found that there are many genuinely talented healers, from many different paths. I also found that healers are ordinary people. While some of us are here to explore language, others to become policemen, and others to become musicians or artists, healers have gone ahead to explore the spiritual dimensions where we all exist, as well.

A healer is not necessarily any wiser or more pure than the rest of us. Some are. Some are not. Healers are as diverse as any other group of people. In addition, their talents and inclinations vary widely. I found that while some healers are "all purpose," others have very specific gifts. Some healers are afraid of cancer or heart disease. Others embrace it. Some people are exceptionally good at shifting emotional patterns; others cannot see their own emotions, or the emotions of others, clearly.

I also came across some extremely gifted people who had not healed fundamental splits in themselves. They might be extremely clairvoyant, they might have a huge amount of *chi* and power at their disposal. But if they do not love themselves, their healings are ultimately going to be limited.

A healer, in the end, is a teacher. He or she can only take their clients as far as they themselves have gone. A healer who takes abuse from his or her mate cannot help someone overcome a pattern of abuse. A healer who has not resolved narcissism cannot heal narcissism in another person. A healer who does not love all of his or her self cannot help someone to embrace his or her own darkness. A healer who needs to control others cannot ultimately help a person release their need to control. A healer who perceives others as competition cannot fully embrace his or her clients or students.

I have come to believe that what sets a few healers apart, including Rosalyn Bruyere, is a profoundly generous spirit. Bruyere is still very much on her journey. But she is clear about the goal. In her mind, it is not about ascension. It is not about communicating with spirits. It is not the number of techniques you know. It is not about being "smarter" or more "powerful" than another person. It is about how you live, moment to moment. "You're not coming here to find the Hope diamond," she once said to me. "It's about being a better person."

Ultimately, what makes healing an important topic is not that it is about a unique group of people, but that it is an investigation that is relevant to each and every one of us. The same qualities that elevate a healer's work are also those that are transformative for those in all other walks of life. The work of a doctor, a lawyer, a politician, a scientist, a corporate executive, a sanitation worker, a postal worker, a cleaning woman and, of course, a parent, will be similarly elevated—inspired, if you will—by anyone holding the intention for the highest good. This is the real lesson of spiritual healing.

It is, in fact, just as Jesus Christ once said (St. Mark 12:30-31), quoting from Deuteronomy and Leviticus in the Old Testament: "And thou shalt love the Lord thy God with all thy heart, and with all thy soul, and with all thy mind, and with all thy strength: this is the first commandment.

"And the second is like, namely this: Thou shalt love thy neighbor as thyself. There is none other commandment greater than these." At the level of the implicate order, after all, we are all one.

Spiritual healing will not cure each and every one of us of physical disease, and physical medicine is not, nor will it ever be, obsolete. But each one of us can choose to be a light in the world. In that, there is grace.

Epilogue

Rosalyn Bruyere warned Dr. Jonathan Kramer that his healing would take time. She was right. It has taken two years for the light to work its way through his system, and even now he feels the transformation is not yet complete.

But recently he began doing energy healings with a few people who have been diagnosed with "terminal" cancer. He eventually plans to go back into medicine, but he wants to return in a way that allows him to continue to work with energy as well. He no longer doubts that subtle energy is real, or that it has the power to transform.

Some of his internal struggles have been resolved, too. As a result, he says, his relationship with his wife, Maria, is better than ever before. "I usually say my relationship is like the stock market," he explains. "There are ups and downs. The general trend is up. And I'm in it for the long haul. But lately it's been much more satisfying. We're much more close, more honest, and more intimate."

Rosalyn Bruyere is also moving toward her destiny. One of the few contemporary teachers of healing who also remains an apprentice, she received one of the most significant teachings of her life in early December 1998.

In a three-day sacred ceremony set in the courtyard of the Healing Light Center Church, His Holiness Lungtok Tenpai Nyima, thirty-third abbot of Men-ri, the spiritual leader of the

Bonpo, honored Bruyere. The Tibetan Bonpo have never honored a woman in this way before.

For most of the previous six months, Bruyere says that she received teachings from the abbot several nights a week in the dream time. Now the abbot and four other monks were in Sierra Madre, California, along with Bruyere's students from across the United States, Europe, and Canada. Dr. Kramer, his wife Maria, and their daughter Rafaella, were among those in the crowd. It was one of the coldest weekends to hit Los Angeles in several years, but the sun was shining.

The highlight of the festivities came on the second day. The abbot crowned Bruyere, who is regarded as an official Bonpo oracle, in a three-hour consecration ceremony normally reserved for newly appointed lamas and abbots.

The monks chanted in their stately, haunting tones and made offerings of fruit, incense, sweets, and sacred objects. Bruyere sat quietly in a vivid blue ceremonial gown, embroidered with gold thread and pearls and lined with red silk. She was just a few feet from the abbot, but she was in a seat that left her several feet lower than the abbot. Her heart radiated waves of golden light. The Abbot's energy was clear and still, like the air from the Himalayan mountain region of Tibet from which he orginally came.

Toward the end of the ceremony, the abbot bestowed on Bruyere a new Dharma (spiritual) name, Yungdrung Rinchen Khadro. Loosely translated: Everlasting Jewel Sky Goer. It was another initiation for Bruyere. "You get the knowledge by sitting in the presence of the one who has that knowledge," explained Healing Light minister Nancy Needham.

It was also an initiation for the students who joined her, according to the abbot. He credited karmic connections over many lifetimes for gathering everyone there under one roof. He urged the students to turn away from negative thinking and negative behavior, to purify themselves and "take refuge in the Buddha Heart."

In other ceremonies, the monks prayed for long life, wealth, empowerment, and purification for all those present. When the ceremonies were over, Bruyere, dressed in street clothes once again, joined the Bonpo abbots and her students for a Mexican-style feast on the patio. Just watching her, it did not seem as if anything about her had changed.

"This is just the most enormous initiation of her life," said Needham. "Here's this woman who started out as a grocery checker. . . . And now she's sitting in her backyard, getting initiated into a major religion as a major 'poobah.'

"I can't begin to speculate about what it means," Needham continued. "The only thing I come up with is: When someone asked of the Buddha, 'What did you do before you were enlightened?' he said, 'I chopped wood and carried water.' And when the person asked, 'What do you do now?' he answered, 'I chop wood and I carry water.'"

Acknowledgments

I thank Rosalyn Bruyere for her wisdom, open heart, and a belief that esoteric knowledge belongs to everyone; Barbara Brennan, a gifted popularizer and innovative educator; Jason Shulman, for delving into the Kabbalah; and Amy Skezas, for connecting to energy at a pure level. They spent many hours discussing subtle energy and healing with me, and also sharing details about their personal and professional evolution. They also opened the doors to their schools. Spending time with each of them was transformative.

This book also would not exist without the extraordinary research work now being done by doctors and scientists. I'd especially like to acknowledge Dr. Robert Jahn and Brenda Dunne at the Princeton Engineering Anomalies Research lab, along with Roger Nelson and Arnold Lettieri. Every time I wondered how the events I was reporting could be true, their research and carefully worked out theoretical models sustained me.

The research and theories of Dr. Elmer Green and his associates Peter Parks and Dr. Steve Fahrion; William Gough, president of the Foundation for Mind-Being Research; Drs. Gary Schwartz and Linda Russek, at the University of Arizona; and Rollin McCraty at the Institute of HeartMath are similarly groundbreaking and inspiring. I feel privileged to have spent many wonderful hours discussing subtle energy and the science behind it with each of them. William Gough and Gary Schwartz were especially enthusiastic and helpful. I also wish to thank Russell Targ, formerly of Stanford

Research Institute, Marilyn Schlitz at the Institute for Noetic Sciences, and David Muehsam.

Dr. Larry Dossey helped set me down this path—taking time to discuss healing when I first stumbled on the subject. His journal *Alternative Therapies*, like *Subtle Energies*, was extremely useful. Heart surgeon Mehmet Oz has been similarly generous in sharing his experiences and ideas. Dr. Elisabeth Targ and Fred Sicher at California Pacific Medical Center have patiently kept me in the loop regarding their study on distant healing and AIDS. Dr. Daniel Benor wrote a truly remarkable book, *Healing Research*, and shared with me what led him to do so. Dr. Lewis Mehl-Madrona is an inspiring clinical innovator. Dr. Deepak Chopra and Dr. Christiane Northrup also shared their insights into healing. I would also like to thank Drs. Steven Amoils, Bruce Harshman, George Lundberg, Frank Livelli, Major Geer, Richard Grossman, Sonal Shah, Mark Russo, and Jerry Whitworth.

Drs. Nancy Reuben, Dan Kinderlehrer, and Ken Kafka shared their unique perspectives as both medical doctors and spiritual healers. They also shared their love, energy, and friendship. I also wish to thank Robert Jaffe, M.D., the founder of the School of Energy Mastery, who gave me beautiful readings about my heart whenever we sat down to do an interview; Emilie Conrad Da'oud, who is doing healing work through movement; Levent Bolukbasi, founder of the IM School of Healing Arts; and Michael Mamas, founder of the School for Enlightenment and Healing.

My very special thanks goes to Gerda Swearengen, for her extraordinary vision—and for spending countless hours initiating me into the mysteries of spiritual healing and into the mysteries of my own soul and psyche. Gerda often saw me more clearly than I saw myself. Healer and fellow yoga practitioner Thomas "T.C." Ayers has also been an astute guide as I made my way through the auric and causal realms. In a very real sense, they have been godparents to this project. This book would be very different without their friendship, wisdom, and support.

Cheryl Bartenberger, too, did her part to initiate me into my own heart. Maria Bartolotta and Catherine Karas shared their experiences at a deep level. I also wish to thank David Grady for his wisdom and honesty and Susan Weiley for her broad perspective.

Dianne Arnold gave me my first experiences of healing and did some heavy lifting, always with love and compassion. Dani Antman helped me to gain a deep personal understanding of how Kabbalistic energy works, and I thank Rabbi Steven Fisdel, Roger Hirsh, Shirley Chambers, and Catherine Vajda, among others, for rounding that understanding out. Don Van Vleet showed me how, as Rosalyn Bruyere always says, "the issue is in the tissue" and literally helped me rewire my nervous system.

I take my hat off to Dr. Jonathan Kramer for sharing the story of his transformation. I also thank Maria and Rafaella. Marilyn Schneider, Joseph Carman, Clark Dingman, Evelyn Perkowski, George Berger, Cheryl Jacobs, Terry Houlihan, Robert Cohen, Fred and Doris Dennard, Warren Nagel, Barbara Sullivan, Diane Munz, Mary Moran, Tracy Nelson, and many others openly, and bravely, shared their personal stories.

Nancy Needham, Jeanne Farrons, Eetla Soracco, Stacy Sabol, Marcella Thompson, Susie Lovett, Deborah East Keir, Pam O'Neil, Tiaia Agri, all of the Healing Light Center Church shared their wisdom and experiences. Amy Wiggins, Alisha White, Susan Brown, Jeanine Sande and Tracey Parker also shared their insights.

Flow Alignment and Connection practitioners Deb Schnitta and Pauline Dishler, Tina Awad, Vinnie Arnold, Judy Eggleston and many others described their explorations in the light realms.

Healers Susan Ulfelder; Nancy Hirsh; Joan Luly; Alan Hayes; Christine Saball-Tobin; Peter Faust; Roseanne Farano; Kate MacPherson; Jim Ambrogi; Dr. Ann Massion; Jan Bresnick; Melanie Brown; Michael Young; Simma Kindelherer; Ginger Bennet; Dr. Martha Harrell; Jane Ely; Donna Evans-Strauss; Phil Marden; Karin Aarons; Loren Stell; Caren Berowsky; Dr. Rob McInnes and Lucie McInnes, Richard Dobson, Connie Myslik, and others at the Barbara Brennan School of Healing, A Society of Souls, and the School for Enlightenment and Healing, shared their insights and experiences.

Mietek and Margaret Wirkus shared their clear vision and devotion to healing. Nan Blake gave me a glimpse of her program,

Divine Unity. Bill Torvund gave me a different understanding of time and space. With Traci Slatton I shared adventures with computer printers, clairvoyance, and poems. Ganga Stone, in her own way, started me on the path that led to this book.

Steven Brill, the founding editor of the *American Lawyer*, *Court TV* and *Brill's Content*, taught me much about writing and reporting and the need to be fearless about searching out the truth—even when it's not popular. A special thanks also goes to Peter Bart, the editor in chief of *Variety*, for his vision and for supporting and encouraging me during this project. In his own way, he was an angel.

Dennis McDougal has been a friend and a colleague at every level, and his editorial input has been invaluable. I'm also grateful to both him and his wife, Sharon, for being such marvelous hosts during my trips to Los Angeles. Ellen Liburt and Elizabeth Marlin read the manuscript in their early stages, as well as being wonderful friends. Ellen also transcribed many hours of interviews.

Bill Gough, Dr. Bob Shacklett, Nancy Reuben, Dan Kinderlehrer, T.C. Ayers, Gerda and Mark Swearengen, Cheryl Bartenberger, Gary Schwartz, and Linda Russek read parts or all of the manuscript and gave me important feedback. T.C. Ayers, in particular, did a very precise and thoughtful preliminary copy edit.

My agent Al Zuckerman went the distance. And I have enjoyed working with everyone at Hampton Roads. Bob Friedman, my editor and publisher, has always seen my book with inspiring clarity. Ken Eagle Feather, the marketing director, has personally supported this project at every level. Publicist Kathy Cooper's genuine enthusiasm has been a pleasure. Jane Hagaman and the design team have been inspired.

As a writer, I have also been influenced by countless other writers, whom I would like to collectively thank. For this book, I found particular inspiration from *The Dancing Wu Li Masters*, by Gary Zukov; *Silent Spring*, by Rachael Carson; *The Hot Zone*, by Richard Preston; and *Autobiography of a Yogi*, by Paramhansa Yogananda.

To my parents, Roslyn and Howard Goldner, I offer a very special thanks, for their love, their encouragement, their teachings, and their support my entire life. I also wish to thank, with love, Stuart, Marcey, Paul, Eric, and Zachary Goldner.

Acknowledgments

On an entirely other dimension, I thank Swami Gurumayi Chidvilasananda and Mother Meera; I have been immeasurably assisted and transformed by their grace. I have also been inspired by the Dalai Lama; His Holiness Lungtok Tenpai Nyima, thirty-third abbot of Men-ri; Jesus Christ; Babaji and Swami Muktananda; Swami Nityananda; and Paramhansa Yogananda. Last, but not least, I wish to thank the saints and sages of all ages for the wisdom and the light they have brought to this world.

Bibliography

Books

Adilakshmi. *The Mother.* Dornberg-Thalheim, Germany: Mother Meera, 1987.

Becker, Robert O., M.D. *Cross Currents: The Promise of Electromedicine. The Perils of Electropollution.* New York: Jeremy P. Tarcher/Putnam, 1990.

Benor, Daniel J., M.D. *Healing Research: Holistic Energy Medicine and Spirituality.* Vol. 1. Southfield, Michigan: Vision Publications, 1999.

Benson, Herbert, M.D., with Marg Stark. *Timeless Healing: The Power and Biology of Belief.* New York: Fireside/Simon & Schuster, 1996.

Berkow, Robert, M.D., ed. *The Merck Manual of Medical Information: Home Edition.* White House Station, N.J.: Merck & Co., 1997.

Bohm, David: *Wholeness and the Implicate Order.* New York: Ark Paperbacks, 1883.

Brennan, Barbara Ann. *Hands of Light: A Guide to Healing through the Human Energy Field.* New York: Bantam Books, 1988.

————. *Light Emerging: The Journey of Personal Healing.* New York: Bantam Books, 1993.

Bruyere, Rosalyn. *Wheels of Light: Chakras, Auras, and the Healing Energy of the Body.* New York: Fireside/Simon & Schuster, 1989.

Chopra, Deepak, M.D. *Return of the Rishi: A Doctor's Story of Spiritual Transformation and Ayurvedic Healing*. Boston: Houghton Mifflin Company, 1988.

Dossey, Larry, M.D. *Healing Words: The Power of Prayer and the Practice of Medicine*. New York: HarperSanFranciso, 1993.

————. *Space, Time & Medicine*. Boulder, Colo.: Shambhala Publications Inc., 1982.

Eisenberg, David, M.D., with Thomas Lee Wright. *Encounters with Qi*. New York: W. W. Norton & Company, Inc., 1995.

Feynman, Richard P. *Six Easy Pieces: Essentials of Physics Explained by Its Most Brilliant Teacher*. Boston: Helix Books/Addison-Wesley Publishing Company, 1996.

Galland, Leo, M.D. *The Four Pillars of Healing*. New York: Random House, 1997.

Giancoli, Douglas. *Physics: Principles with Applications*. Englewood Cliffs, N.J.: Prentice Hall, 1991.

Goldberg, Jane. *Deceits of the Mind and Their Effects on the Body*. New Brunswick, N.J.: Transaction Publishers, 1991.

Goswami, Amit, with Richard E. Reed and Maggie Goswami. *The Self-Aware Universe: How Consciousness Creates the Material World*. New York: Jeremy P. Tarcher/Putnam, 1995.

Halevi, Z'ev ben Shimon. *Kabbalah: Tradition of Hidden Knowledge*. New York: Thames & Hudson, 1979.

Jahn, Robert, and Brenda Dunne. *Margins of Reality: The Role of Consciousness in the Physical World*. New York: Harcourt Brace & Company, 1987.

Kaku, Michio. *Hyperspace*. New York: Anchor Books, Doubleday, 1995.

Kaplan, Rabbi Aryeh. *Inner Space*. New York: Moznaim Publishing Corp., 1990.

————. *Sefer Yetzirah: The Book of Creation, in Theory and Practice*. York Beach, Maine: Samuel Weiser, Inc., 1997.

Kuhn, Thomas. *The Structure of Scientific Revolutions*. 3d ed. Chicago: The University of Chicago Press, 1996.

Morehouse, David. *Psychic Warrior: Inside the CIA's Stargate Program; The True Story of a Soldier's Espionage and Awakening.* New York: St. Martin's Press. 1996.

Muktananda, Swami. *Play of Consciousness: A Spiritual Autobiography*. South Fallsburg, N.Y.: SYDA Foundation, 1994.

Northrup, Christiane, M.D. *Women's Bodies, Women's Wisdom: Creating Physical and Emotional Health and Healing*. New York: Bantam, 1994.

Ornish, Dean, M.D. *Love & Survival: The Scientific Basis for the Healing Power of Intimacy*. New York: HarperCollins, 1998.

Pert, Candace. *Molecules of Emotion: Why You Feel the Way You Feel*. New York: Scribner, 1997.

Radin, Dean. *The Conscious Universe: The Scientific Truth of Psychic Phenomena*. New York: HarperSanFrancisco, 1997.

Sheinkin, M.D. *Path of the Kabbalah*. New York: Paragon House, 1986.

Siegel, Bernie, M.D. *Love, Medicine & Miracles: Lessons Learned about Self-Healing from a Surgeon's Experience with Exceptional Patients*. New York: HarperPerennial, 1986.

Targ, Russell, and Jane Katra. *Miracles of Mind: Exploring Nonlocal Consciousness and Spiritual Healing*. Novato, Calif.: New World Library, 1998.

Weil, Andrew, M.D. *Spontaneous Healing: How to Discover and Enhance Your Body's Natural Ability to Maintain and Heal Itself*. New York: Alfred A. Knopf, 1995.

Wolman, Benjamin, and Motague Ullman, eds. *Handbook of States of Consciousness*. New York: Van Nostran Reinhold Company, 1986.

Yogananda, Paramahansa. *Scientific Healing Affirmations: Theory and Practice of Concentration*. Los Angeles: Self-Realization Fellowship, 1958.

———. *Where There Is Light: Insight and Inspiration for Meeting Life's Challenges*. Los Angeles: Self-Realization Fellowship, 1988.

Zukav, Gary. *The Dancing Wu Li Masters: An Overview of the New Physics.* New York: Bantam Books, 1980.

Periodicals

"Adverse Drug Reactions May Cause over 100,000 Deaths among Hospitalized Patients Each Year." *Science News Update*, 15 April 1998.

Altman, Lawrence K. "Drug Shown to Shrink Tumors in Type of Breast Cancer by Targeting Gene Defect." *New York Times*, 18 May 1998.

Azavedo, E., G. Svane and B. Nordenstrom. "Radiological Evidence of Response to Electrochemical Treatment of Breast Cancer." *Clinical Radiology* 43 (1991): 84–7.

Bates, David, M.D. "How Worried Should We Be?" *Journal of the American Medical Association* 279 (1998): 1216–17.

Benor, Daniel, M.D., "Psi Healing Research." *The International Society for the Study of Subtle Energies and Energy Medicine Newsletter* 2, no. 2 (Summer 1991): 11–12.

———. "Lessons From Spiritual Healing Research & Practice." *Subtle Energies* 3, no. 1 (1992): 73.

Braud, William, and Marilyn Schlitz. "Consciousness Interactions with Remote Biological Systems: Anomalous Intentionality Effects." *Subtle Energies* 2, no. 1 (1991): 1–46.

Brody, Jane E. "A Cold Fact: High Stress Can Make You Sick." *New York Times*, 12 May 1998.

———. "Relaxation Method May Aid Health." *New York Times*, 7 August 1996.

Browne, Malcolm W. "Far Apart, 2 Particles Respond Faster Than Light." *New York Times*, 22 July 1997.

Colt, George Howe. "The Healing Revolution." *Life* (September 1996): 35–50.

Dossey, Larry, M.D. "Healing Happens: The Miracle of Distant Healing." *Utne Reader* (September-October 1995): 52–9.

———. "Notes on the Journey." *Alternative Therapies* 1, no. 1 (March 1995): 6–9.

Dunne, Brenda J., "Gender Differences in Human/Machine Anomalies." *Journal of Scientific Exploration* 12, no. 1 (1998): 3–55.

Eisenberg, David, M.D., R. Davis, S. Ettner, S. Appel, S. Wilkey, M. van Rompay, and R. Kessler. "Trends in Alternative Medicine Use in the United States, 1990–1997." *Journal of the American Medical Association* 11 (1998): 1569–75.

Fahrion, Steven, Mietek Wirkus, and Patricia Pooley. "EEG Amplitude, Brain Mapping & Synchrony in & between a Bioenergy Practitioner & Client During Healing." *Subtle Energies* 3, no. 1 (1992): 19–52.

Grady, Denise. "As Silent Killer Returns, Doctors Rethink Tactics to Lower Blood Pressure." *Science Times* section, *New York Times*, 14 July 1998.

Green, Elmer. "Mind Over Matter: Volition and the Cosmic Connection in Yogic Theory." *Subtle Energies* 4, no. 2 (1993): 151–70.

Green, Elmer., Peter Parks, Paul Guyer, Steven Fahrion, and Lolafaye Coyne. "Anomalous Electrostatic Phenomena in Exceptional Subjects." *Subtle Energies* 2, no. 3 (1991): 69–94.

Heermeier, K., M. Spanner, J. Trager, R. Gradinger, P. G. Strauss, W. Kraus, and J. Schmidt. "Effects of Extremely Low Frequency EMF on Collagen Type I mRNA Expression and Extracellular Matrix Synthesis of Human Osteoblastic Cells." *Bioelectromagnetics* 19 (1998): 222–31.

Horrigan, Bonnie. "Delores Krieger, R.N., Ph.D.: Healing with Therapeutic Touch." *Alternative Therapies* 4, no. 1 (January 1998): 86–92.

Jahn, Robert G. "Information, Consciousness, and Health." *Alternative Therapies* 2, no. 3 (May 1996): 32–8.

Jahn, Robert G., and Brenda Dunne. "Science of the Subjective." *Journal of Scientific Exploration* 11, no. 2 (1997): 201–24.

Kolota, Gina. "2d Breast Cancer Gene Found In Jewish Women." *New York Times*, 1996.

————. "Paradox in Ovarian and Breast Cancer Risk Intrigues Scientists." *New York Times*, 7 November 1996.

Langreth, Robert, and Andrea Petersen. "A Stampede Is on for Impotence Pill." *Wall Street Journal*, 20 April 1998.

Lazarou, Jason, Bruce Pomeranz, M.D., and Paul N. Corey. "Incidence of Adverse Drug Reactions in Hospitalized Patients." *Journal of the American Medical Association* 279 (1998): 1200–5.

May, Edwin, and L. Vilenskaya. "Overview of Current Parapsychology Research in the Former Soviet Union." *Subtle Energies* 3, no. 3 (1992): 45.

McCraty, Rollin, Mike Atkinson, and William Tiller. "New Electrophysiological Correlates Associated with Intentional Heart Focus." *Subtle Energies* 4, no. 3 (1993): 251.

McCraty, Rollin, Mike Atkinson, William Tiller, Glen Rein, and Alan Watkins. "The Effects of Emotions on Short-Term Power Spectrum Analysis of Heart Rate Variability." *American Journal of Cardiology* 76, no. 14 (15 November 1995): 1089–93.

McCraty, Rollin, Bob Barrios-Choplin, D. Rozman, M. Atkinson, and A. Watkins. "New Stress Management Program Increases DHEA and Reduces Cortisol Levels." *Integrative Physiological and Behavioral Science* 33, no. 2 (1998): 151–70.

McNeil, Donald. G., Jr. "AIDS Stalking Africa's Struggling Economies." *New York Times*, 15 November 1998.

Mehl-Madrona, Lewis. M.D. "Native American Medicine in the Treatment of Chronic Illness: Developing an Integrate Program and Evaluating Its Effectiveness." *Alternative Therapies* 5, no. 1 (January 1999): 36–44.

Moore, Nancy G. "A Review of Alternative Medical Courses Taught at U.S. Medical Schools." *Alternative Therapies* 4, no. 3 (May 1998): 90–101.

Morrow, David J. "The Elixirs of Life Style." *New York Times*, 11 November 1998.

Bibliography

Muehsam, David; M. S. Markhov; P. Muehsam, M.D.; A. Pilla; R. Shen; and Yi Wu. "Effects of QiGong on Cell-Free Myosin Phosphorylation: Preliminary Experiments." *Subtle Energies* 5, no. 1 (1994): 93–108.

Nelson, R. D., G. J. Bradish, Y. H. Dobyns, B. J. Dunne, and R. G. Jahn. "FieldREG Anomalies in Group Situations." *Journal of Scientific Exploration* 10, no. 1 (March 1996): 111.

Nordenström, Björn. "The Paradigm of Biologically Closed Electric Curcuits (BCEC) and the Formation of an International Association (IABC) for BCEC Systems." *European Journal of Surgery* Supplement 574 (1994): 7–23.

Nuland, Sherwin B. "Medicine Isn't Just for the Sick Anymore." *New York Times*, 10 May 1998.

Pyatnitsky, L. N., and V. A. Fonkin. "Human Consciousness Influence on Water Structure." *Journal of Scientific Exploration* 9, no. 1 (March 1995): 89.

Rauscher, Elizabeth. "Human Volitional Effects on a Model Bacterial System." *Subtle Energies* 1, no. 1 (March 1990): 21.

Rein, Glen, M. Atkinson, and R. McCraty. "The Physiological and Psychological Effects of Compassion and Anger." *Journal of Advancement in Medicine* 8, no. 2 (1996): 87–105.

Rosa, Linda, Emily Rosa, Larry Sarner, and Stephen Barrett, M.D. "A Close Look at Therapeutic Touch." *Journal of the American Medical Association* 279 (1998):1005–10.

Rosenthal, Elisabeth. "In North Korean Hunger, Legacy Is Stunted Children." *New York Times*, 10 December 1998.

Rubik, Beverly. "Energy Medicine and the Unifying Concept of Information." *Alternative Therapies* 1, no. 1 (March 1995): 34–9.

Russek, Linda, and Gary Schwartz. "Energy Cardiology: A Dynamical Energy Systems Approach for Integrating Conventional and Alternative Medicine." *Advances: The Journal of Mind-Body Health* 12, no. 4 (Fall 1996): 4–24.

———. "Interpersonal Heart-Brain Registration and the Perception of Parental Love: A 42-Year Follow-up of the Harvard Mastery of Stress Study." *Subtle Energies* 5, no. 3 (1994): 195–208.

Schlitz, Marilyn, and W. Braud. "Distant Intentionality and Healing: Assessing the Evidence." *Alternative Therapies* 3, no. 6 (November 1997): 62–73.

Schwartz, Gary, and Linda Russek. "The Challenge of One Medicine: Theories of Health and Eight 'World Hypotheses.'" *Advances: The Journal of Mind-Body Health* 13, no. 3 (Summer 1997): 7–30.

———. "Dynamical Energy Systems and Modern Physics: Fostering the Science and Spirit of Complementary and Alternative Medicine." *Alternative Therapies* 3, no. 3 (May 1997): 46–56

———. "Interpersonal Registration of Actual and Intended Eye Gaze: Relationship to Openness to Spiritual Beliefs and Experiences." *Journal of Scientific Exploration* (1998), in press.

———. "Previously Published Research May Help to Deflate TT Controversy." *Alternative Therapies* 4, no. 5 (September 1998): 112–3.

Schwartz, Gary, Linda Russek, and Justin Beltran. "Interpersonal Hand Energy Registration: Evidence for Implicit Performance and Perception." *Subtle Energies* 6, no. 3 (1995): 183–200.

Shell, Ellen Ruppel. "The Hippocractic Wars." *New York Times Magazine*, 28 June 1998.

Shorto, Russell. "Belief by the Numbers." *New York Times Magazine*, 7 December 1997.

Sicher, Fred; Elisabeth Targ, M.D.; D. Moore II; and Helene Smith. "A Randomized Double-Blind Study of the Effect of Distant Healing in a Population with Advanced AIDS—Report of a Small Scale Study." *Western Journal of Medicine* 169, no. 6 (December 1998): 356–63.

Stolberg, Sheryl Gay. "Gay Culture Weighs Sense and Sexuality." *New York Times, Week in Review*, 23 November 1997.

———. "Gifts to Science Researchers Have Strings, Study Finds." *New York Times*, 1 April 1998.

Sugano, Hisanobu, Seiya Uchida, and Itsuo Kuramoto. "A New Approach to the Studies of Subtle Energies." *Subtle Energies* 5, no. 2 (1994): 143–66.

Bibliography

Targ, Russell. "Remote Viewing at Stanford Research Institute in the 1970s: A Memoir." *Journal of Scientific Exploration* 10, no. 1 (March 1996): 77.

Targ, Russell, and H. Puthoff. "Investigating the Paranormal." *Nature* 251 (18 October 1974): 559.

Tiller, William, E. Green, Peter Parks, and Stacy Anderson. "Towards Explaining Anomalously Large Body Voltage Surges on Exceptional Subjects, Part I: The Electrostatic Approximation." *Journal of Scientific Exploration* 9, no. 3 (September 1995): 331.

Tiller, William, Rollin McCraty, and Mike Atkinson. "Cardiac Coherence: A New Noninvasive Measure of Atuonomic Nervous System Disorder." *Alternative Therapies* 2, no. 1 (January 1996): 52–6.

Wallis, Claudia. "Faith and Healing: Can Spirituality Promote Health? Doctors Are Finding Some Surprising Evidence." *Time* (24 June 1996): 58–64.

Weinstein, Michael. "Checking Medicine's Vital Signs." *New York Times Magazine*, 19 April 1998.

"What You Need to Know about Cancer." *Scientific American*, Special Issue (September 1996).

Wirth, Daniel. "The Effect of Non-Contact Therapeutic Touch on the Healing Rate of Full Thickness Dermal Wounds." *Subtle Energies* 1, no. 1 (1990).

Wirth, Daniel, Cathy A. Johnson, Joseph Horvath, Jo Ann D. MacGregor. "The Effect of Alternative Healing Therapy on the Regeneration Rate of Salamander Forelimbs." *Journal for Scientific Exploration* 6, no. 4 (December 1992): 374.

Yan, Xin, Zuyin Lu, Sizian Yan, and Shengping Li. "Measurement of the Effects of External Qi on the Polarization Plane of a Linearly Polarized Laser Beam." *Nature Journal* (China) 11 (1988): 563–6.

Yan, Xin, Zuyin Lu, Tianbao Zhan, Haidong Wang, and Runsheng Zhu. "The Influence of the External Qigong on the Radioactive Rate of 241 Am." *Nature Journal* (China) 11 (1988): 809–12.

Yun Yen, Jian-Ren Li, Bing Sen Zhou, Fernando Rojas, J. Yu, C. K. Chou, "Electrochemical Treatment of Human KB Cells in Vitro. *Bioelectromagnetics* 20 (1999): 34–41.

Audiovisuals

Cooper, Rabbi David A. *The Mystical Kabbalah.* Boulder, Colo.: Sounds True Audio, 1994. Videotape.

Packer, Duane, and Sanaya Roman, with DaBen and Orin. *Awakening Your Light Body: A Course in Enlightenment,* Vol 1–6. Medford, Oreg.: LuminEssence Productions. Audiotape.

———. *Radiance: Filling in the Frequencies.* Vol 1–6. Medford, Oreg.: LuminEssence Productions. Audiotape.

Skezas, Amy, with Athabascar and the Communities of Light. *Flow Alignment and Connection Practitioner's Foundations.* San Rafael, Calif.: Roselight, 1996. Audiotape.

———. *Physical, Atomic and Cellular Evolution.* San Rafael, Calif.: Roselight, 1998. Audiotape.

———. *Teaching with Light.* San Rafael, Calif.: Roselight, 1994. Audiotape.

Wirkus Bioenergy Foundation. *Bioenergy: A Healing Art.* Bethesda, Md.: New World Media Alliance, 1992. Videotape.

Other

AIDS Medical Glossary. Treatment Issues. New York: Gay Men's Health Crisis, June 1997.

American Cancer Society. *Cancer Facts & Figures.* 1997.

American Heart Association. *Heart and Stroke Facts: 1997 Statistical Supplement.* New York: American Heart Association, 1997.

Dunne, Brenda J. "Co-Operator Experiments with an REG Device." Technical Note PEAR 91005. Princeton, N.J.: Princeton University Press, 1991.

Fahrion, Steven. "Final Report to Office of Alternative Medicine on the Grant: Application of Energetic Therapy to Basal Cell Carcinoma." A report prepared for the National Institutes of Health, October 1995.

"Got Sex?" *B-2K: Beyond 2000, 98/99* New York: Gay Men's Health Crisis.

Gough, William. *Proposal for QiGong: Scientific and Medical Research.* Los Altos, Calif.: Foundation for Mind-Being Research, 1989. Unpublished.

———. "Science and Sufism." Proceedings of the fourteenth International Conference on the Study of Shamanism and Alternate Modes of Healing. San Rafael, California, September 1997.

Gough, William, and Robert Shacklett. "The Science of Connectiveness." Report at Fifth Annual Conference, International Society for the Study of Subtle Energies and Energy Medicine. Boulder, Colorado, June 1995.

———. "Outer and Inner Light." Proceedings of the Twelfth International Conference on the Study of Shamanism and Alternate Modes of Healing. San Rafael, California, September 1995.

———. "Keys to an Expanded Scientific Paradigm." Proceedings of the Thirteenth International Conference on the Study of Shamanism and Alternate Modes of Healing. San Rafael, California, September 1996.

Green, Elmer. *Alpha-Theta Brainwave Training: Instrumental Vispassana?* Report at Montreal Symposium, June 1993.

HIV/AIDS Facts. New York: Gay Men's Health Crisis, October 1998.

Kabat-Zinn, Jon. "Mindfulness Meditation: What It Is, What It Isn't, and Its Role in Health Care and Medicine." University of Massachusetts Stress Reduction Clinic Web site, http://www.reduceyourstress.com/research.htm. Accessed December, 1998.

McCraty, Rollin. "Head/Heart Entrainment." Brain-Mind Applied Neurophysiology and EEG and Neurofeedback Proceedings. Key West, 1996.

National Institutes of Health. *Alternative Medicine: Expanding Medical Horizons; A Report to the National Institutes of Health on Alternative Medical Systems and Practices in the United States.* Washington, D.C.: GPO, 1992.

Nelson, R. D., R. G. Jahn, B. J. Dunne, Y. H. Dobyns, and G. J Bradish. "Fielded II: Consciousness Field Effects: Replications and Explorations." Technical note PEAR 9700. Princeton, N.J.: Princeton University Press, June 1997.

Research Overview: Exploring the Role of the Heart in Human Performance. Boulder Creek, Colo.: HeartMath Research Center, 1997.

Shah, Sonal; A. Ogden.; C. Pettker; A. Raffo; S. Itescu, M.D.; and M. Oz, M.D. "A Study of the Effect of Energy Healing on In vitro Tumor Cell Proliferation." Unpublished paper.

Solman, Paul. "Seeking an Alternative." *The Newshour with Jim Lehrer,* Transcript. 27 August 1998.

Targ, Elisabeth, M.D. "Evaluating Remote Healing: A Research Review." Unpublished paper.

Index

A

Aarons, Karin, 150–51
abortion, 90–91
acupuncture, 122–23
AIDS, 154–55, 236–38. *See
    also* HIV
  anger and, 243–45
  and dying, 242, 244, 247,
      252–54
  emotional issues and,
      241–45
  energy signature, 257
  feeding on fear, 257–58
  research on distant healing
      of, 31, 254–63
  sexual abuse and, 243
  sexual attitudes and,
      238–41
  as spiritual path, 236–41,
      246–47, 250, 263
  stabilization through
      spiritual healing, 242,
      244–45, 247–52,
      258–62

  in Third World, 239
AIDS-related illnesses, 259,
    262
  Kaposi's sarcoma, 248–51
alternative medicine. *See also
    specific illnesses and
    treatments*
  increasing utilization of, 17
"Alternative Medicine:
    Expanding Medical
    Horizons," 21
Ambrogi, Jim, 258
American Medical Association
    (AMA), 17, 20, 21
  ignoring of research
      findings, 15–17
Amoils, Steven, 95–97
angels, 144–45
anger
  affecting others, even at a
      distance, 296–97
  effect on physiology, 76. *See
      also* heart disease
  electrical equipment
      breaking in response
      to, 296

296, 307
Grad, Bernard, 122
Grady, David, 102, 154
Gray, Bill, 117
Green, Elmer, 47–48, 73, 75,
  296, 297, 301, 304–5
grids, 278
Grossman, Richard, 123–24
group consciousness. *See*
  consciousness, collective
guidance, 274
Guided Self Healing, 179–80

H

hands, 97
  felt inside body, 36
hara healing, 103, 140, 153,
  259
Harrell, Martha, 162
Harshman, Bruce, 197, 198
Hasidic movement, resurgence
  of healing in, 161
Hastings, Arnold, 197
Hayes, Alan, 36, 67, 99, 151
head injuries, 64
headaches, 14, 33, 35, 92–93
healer-client relationship,
  69–71
healers, 305
  changed in the healing
    process, 70
  importance of
    self-knowledge,
    103–4
  key to effectiveness
    Bruyere, 130
  love and devotion to
    God, 47, 68–70,
    305, 306

need for training, 302
physiology during healing,
  47–48, 71–72, 301–2
range of abilities, 305, 306
sense of union with other,
  71, 269, 278
as teachers, 306
healing, spiritual/energy,
  54–58. *See also specific*
  illnesses and types of healing
advice to people obtaining,
  4–5
combined with medical
  treatment, 4–5,
  37–38, 220, 233
vs. curing, 88, 234
essential elements, 67–70.
  See also intention;
  love; resonance;
  surrender
as expansion of
  consciousness, 9, 34,
  57–58, 67, 117–19,
  125–27
growing popularity of, 14,
  20, 298–99
history, 120–23
learning and teaching, 98,
  100, 101, 103–5, 272
media coverage of, 14–17
names for, 23
physiological aspects, 48,
  72–77, 79, 301. *See*
  also electromagnetic
  frequencies
quantum physics and, 46
spiritual *vs.* energy healing,
  81, 85
trademarking techniques of,
  5, 141
transcendent experiences

Hampton Roads Publishing Company

. . . for the evolving human spirit

Hampton Roads Publishing Company
publishes books on a variety of subjects including
metaphysics, health, complementary medicine,
visionary fiction, and other related topics.

For a copy of our latest catalog,
call toll-free, 800-766-8009,
or send your name and address to:

Hampton Roads Publishing Company, Inc.
134 Burgess Lane
Charlottesville, VA 22902
e-mail: hrpc@hrpub.com
www.hrpub.com